Boeing Versus Airbus

Boeing Versus Airbus

THE INSIDE STORY OF THE GREATEST
INTERNATIONAL COMPETITION IN BUSINESS

JOHN NEWHOUSE

Alfred A. Knopf · New York · 2007

THIS IS A BORZOI BOOK
PUBLISHED BY ALFRED A. KNOPF

Copyright © 2007 by John Newhouse

All rights reserved. Published in the United States by Alfred A. Knopf,
a division of Random House, Inc., New York, and in Canada
by Random House of Canada Limited, Toronto.
www.aaknopf.com

Library of Congress Cataloging-in-Publication Data
Newhouse, John.
Boeing versus Airbus / John Newhouse.—1st ed.
p.   cm.
Includes bibliographical references and index.
ISBN-13: 978-1-4000-4336-1
1. Boeing Company.   2. Airbus Industrie.   3. Aircraft industry–United States.
4. Aircraft industry—France.   5. Competition, International.   I. Title.
HD9711.U64B646 2007
338.7'629133340944—dc22   2006030611

Manufactured in the United States of America
First Edition

*To Symmie and to the memory of
Hugo Young and of Warren Zimmermann*

CONTENTS

PROLOGUE

Back in the 1970s and early 1980s, four companies divided the turbulent business of making and selling passenger airplanes. One of them, the Boeing Company, was dominant. The other two big American players—the Lockheed Aircraft Corporation and the McDonnell Douglas Corporation—labored in the wake of their own mistakes. Lockheed's were terminal, and McDonnell Douglas, known in the trade as McDac, hadn't come to terms with reality. The reality was that a small European company called Airbus Industrie, generally known only as Airbus, had abruptly become not just a player but a mortal threat. Simply put, Airbus was eating McDac's lunch.

Although steeply uphill, this business has never lacked bold, entrepreneurial spirits. Many have tried, few successfully. Some of the high rollers never learned to read the market. The airplanes they built were too big or too small, or cost more to operate than airlines were willing to pay. Or the airline market might have moved on. Or the new airplane might have been mated with the wrong engine, or just been unlucky.

An example of bad luck was Lockheed's L-1011, a three-engine, wide-bodied airplane built in the late 1960s and also known as the Tristar. In its time it may have been the best of the double-aisle airplanes, probably the most admired by aerodynamicists. But the combination of bad luck and bad timing victimized the airplane and its maker. The L-1011 had lost $2.5 billion when it was retired in 1981.

Suppliers of these large commercial aircraft (LCAs, as they are known in the trade) have goals that draw on spongy assumptions, political hubris, and industrial savoir faire. They mix great expectations with huge uncertainties. They grapple with uncertainty by dispensing smoke and mirrors. Every transaction becomes the most important until the next one.

Reading the market is largely guesswork. An airline may plan to use a new airplane for twenty, possibly thirty years, but can't predict how many times the market will change direction along the way. In market forecasting, the airline must guess what size bucket (the airplane) will be needed to carry an unknown quantity of sand (the passengers). The supplier guesses when to launch an airplane and must then continue betting that it's one that will meet both the short- and long-term needs of the unforgiving market.

The decision to build a new LCA alerts boards of directors and shareholders to impending deficits, big ones. Indeed, the costs of any such venture can amount to betting the company, literally. A single deal with one airline can determine the fate of an airplane on which billions of dollars have been invested. And the returns, if any, lie far ahead. The break-even point of a new program is invariably a made-up number and is rarely, if ever, pinned down.

No airline will pay the list price for an airplane, if there is such a thing. The massive discounts offered to launch customers tend to establish the price, or come close to establishing it. The business is tougher than most, largely because it's more about instinct and psychology than economics. When airlines feel confident about the future, they order airplanes. When they lose confidence, they stop buying. In good times, the airlines purchase too many airplanes, but all too often they take deliveries in the economy's troughs, which always lie just ahead—when they may cancel or postpone deliveries. Timing is the key variable for buyer and seller.

Ironically, McDac, or more exactly its founder, James McDonnell, blundered by refusing to build the very airplane—a small, twin-engine wide-body—that Airbus did build and that allowed this European upstart to acquire a foothold in the global airline market. The A300, as Airbus called its first airplane, was an ideal fit for a hole in the market that all the suppliers could see and that any one of them could have filled. But Mr. Mac, as he liked to be called (by family members as well as others), decided to compete with Lockheed by building not what the market wanted but his own three-engine wide-body. He called it the DC-10. It appeared indistinguishable from the L-1011 but was inferior in ways that mattered. Indeed, the DC-10, an ill-conceived and rather hurried project, was to acquire some notoriety. Building it was a foolish move. The market for these look-alike aircraft wasn't there; predictably, they killed each other.

They did more than that. Neither of the two companies would build another LCA, and at different speeds, each would abandon the commercial end of the business. McDac's exit meant the demise of a truly great company, the Douglas Aircraft Corporation. At one time, it had been the most respected of LCA suppliers, and had the confidence of more of the world's airlines than either Boeing or Lockheed. In the early days of the jet age, Douglas had been Boeing's only peer, but the company's leadership had also become steadily less rigorous and disciplined in holding down costs. By 1966 it had lost the confidence of its bankers and become a takeover target for Mr. Mac, who saw every reason to join his highly profitable military aircraft business with the world's most illustrious LCA producer.

The marriage never worked. Mr. Mac foolishly tried to bend Douglas to his ways of making and selling a very dissimilar product line. His ignorance, judgment, and timing—all three—took the venture straight downhill. Douglas had been the airlines' preferred producer of propeller-driven LCAs, and its first jet-powered models—the DC-8 and DC-9—were revered, but Boeing had invested more heavily and judiciously in jet airliners and had begun to take control of a burgeoning market for them.

AN EXISTENTIAL PENDULUM governs the fortunes of the companies that struggle to gain an edge in this unsteady business. At one time, the advantage might have drifted now to Douglas, now to Lockheed, now to Boeing. Then, in the years between 1985 and 2005, the gestalt changed. As the weaker players fell away, the focus shifted to a hardier but dissimiliar pair: mighty Boeing and the arriviste Airbus.

For much of that time, Boeing held a commanding lead, its supremacy not really contested. Nevertheless, by the mid-1990s, if not before, the gallery could see this twosome's fortunes start to converge, as Boeing, complacent and risk averse, became less committed to the fundamentals of its trade—building new and better models and treating airline customers with care. Airbus, on the other hand, was stressing the fundamentals, gaining credibility, making a dent in the market, and even beginning to scent blood. With the passage of not much more time, the seemingly fanciful notion of Airbus catching up with and even moving ahead of Boeing in market share acquired reality.

In making airplanes of 150 or more seats, Airbus and Boeing controlled the market. Both had successful product lines. Together they constituted a maturing duopoly—an anomaly in this marketplace. Still, nothing stays the same for very long in this business. In just eighteen months, from January 2005 to June 2006, Airbus tumbled off the comfortable plateau it was sharing with Boeing. Its fortunes fell steeply, more so than Boeing's had fallen during the decade in which it had lost the leadership role. The top tier of Airbus's management had become nearly as complacent and risk averse as Boeing's had been then. Moreover, Boeing had put on offer a new and highly innovative midsize airplane called the 787, one that might all but dislodge Airbus from the richest segment of the market unless Airbus acted swiftly to match its rival's aggressive move. In failing to do that, Airbus is paying, and will continue to pay, a heavy price. That much had become clear by mid-2005.

Not until one year later, at the Farnborough International Air Show, did Airbus management finally unveil a new midsize airplane, the A350, which was designed to compare favorably with Boeing's 787. Airbus did have one new product on the market then, its superjumbo A380, but that airplane had been buffeted by production problems and was draining away financial resources.

On June 14, 2006, those problems suddenly escalated into a full-blown crisis as Airbus announced a six- to seven-month delay in the delivery schedule for the A380. The problem, it seemed, was installing 310 miles or so of wiring in the right places, notably in the in-flight entertainment systems and kitchen galleys. The announcement came as a nasty shock to customers of the A380, who had expected deliveries of the huge airplane to begin in the first half of 2007. These airlines had already experienced a similar delay the previous year, one that had cost Airbus tens of millions of dollars in penalties. The company's announcement on June 14 was coupled with a warning that its operating income would fall by $625 million each year between 2007 and 2010.

The blowback this time was far more serious, and the ripple effect much wider. EADS (European Aeronautic Defense and Space Company), Airbus's parent company, saw almost $7 billion in market capitalization disappear on the day following the announcement. And while EADS's shares fell by 26 percent, Boeing's rose 6.5 percent on the New York Stock Exchange. Some potential A380 users, besides demanding compensation for the delays, threatened to cancel orders.

Questions about the A380's future and whether it had one were immediately linked with larger, far more complex issues involving management and company strategy. Airbus's central problem, and the crippling one, is a jerry-built corporate structure that is aimed at satisfying the narrowly focused political interests of the company's French and German stakeholders. In order to balance these interests, the structure seems to require two chief executives and two chairmen. Not surprisingly, this dual management arrangement has over the years become steadily less functional and less competent. Airbus is unlikely to compete again on even terms with Boeing unless it can substitute a simple, straightforward managerial structure for what it is saddled with now.

Boeing Versus Airbus

CHAPTER ONE

Being Number One

IN THE AIRCRAFT BUSINESS, as in a Trollope novel, things are often not what they seem. In the 1980s, Boeing still reigned supreme. Its airplanes covered the market. Its product support was exemplary. Boeing was universally judged one of America's best and most admired companies, partly because its sales abroad of large commercial airplanes were the country's biggest export, and partly because it had learned to build these airplanes better, faster, and cheaper than anyone else had done. "World-class" was Boeing's lofty but accurate characterization of itself.

The competition was barely visible. McDac had entered its steady but terminal decline, and in Seattle, Boeing's home base, Airbus was seen as just another in a long line of European wannabes that would stay in the game only as long as a consortium of governments remained willing to throw vast sums of money at a seemingly certain loser. Today, things have turned around. Boeing and Airbus are the sole suppliers of big airliners, but over many of the past twenty years, the two companies were moving in opposite directions. Boeing's multiple troubles, most of them self-inflicted, signaled an end to its dominance and pointed up Airbus's methodical rise.

Things had begun to change in the late 1980s. And it was no joke when, on April 1, 1993, Moody's downgraded Boeing's debt rating for the first time in the company's seventy-six-year history. Still, as late as

1990, Boeing held 62 percent of the market, McDonnell Douglas 23 percent, Airbus just 15 percent. Today it's very different. McDonnell Douglas is gone, having been absorbed by Boeing in August 1997. In 2004, Airbus outsold Boeing, and did so again in 2005.

Boeing's troubles were traceable partly to arrogance—a tendency to take the market for granted, to coast on its laurels—and partly to changes that developed in the corporate culture. These changes began to dull Boeing's feel for the game, a game in which the supplier must either take large risks with operating margins or make way for the competition. Then there is the legacy of obsolescence. So much is invested in existing systems that a Boeing or an Airbus cannot absorb the new technologies except in small bites. Nevertheless, whatever the cost, they must invest in these technologies, even while being manipulated in a way that drives down the cost of new airplanes to a point at which the financially strapped airlines can afford to buy them. "You can't win, you can't break even, and you can't quit," said Jean Pierson, a former CEO of Airbus, who understood the need to invest in research and technology.

The industry has produced few more interesting figures than Pierson. He is a legend. Experienced people at the Airbus offices in Toulouse agree that without Jean Pierson, who retired in 1998, there would be no Airbus. This is a people industry, even if it is technology driven. Those who succeed are individuals with vision and guts and a sure sense of their company's interests, as distinct from their own (or even those of their stockholders). Pierson defined the model of what it takes. He had the requisite vision, guts, common sense, and the personal force to persuade colleagues at Airbus to do things his way and to persuade customers—including wary, skeptical American carriers—to buy his airplanes instead of Boeing's.

Pierson was known as "the bear of the Pyrenees." He now spends some of his time in Nice and the rest in Corsica—in the mountains behind a small port not far from Bastia. He keeps a small boat there, a farewell gift from Airbus. And he does some indifferent fishing, not with tackle but with a string tied to his finger to which he attaches bait.

Pierson arrived as boss of Airbus in 1985, just when T. Wilson (the

T is for Thornton, but he was known throughout the aviation world and beyond as "T"), a figure very like him in a number of ways, retired as Boeing's chief executive. Wilson, like Pierson, was a vivid, dominating, sure-handed leader. And just as Pierson's arrival marked the start of Airbus's ascent, Wilson's departure marked the start of Boeing's decline. The fortunes of Boeing and Airbus were both closely tied to the style and the aura of these two remarkable leaders whose paths barely crossed.

Each of them got on well with and had the respect of his opposite numbers in the airline and engine businesses, partly because they were both hands-on managers who knew airplanes from the wheels up. Both had been factory-floor guys who knew what was involved in the various blue-collar jobs. At Airbus, they say, Pierson would talk to employees in these jobs and then, based on what he'd learned, might say to his staff, "We are going to be ten days late in delivering this or that airplane"—meaning, "You guys better shape up right now or we will be paying heavy penalties for missing delivery dates."

Wilson would sit down with factory workers at lunch in the cafeteria and find out what was going on in their various operations; and then, if it was advisable, he would take up what he'd learned with the relevant managers. He wasn't Boeing's founder, but he was called "the founder" by some of his people. "He ran the company," says one former executive. "It did not run him. Wilson overrode the system whenever he had to."

Like Pierson, Wilson had an intuitive feel for his company's larger interests. He knew that Boeing had the world's greatest commercial aircraft franchise. He would do whatever it took to protect that. He never liked diversifying if it meant moving the company onto ground it knew less well or not at all. The point is best illustrated by anecdotal evidence. For example, Robert R. Kiley (an American who in 2001 would become the surprise choice to take over management of the London Underground) had a remarkable encounter with Wilson in 1975, when Kiley had just been named chairman and chief executive officer of the Massachusetts Bay Transportation Authority (MBTA).

The MBTA had recently bought new trams, or streetcars. These vehicles had been supplied by Vertol, at the time a subdivision of Boeing, which had acquired it in 1960 (nearly a decade before Wilson took on major responsibilities). Kiley recalls the new equipment "as having quickly become a big and constant problem—a horror story. It was sleek-looking and very high-tech, too much so. The doors were a special problem. They had about a thousand moving parts, some of them electronically driven. The press reaction was awful. We intended to sue Boeing.

"One Saturday morning," Kiley continues, "I was alone in my office in Boston, and a guard downstairs called to say that a man named Wilson was there and wanted to see me. When I discovered it was T. Wilson, Boeing's CEO, I went down and brought him to my office. He was upset about what had happened, noting how sorry he was not to have stopped this move by Boeing into a technology it knew nothing about. He made clear his feeling that Boeing should not stray from the business it knew. He said, 'Mr. Kiley, my only interest is preserving my company's good name. I'll do whatever you want us to do.' He offered, in effect, to fix the trains or, failing that, repay the MBTA's investment—about $45 million in mid-1970s dollars."[1]

The trams, which had never worked, couldn't be fixed, and so Boeing repaid the MBTA. For the company, it was the sensible and cost-effective solution to the problem. Not so long after Wilson stepped down, Boeing began to ignore the lesson it had learned with the MBTA: to keep the company focused on the business it knew best.

Boeing had prospered by concentrating on product development and the customer, assuming, correctly, that doing so would best protect shareholder interests. Movement away from these priorities was slow, but within ten years of Wilson's departure, Boeing had changed direction.

AIRLINERS, like T-shirts, come in different sizes—small, medium, large, and extra-large. But they have more variety than T-shirts, because the suppliers build each of their products into families; in turn, the family members, the airplanes, vary somewhat in size, range, and other characteristics, the better to fill each of the airline market's crevices.

The low end of the market is covered by two single-aisle airplanes, Boeing's 737 and Airbus's A320. They are roughly the same size, seating up to 190 people. Both are exceptionally successful, having exceeded the most optimistic forecasts of their respective companies. The 737 is older and has been steadily improved over the years. But the A320, a newer, slightly larger, and more comfortable aircraft, is outselling the 737, not least in the low-cost market that Boeing had monopolized. In December 2004, the surge in orders for A320's from low-cost carriers caused Boeing to shake up its sales force and replace its chief salesman, Toby Bright.

The biggest revenue earners are airplanes with 200 to 300 seats. For many years, Boeing had this so-called middle market largely to itself with the 757, a long, single-aisle airplane, and the double-aisle 767. The narrower and less comfortable of the two, the 757, could seat up to 239 passengers, while the more popular 767 carries 218 to 304, depending on the version. The extended-range version of the family became the most profitable of all Boeing aircraft (a distinction widely but wrongly thought to belong to its 747 jumbo). This airplane's other distinction lay in becoming the first long-range, transatlantic, twin-engine airliner. It was quietly followed by the Airbus A310, which was less popular.

Then, in the mid-1990s, Airbus moved aggressively into this Boeing fiefdom with the A330-200, a new medium-size airplane that quickly became very popular with airlines as a vehicle for moving both people and cargo. The heavy demand for the A330-200 drove Boeing out of the middle market, the richest segment. In October 2003, it announced that too few orders for its single-aisle 757 had dictated a decision to end production of the aircraft by the end of that year; the news foreshadowed serious job cuts. As for the 767, its days, too, were clearly numbered.

Between these middle-sized vehicles and the high-end jumbos lay a hole in the market for which Boeing and Airbus began competing vigorously in the 1990s. Boeing entered the fray with the 777, a high-quality and very popular airplane. The 777 in a standard configuration seats between 300 and 370 passengers. Its launch customer, United Airlines, began flying it in 1994. Airbus's counterpart aircraft in this market, the A340, began life commercially a bit earlier, with Air France and Lufthansa, in March 1993.

Predictably, these minijumbos—the 777 and the A340—became minifamilies of aircraft with varying ranges and other features. Each of the two product lines flourished for a time, until the 777 began to take control of the market. It is judged marginally more comfortable than the A340 (and most other aircraft, too) and is believed to have slightly lower operating costs. In most ways that matter, the 777 is much the better airplane.

More important, the 777, in its early standard version, may have trailed the A340, but Boeing had thoughtfully begun to design and build an extended-range member of the minijumbo family before Airbus got going with a similarly long-range A340. This meant that the competitive edge in what became a highly profitable market for the longest-range versions of these big airplanes belongs to Boeing.

The market's extra-large segment—the high end—has belonged to Boeing since the late 1960s, when it built and began selling the 747, an airplane that was two and a half times larger than the 707, the next-biggest LCA. Thirty years later, Airbus, perhaps unwisely, chose to overtake and even oust Boeing from this market by building a new and even bigger airplane. This superjumbo, the A380, had been scheduled to begin its commercial life with Singapore Airlines (SIA), the launch customer, in the spring of 2006. But Airbus, aware that the airplane couldn't meet performance guaranties, pushed the delivery date back to the fall of that year, and then was obliged to postpone it thanks to repeated and deeply injurious delays. The airplane's prospects had become unclear.

DURING THAT SMALL WINDOW in the mid-1980s when T. Wilson was disengaging from his company and Pierson was taking charge of his,

Airbus swiped Boeing's playbook. It set about building families of airplane types that would span the entire market and demonstrate a stronger commitment to staying even with technology creep. Boeing was still covering the low end of the market with the 737, a 1960s design, and the high end with the 747, a model of the same vintage. Most of Boeing's production methods not only lagged behind those of Airbus but were traceable to the era of big World War II bombers.

Starting in the 1980s, Boeing's arrogance began to coexist with a concern that it was losing its edge, that it was no longer as good at making airplanes more productively than the competition. Its concern about itself deepened. It began to take the threat from Airbus more seriously, while still avoiding risks of the sort it had once taken and that had accounted for its success.

Airbus had started to exude confidence. The talk from Airbus people was reminiscent of Boeing engineers' and senior executives' talk when there was no serious competitor. Airbus then became a metaphor for how Europe could compete against the best and most successful of American industries. And that alone is a big, possibly historic, reversal of attitude. Not long before, European suppliers had been known for making aircraft that were short both on market appeal and on reliable product support.

Airbus wasn't launched because some person, or persons, had an original and creative idea. Instead, its origins reflected the deep anxiety of Britain, France, and Germany, each of which wanted to preserve its aircraft industry. No one of these industries was any longer strong enough to compete with American companies, and the Europeans saw this multiparty approach—the still nascent European idea—as the only way.

As for Airbus, until recently it was seen by its American counterparts as bearing the stigma of being French (it's centered in Toulouse) and, worse, socialist—just another jobs program built upon government subsidies that made possible the development of all the new aircraft. Moreover, given Airbus's apparent reliance on direct government support, American companies used to tell themselves that this oddly configured new player would be slow-moving and unable to match the standards of, say, Boeing. This line helped to breed complacency in Seattle. Boeing people didn't look beyond, or contest, their own dogma. Even now, one can hear Airbus described dismissively by some current and former Boeing staff as "just socialism."

Describing Airbus as a jobs program is simplistic. Europe's aerospace industry has traditionally performed that role while producing equipment ranging in quality from acceptable to high. But most labor forces there are protected by a munificent safety net, which, along with Europe's most serious problem—the demography gap—bedevils governments.

Airbus employees are critical of Boeing's habit of laying off thousands of highly trained mechanics in slack periods and then rehiring those that haven't slipped away to work for a competitor. Europeans profess to see this pattern as hard to understand.

The challenge for Airbus in its early days was getting labor and manufacturing costs under control. The company succeeded in doing so, and starting in the early to mid-1990s, it was costing Airbus less to build airplanes than it was costing Boeing.

Airbus began as a consortium of four European national aircraft corporations. France, Germany, Britain, and Spain were each represented. In the summer of 2000, three of the four partners became a unified commercial enterprise and part of the huge, publicly traded corporation called EADS, which is based in Paris. Today, 22.5 percent of EADS is owned by DaimlerChrysler. The French state and the Lagardère aircraft group, also French, divide another 30 percent share. Spain holds a 5.5 percent share, and the balance is traded on European stock exchanges. British Aerospace—later reinvented as BAE Systems—did not join EADS, but did retain its 20 percent share in Airbus.

Airbus-EADS is a curious and badly flawed structure. EADS owns most of Airbus, but its Airbus component amounts to most of EADS. The top jobs at EADS are held by two co-chairmen, one French, one German. Their operational supervision of Airbus is nominal, however, possibly because it accounts for roughly 65 percent of the Paris-based parent company's turnover and 80 percent of its revenue. In short, Airbus has more or less run its own show, a freedom that probably contributed to its steep ascent.

But Airbus staffers chafe at being, at least technically, an appendage of EADS. "Why do we need EADS?" they ask. "We are a stand-alone company. We supply half of all the corporation's labor, seventy percent of its revenue, and most of the profits. So why not float shares in Airbus?" The tail, they think, wags the dog.

AIRBUS IS A CURIOUS ANIMAL—an unlisted company that once a year holds a meeting in New York City with financial analysts called the Airbus Wall Street Forum. The question arises: Why is a company that is not listed, but part of one that is listed, going directly to people who rate listed companies? Why shouldn't Airbus become a listed company? Listed or unlisted, the point about Airbus is that a group of diverse Europeans managed to get out of one another's way and, despite the company's curious structure, were able to make major success of it.

It is still a new company, having just begun life as an integrated corporate entity in 2000. There remain few traces of the rough-and-tumble style that divided Airbus when it was a consortium of four companies with very different business cultures and different approaches to building airplanes, which in turn reflected different levels of experience with the process.

Pierson, unlike T. Wilson, wasn't betting the company on a new airplane, but he and his colleagues had to reconcile France's first priority, market share, with Germany's overriding concern, the bottom line. And there was Britain's congenital ambivalence regarding European projects, driven in this case by a concern that taking part in Airbus might harm British interests in the United States. Also, Wilson was running a company that possessed the strongest commercial franchise the industry had seen. He was the undisputed boss, surrounded by like-minded colleagues with whom communication could be held to a few words.

In those early days, Airbus was a loosely strung sales-and-marketing organization without much in the way of a product line to do something with. The member companies could lobby the Airbus case for building an airplane with the Commission of the European Union, but were forbidden by these firms from lobbying their governments. The industrial assets of the companies were not pooled, and none of them knew anything about the financial details of its partners' Airbus-related operations.

If Airbus had a founding father it was Roger Beteille, a brilliant French engineer and the first director. Beteille had a flair for making things happen and a shrewd business sense. When he began maneuvering the fortunes of Airbus in 1967, with just a secretary to help, this gifted, multirole figure probably didn't presume to think that he was seeding another version of Boeing or Douglas. But he did believe strongly in what he was doing and in what the various European aircraft companies could bring to a contest with their more successful and robust American counterparts.

Beteille understood that the airlines needed competition among suppliers of LCA. By early 1980s, he could see that Lockheed was finished as a supplier and that McDonnell Douglas was making the wrong moves. Now, of course, the airlines have only Airbus and Boeing to play off and beat down on price. Although the carriers would much rather have three or four suppliers, having two is far better than being at the mercy of one.

Airbus is a large and impressively modern assemblage of facilities located in Blagnac, a suburb of Toulouse. Until a combination of bad decisions and managerial strife within EADS took its toll, the company exuded a strong sense of being comfortable with itself. Since the 1980s, Airbus has done many things right, whereas in this same period Boeing got a great many of them wrong.

Airbus did things that saved money and appealed to airlines. For example, it standardized the cockpits in its family of airplanes, a feature called "commonalty" that airlines especially like, yet one that Boeing was reluctant to emulate, mainly because of the costs involved, but will adopt with its new midsize airplane, the 787.

Creating families of aircraft types that prospered in the marketplace has enabled Airbus to reduce labor costs. The more airplanes a supplier builds, especially those with similar features, the more rapidly its labor force descends the learning curve. Since workers learn as they work, both costs and mistakes decline with numbers of units produced. Boeing was a beneficiary of this first principle when it was building bombers in World War II and later when it created a first-generation family of jet airliners.

Although Boeing remained a well-organized and reasonably well disciplined company into the 1990s, it had grown more hierarchical and less flexible. A similar judgment of the Boeing company can still be heard from its airline customers, engine makers, other big suppliers of airplane parts, and a great many of its own people. Boeing, they say, is more bureaucracy-laden than other companies—according to some former Defense Department officials who now observe Boeing from the private sector, even more so than the Pentagon.

These are major flaws in a trade that draws heavily on instinct and seat-of-the-pants decisions. The arrogance remains, and, until recently, so did the tendency to take the customer for granted. Boeing's critics, in-house as well as external, complain about a heavy presence of inexperienced business-school types and too little listening to the airline market.

Some of the harshest comment was heard from people serving in companies that have worked most closely with Boeing. General Electric Aircraft Engines is an example. Boeing has in recent years aligned, or tried to align, its corporate culture with GE's; indeed, Airbus people feel that GE has at times shown a strong pro-Boeing bias in negotiations involving the engine and airframe companies. Still, GE people describe Boeing as indifferent to costs (indeed, extravagant), mired in layers of bureaucracy, and insensitive to customers' needs. Many, if not most, of those customers are also GE customers.

An incident that caused special pain to various GE people involved a Chinese-American executive, Li Hsi, who had handled the company's engine sales in Taiwan and then became regional general manager in China. Li was highly regarded by his company. His view of the Boeing people whom he saw working on aircraft sales, some of which involved both companies, was that they lacked a feel for dealing with Chinese customers. Li's informal suggestions for changes in Boeing's modus operandi were passed to Boeing as well as to his own company, and they were entirely well intentioned and constructive, according to GE people.

However, senior Boeing executives reacted by accusing Li of being pro-Airbus and asking that he be removed. His company obliged Boeing, and transferred Li to Cincinnati and a job that had little appeal for him. The incident angered several GE people at various levels. "He was very unhappy," one of them said. "Boeing pressure caused GE to make a stupid decision. Li had been trying to help Boeing."[2]

During the 1990s, Airbus came to resemble the Boeing of old: predatory and conveying a relentless energy and commitment to the hunt for buyers of its wares. Airbus people appeared to be more comfortable with their company than is the case with Boeing staff that one encounters. And there are fewer of them. A part of Jean Pierson's legacy was a much leaner bureaucracy, leaner than at other aerospace companies.

In recent years, the adversary companies acquired different body language. The Airbus style was forward leaning. Boeing's became wary and defensive, the arrogance a little less transparent. The people in Toulouse were looser and more discursive, less likely to adopt the glossy-brochure approach to describing an aircraft that one might encounter in Seattle. Boeing executives are far more scripted, and some of them, like many political types, respond to questions that have not been asked.

The companies blow the same amount of smoke at visitors—a lot. Each tends to maximize the prospects for its product line and to plant or reinforce doubts about the other side's. Each puts down the other's strategic approach to the market. Each expresses wonder, or puzzlement, about why the other is basing its plans on this or that.

But Airbus, because it was playing catch-up over the years—climbing a steep hill—learned to be more or less honest, at least with itself. Also, with four national players taking part, the process of building consensus on issues was often difficult, but exacting, and probably generated a number of good decisions. Meanwhile, Boeing was trying to assign blame for things going wrong. It would blame not itself but external forces, starting with weak, unreliable airlines, and also emphasize the subsidies that European governments were giving Airbus.

There was something to that, but less than Boeing claimed. Luck plays a major part in this exigent business, as it does in so many endeavors. Airbus had the great good fortune to be well run at a time when Boeing was undergoing a stretch of serious mismanagement.

"Provincial" is among the terms widely used to describe Boeing, and for a company that sells 70 percent of its aircraft overseas, it is a reproach. Some Boeing watchers have recommended that each of its executives be required to live abroad for a period of no less than six months. But Boeing has always been an unworldly company, even in the days when its chief competitors were Lockheed and Douglas. In any case, whether provincial or worldly, Boeing's marketing and sales staffs are seen as less accomplished than Airbus's, its cadre of talented executives smaller.

As for the design and composition of airplanes, Boeing and Airbus have similar pools of accomplished—indeed, brilliant—aerodynamicists. And each company is carpeted with executives who began life as engineers. Otherwise their corporate cultures are dissimilar. Boeing's management is layered, awkward, and in some sectors abnormally quarrelsome.

Airbus was forced to acquire discipline, partly by the so-called tyranny of the dollar. Contracts are negotiated in dollars, and as the currency weakened, Airbus had to drain some of the cost out of its system. Doing so added to the competitive tension between the various Airbus companies but did breed a higher level of efficiency, and hence productivity.

Boeing's homogeneity contrasts sharply with Airbus, a collection of forty or so nationalities and, one is told, no sense of hierarchy. Airbus flatters itself on being a model of cohesiveness. A visitor is told repeatedly that the company's diversity induces a collegiality among people who have had to reconcile different styles and perspectives on how best to get the job done. (Language differences are not a problem. Staff people are in many cases multilingual, and those who are not are in any case wholly comfortable with English; it has become the working language.)

The assumption in the 1980s and much of the 1990s was that Boeing's monoculture would have little difficulty in overpowering Airbus's multiculture. But it didn't. Again, much, if not most, of the credit goes to Pierson, who took control of a group of companies beset by divergent business cultures and, even worse, by the sharply contesting priorities of their patrons, the four governments. In Airbus's early days, each government felt it had to agree on a new project; the acquiescence of a national airline—such as Air France or Lufthansa—was also required. And there was the question of who would run the project. Since each project involved four different companies, a cooperative team—indeed, a team spirit—had to develop, and it did. The process is said by industry analysts to have generated high-quality decisions, although not always promptly.

"There was constant bickering," says Pierson, "a constant need to find consensus. That wore me down."[3] He was just fifty-eight when he retired. He doesn't say much about his decision to retire early. It was generally thought that while he may have been very tired (he had said as much, and was keenly aware of the heart attack he had recently experienced), he was also reluctant to begin having to deal with the politics of a very different corporate structure, this one spearheaded by companies and operating under dual CEOs, one French, one German. "Imagine a company with two CEOs," he could be heard observing after he left. The comment turned out to be far more telling than he may have thought.

Much of Pierson's energy over the years was used to settle disputes and smooth rough edges. He not only succeeded but had presided over the creation of more jet transport programs than any similar figure, American or European. "Airbus needed the combination of Pierson and Boeing's ineptitude," says Robert (Bob) Alizart, who worked closely with him for most of that time and who has also retired.[4] This view is shared by most Airbus people, some of whom began worrying a few years ago that their own company had gotten just a little *too* comfortable—too willing to write Boeing off as a serious competitor. Boeing's commercial aircraft division, they knew, had always been and remains a reservoir of surpassing talent, of people who remain dedicated to building airplanes of the highest quality.

A great many of Boeing's gifted people, however, felt they had been let down by management, which in the late 1990s was taken over by a strongly risk-averse faction. This leadership was seen elsewhere in the company as having been narrowly focused on shareholder interests and reluctant to invest in new technology and new products. And since John McDonnell, the chairman, and Harry Stonecipher, the former CEO, are the largest individual stockholders, questions about motives, whether fair or unfair, were raised by people in and beyond Boeing.

"We are not the company we were fifteen years ago. We are a company very much focused on our shareholders." That comment was made as recently as February 9, 2005, by a senior vice president of Boeing. He and others always thought that putting product and customer support ahead of shareholder interests, as narrowly defined, was the best way to promote those interests.

"Boeing has struggled with the development work needed to take the company into the 21st century," said Tim Clark, president of Emirates, the Dubai airline that is one of the world's major buyers of long-haul aircraft. "Airbus," he told the *Financial Times* in January 2005, "has been braver, more brazen, more prepared to push the boat out. Boeing was more concerned about shareholder returns."[5]

ALL THAT WAS LARGELY TRUE, but the talk of Airbus's ascendancy or Boeing's irreversible slide was exaggerated and deeply misleading, as events occurring just a few months later would richly illustrate. These companies struggle for advantage in a business where a single transaction can and often does loosen an airframe maker's purchase on a major segment of the market. Handicapping long-term winners and losers is a dicey exercise. A new airplane may look highly promising in the conceptual phase, draw a fair amount of encouragement, make a promising entry into the market, and then flounder. Or it may succeed beyond reasonable expectations.

By committing itself to building a new middle-sized airplane in December 2003, Boeing's management softened the criticism. It had been far from obvious that management and the board would decide in favor of the new product. The skepticism in-house and beyond didn't then go away, but was less pronounced and disconcerting than before the decision.

Boeing got lucky—very lucky—with this new airplane. It had flirted for two years with a conceptually silly plane that did not arouse the interest of even one of the world's airlines. Corporate management, which over a decade had gotten most things wrong, then decided, without much enthusiasm, in favor of a fundamentally different variant that should have been the choice from the beginning, because it was just the right airplane—one that offered Boeing a clear path back to the middle market.

In the spring of 2005 Boeing began making inroads on Airbus's customer base by selling this new airplane, the 787, in large numbers and selling it to carriers that Airbus was counting on to help sustain its hold on the middle market. In June, Air Canada's chief executive, Robert Milton, called the airplane "a game changer." Not long before, he had appeared in an Airbus sales video saying that any carrier flying non-Airbus planes would be "left in the dust."[6]

The 787 was still a "paper airplane" then, not yet out of the larval stage and not scheduled for delivery to customer airlines until the summer of 2008. However, in outline it impressed all sides, and its early success in the market indicated that Boeing had a winner, *if* the production phase proceeded without a serious stumble. Company morale improved, and so did shareholder returns.

Then, seemingly overnight, the sharp turnabout in Boeing's fortunes was bolstered by a sea of troubles that befell Airbus on multiple fronts. These surfaced publicly in the run-up to the Paris Air Show in mid-June 2005. Airbus was compelled to announce then that the first deliveries of the A380 superjumbo would be delayed up to six months—from mid-2006 until early 2007. Airbus, it appeared, needed more time in which to align this huge airplane with the specifications and performance guaranties that had been promised. But delaying deliveries was likely to cost the company tens of millions of dollars in penalties owed to customer airlines.

The costs to Airbus were underlined by Chew Choon Seng, Singapore Airlines' chief executive. "The late delivery," he said, "extremely disrupts our capacity planning. Preparations were ready for the training of pilots, flight attendants and technicians. I am not going to get into a fight with Airbus. . . . I am a serious client. And I would like to think that Airbus is a serious company. Unless, of course, Airbus wants to send me a signal that I shouldn't buy a single aircraft from them again . . . according to our contract, we are entitled to compensation. It is comparable to a taxi ride: the longer the ride, the more it costs. Each additional month delay will be more expensive for Airbus."[7]

Then, Airbus had to disclose another painful postponement, this one the launch of a new airplane whose design hadn't been settled on but was already being offered to airlines as a rival to the 787. The postponement, reflecting as it did an apparently soft market for this paper airplane, was an embarrassing setback. The talk was that the company's engineering resources were so taken up by the A380 that it wasn't ready to take on a new and highly advanced project.

Worse yet, perhaps, the leadership of EADS, Airbus's parent company, was imploding. Over a period of several months preceding the air show, senior French and German officials, not to mention boardroom heavyweights, had been quarreling bitterly. The parties were supposed to have coequal roles. EADS has two co–chief executives and two co-chairmen. However, the Germans saw the French as engaged in trying to seize de facto control.

Noel Forgeard, Pierson's successor at Airbus, had been chosen by the French at the end of 2004 to become the next co–chief executive of EADS. However, Forgeard, with strong encouragement from French president Jacques Chirac, was lobbying hard to replace the dual-management system with a single CEO, namely himself. Forgeard had at one stage served as Chirac's industrial adviser.

The Germans dug in their heels, not because they were opposed to having a single CEO but because they felt that Forgeard was overplaying his political connections in Paris and because they didn't think he was the right choice. Instead, DaimlerChrysler was believed to have favored an arrangement whereby Philippe Camus, a highly regarded French joint CEO of EADS who lost a bruising public battle with Forgeard and was ousted, would have become its sole chief executive. In turn, a senior executive from DaimlerChrysler would have been named sole chairman of EADS.

Around this time, Forgeard made a point of saying that the effort to block his bid for unitary leadership amounted to a vicious struggle by others to acquire the role he sought. He spoke of having just reread the memoirs of Saint-Simon, with its tales of intrigue and struggles for advantage in the court of Louis XIV. The campaign against him, he said, was orchestrated by a small Parisian clique (presumably supporters of Camus) operating between "the Café Flore [on the Boulevard Saint-Germain] and Fouquets restaurant" (on the Champs-Elysées) and a similar gathering place in Munich.[8]

Neither side gave way. The impasse became the most acute of Airbus's midyear embarrassments and a deeply disruptive internal problem. EADS-Airbus appeared to be bereft of coherent decision-making procedures. In late June 2005, the management battle was settled. It was agreed that Forgeard and Thomas Enders, the head of the EADS defense division, would of become co–chief executives of EADS. The balance of nationalities would be maintained. Or so it seemed. It appeared to be a victory for Chirac: not only had his favorite, Forgeard, survived, but the division of labor left him presiding over Airbus.

Much of what lay behind the outcome probably had more to do with France's resounding *non* to the European Union's constitution than to the merits or the strengths of the personalities. For Chirac, who had campaigned strongly for it, this rejection was a stunning setback. To have lost ground to the Germans over the EADS-Airbus management issue immediately thereafter would have been a second political blow that his German partners were reluctant to deliver. Moreover, while the two parties are equal partners, the French continue to regard Airbus as a fiefdom.

A year later, in June 2006, the issue of corporate governance flared up again as the second and more injurious crisis involving the A380 struck Airbus/EADS. The production problems that were slowing down the program and that management should have disposed of had become enmeshed in cross-border politics and political infighting. This time, Forgeard was in the crosshairs, especially after he initially sought to hang the blame on the German factories, then, under pressure, included a French site in his critique, and still later expressed regret at having said anything at all.

Even worse for Forgeard, the storm broke amid revelations that three months earlier he had exercised options to sell EADS shares worth 2.5 million euros ($3.4 million). Three of his children also sold shares at the same time, as did two board members. Talk of insider trading ensued, and, predictably, an investigation was launched.

The gallery was less interested in whether Forgeard would be proved culpable than in when he would leave and who would replace him. Although he struggled to stay on, Chirac, quite clearly, couldn't continue to protect him. And so on July 2, eight years after Pierson's departure, his deeply flawed successor did go at last. However, the binational equlibrium held. The *Wall Street Journal* reported that "because decision-making power is split between French and German shareholders, the French side will request that a German executive [also] be dismissed. If Mr. Forgeard steps down . . . Airbus chairman Gustav Humbert could pay the price of such bargaining."[9] And he did. Humbert took responsibility for the A380 fiasco, although he had inherited the production problems from Forgeard.

Forgeard was replaced by Louis Gallois, chairman of SNCF, France's national railroad company, and a member of the board of EADS. Before then, he had been chairman of Snecma, the French aero-engine company. Humbert's successor at Airbus was Christian Streiff, a former chief operating officer of the Saint-Gobain Group, the glass and building materials group. Streiff had no previous experience in his new trade. Tom Enders would remain co–chief executive of EADS.

Gallois, like Forgeard, is politically astute, but his focus isn't politics. Nor is it money and position. He is seen as a safe pair of hands and, unlike Forgeard, personally disinterested. Both are products of France's so-called *grandes écoles,* and both belong to a hierarchy, but one that doesn't bend easily to dynamic change and does have a statist tendency. Gallois is seen on all sides as blending decency with relevant experience. But at sixty-one, he is within three years of mandatory retirement and hence a transitional figure.

Within and beyond Airbus, the crisis seemed to present a golden opportunity to put an end to the politics and infighting and to streamline the company's leadership. Instead, the uneasy French-German combine sustained what amounts to a corporate anomaly, dual sovereigns with limited commercial reach.

The changes appear to portend no less political tension of distrust between them. DaimlerChrysler, the single largest EADS shareholder, with 22.5 percent, is worrying aloud about interference by the French government, which has a 15 percent share and is said to be pressing to enlarge its right to intervene in company affairs. Tom Enders, the German co–chief executive of EADS, knows the military side, not the commercial. But he has insisted that Streiff report directly to him, not to Gallois, who does know the commercial side.

Enders wants to integrate Airbus more closely with EADS, and from his point of view, why not? Airbus is the engine that drives EADS, and Enders, along with various colleagues, wants to be sure that it is doing what they think it should be doing. But Airbus, not suprisingly, thinks that "integration" with EADS will kill the golden goose.

If asked how best to operate within the current management structure, numerous Airbus people would say: "We need someone who knows the commercial aircraft industry as well as anyone and is trusted in the places that matter." Some of them, along with many Airbus watchers, do not hesitate to suggest that Jean Pierson comes closest to fitting these criteria. A decision to return Pierson to Toulouse with full control of Airbus would stretch but not exceed the political tolerances of the dual sovereigns. Although he is French, he was always seen first and foremost as a company man, and he was widely respected in relevant German circles. Having him back might be the best way to restore the company's strategic focus, not to mention customer confidence. Airbus continues to live off his product line—his legacy.

Would Pierson do it? Alizart, who for many years was Pierson's executive assistant and confidant says, "He might, provided he could set a limit of no more than two years on his term and would be reporting to Gallois."[10] Reached in Corsica, Pierson says that he would not have considered coming back, citing age as the reason. "I am over sixty-five," he said. "That is too old." And he does seem comfortable with the changes made at the top. "Gallois," he said, "is a friend." And he had heard good reports about Streiff, whom he was planning to see in a few days. Quite clearly, Pierson is going to be consulted regularly, and he seems happy to be reengaged but in a nonstressful role.[11]

IN JUNE 2005, with the management issue in play, Boeing gave the edgy partners in the French and German combine a strong reason to begin trusting each other and doing something sensible. Just one week after Forgeard's narrow escape, Boeing named a new leader, W. James McNerney, the highly regarded chairman and chief executive of 3M (Minnesota Mining and Manufacturing Co.). McNerney, then fifty-five, is a native of Providence, Rhode Island, who did his undergraduate work at Yale and went on to the Harvard Business School.

Boeing had wanted McNerney to become its leader for the long term and had pursued him unsuccessfully for some time. After periodically saying no to Boeing, once publicly, and insisting that he wanted to remain at 3M, McNerney changed his mind and took the job. He then said, "I was reluctant to leave 3M after only 4½ years with a great management team in place, but Boeing is such a special company in an industry I love. I figured I might never have another opportunity to run a company so crucial to the U.S. economy. The timing just seemed to be right."[12]

Boeing rejoiced. In various jobs over the years, including management of GE's aeroengine group, McNerney had made a uniformly strong and favorable impression on the aircraft industry and beyond. Indeed, within GE, he had been expected to succeed Jack Welch. But in 2000, Welch, a poor judge of talent by most accounts, instead chose Jeffrey R. Immelt. McNerney then left and became the first outsider to run 3M.

Although McNerney's decision to take the Boeing job surprised the industry, a few of those who knew him best had expected it. One of them was Bob Conboy, who had worked closely with McNerney in the GE jet engine unit. "I think that in the end Jim will take the job," he said several weeks before the event. "He knows he's qualified and can do it. And given his age, he will see the job as the last big challenge he will face."[13]

As he had been at 3M, McNerney became the first outsider to run the Boeing Company. And he had acquired broader business experience both within and beyond the industry than his predecessors there. "A corporate superstar," said the *Seattle Times* in its report on the appointment. On June 30, the day McNerney's decision was announced, investors sent Boeing's share price up $4.29, or 7 percent, to close at a four-year high. On the same day, 3M's share price fell $3.74, or 4.9 percent.

Perhaps better than anyone, McNerney would be able to set about ridding Boeing's corporate culture of the mold that had set in over the past decade. In Toulouse a year earlier, John Leahy, an American who is a senior vice president of Airbus and the remarkably successful director of its sales operations, talked about Boeing's quest for a leader and the possible candidates, starting with McNerney. "We light candles in the hope that he stays at 3M," Leahy said.

Cautionary voices within Airbus who had warned at about that time, when the company was riding high, against reading too much into its good news had turned out to be right. One of them was Jean Pierson. In June 2004, retired and sitting on his boat in Corsica, he said, "Arrogance has changed camps now. It is in Toulouse. But it is harder to be number one and easier to chase number one. Our product strategy was easy, because there was nothing to protect. When you have a full product line it is different. Do you protect what you have, or do you build a new airplane. Do I protect? Or do I invest?"[14]

One year later, in almost the same words, Henri Courpron, who was then president and CEO of Airbus North America and is now senior vice president for procurement and a figure who resembles Pierson in attitude and style, said: "We failed to manage being number one. We told ourselves it would be more difficult to be number one than to try to be that. And we were right. It is more difficult. The problem in managing a lead is that you look back, not forward. We got caught looking back. When we killed the 767 with the A330, Boeing began looking ahead. We didn't."[15]

CHAPTER TWO

Trading Places

THE THINKING THAT SHAPES air travel has changed, as have the companies that are most directly involved with it. Besides Boeing and Airbus, they include the suppliers of smaller regional aircraft, the airlines of the world, and the three big engine makers—GE Aircraft Engines, Rolls-Royce, and Pratt & Whitney (United Technologies).

Their ritual mantra used to be HIGHER, FASTER, FARTHER. Airbus actually affixed a sticker with those three words on the tails of several A320's earmarked for United Airlines. (In the early 1990s, Airbus surprised itself, not to mention Boeing, by selling these airplanes to its competitor's most conspicuously loyal customer.) Not long afterward, however, the fashion began to change. The premium on speed, for example, shifted to an outcry for *efficiency,* a euphemism used by airlines that were beset by difficulties and were insisting on airplanes that cost less to operate. High-speed flight, it seemed, was strictly for the military. Airlines couldn't make a living that way. The demise of the Concorde proved it, as had the failure of Boeing's Sonic Cruiser program in 2002.

Holding down "seat mile costs" meant designing airplanes with the right number of seats for certain airlines and their route structures, thereby maximizing the chances of being able to fill these seats with customers. It meant blending airframes and engines in a way that would control fuel burn and produce other economies.

Boeing and Airbus are both bent on shoring up positions in the section of the market where each is weakest (or not even present). With its behemoth, the A380, Airbus has challenged Boeing's long-run dominance in the so-called very-large-aircraft market that the 747 had provided. And Boeing, after an absence of fifteen or so years from its core business, is developing another market-driven better mousetrap. The company's radically different new airplane was at first called the 7E7, the *E* standing for "efficiency." It was then rechristened the 787, a more logical designation for a stable mate of Boeing's first long-haul jet airliner, the 707, and its latest, the 777. Many Boeing executives studiously refer to the 787 as the Dreamliner, an artful nickname that a few of Airbus's public relations people admit to envying and even worrying about.

The 787 is intended to erase Airbus's huge advantage in the medium-range segment of the airline market, partly by offering lower operating costs than today's other airplanes. The 787, Boeing says, is based on a new approach that will keep design and production costs low and improve the fuel and aerodynamic efficiency of the plane. The 787 will also heighten comfort by offering larger windows and higher humidity in the cabins. It will be a "game changer," Boeing people say. They could be right.

Development costs are uncertain but will be high. A figure of $8 billion has been waved around by Boeing, but that has to be a lowball estimate, since the less advanced 777, the company's last LCA, is judged to have cost nearly $14 billion to develop. But Boeing left itself a hard choice: either quit the commercial aircraft business altogether or build a very advanced airplane, one that would appeal strongly to a wide variety of airline customers.

Going forward with the Dreamliner, said Walter Gillette, who was then Boeing's vice president for engineering, "is the biggest step we have taken in 50 years."[1] With this airplane, Boeing has radically altered—indeed revolutionized—its approach to designing, building, and financing new products. Its role is that of "systems integrator," coordinating the design and development efforts of a group of largely non-U.S. partners.

Never before had Boeing outsourced the responsibility for a wing; the wing and the flight deck are the clever parts of any airframe. "We Build Wings," Boeing once proclaimed to the world. It regarded itself, probably correctly, as without peer in designing wings and building them within tight budgetary constraints, a prowess of which T. Wilson was manifestly proud.

That was then, however. The major responsibilities for designing and building the 787 wing have been outsourced to Japan. Together, three Japanese companies, backed by their government, are at least as directly involved in building the 787 as Boeing itself. They are known as the "three heavies." Mitsubishi Heavy Industries is doing a large part of the work on the wing, along with Fuji Heavy Industries, which will build the center wing box and integrate the wings with the plane's landing gear. Kawasaki Heavy Industries is building a section of the fuselage behind the cockpit as well as the trailing edges of the wings.[2]

Briefly, Japan is becoming a risk-sharing partner responsible for creating 35 percent of Boeing's first new airplane in thirteen years. In addition, Italy's chief aerospace firm, Alenia, and an American company, Vought, are doing much of the work on the fuselage panels.

Japan's role is controversial. Boeing's engineers are in the main hostile to "farming out tribal knowledge," as some of them put it. The Japanese have never built a wing for a big airliner, and no one has developed a wing box made of composites for such an airplane. Actually, Boeing says, half of the 787's primary structure, including the entire fuselage, will be built of composites, an industry first.

Composites are a class of materials that include fiberglass, Kevlar, and other fibers, notably carbon fiber. These are held in shape by a hardened resin, usually epoxy. The composites offer advantages: they are lighter and stronger; they don't corrode or fatigue as metal does. The 787's fuselage skin will be a single piece of layered carbon fiber reinforced plastic (or CFRP) in place of several hundred sheets of aluminum. CFRP will also be used to build the floor beams, and the frames from nose to tail. Most of the center section of the airplane's wing will be made of CFRP as well. This section is considered the "keystone" that holds the airplane together. The outboard wing box, the airplane's strongest structure, will be made mostly of CFRP. Other parts of the 787—too numerous to mention—will be built with composites too.

"Building a wing is an art," says Gordon McKinzie, who for many years managed United Airlines' new technology division and was closely involved in his company's selection of new aircraft, most of them Boeings. "Building it out of a new material is a major challenge. If anyone told a Boeing guy a few years ago the company would try it, he'd have said, 'Over my dead body.' And I never thought I'd see the day when Boeing was farming out the engineering. Boeing hates losing control. It used to be called a schedule-driven company."[3]

In the past, Boeing's approach to building its airplanes was conservative, pragmatic, and self-sustaining. Besides the wing, however, Boeing is depending on suppliers, European and American, along with Japan's heavies, to build several of the 787's other sections. In outsourcing, Boeing is really doing what once would have been unthinkable: copying the Airbus model. But Airbus has made a virtue of necessity. None of its member countries possessed a major American-size aerospace company. But each of its companies insists on having a share in building the airplanes. So Airbus has spent close to thirty-five years creating a network of suppliers and coordinating it. And at least half of Airbus's A350 will consist of composites, although of a different and less challenging type than Boeing is using.

Instead of building its new airplanes, Boeing will assemble their various parts. Close to 70 percent of the 787's parts are being made outside the United States. Most of them will be conveyed to the Puget Sound area in huge cargo aircraft. Boeing expects to be able to snap the parts together in just three days.

AIRBUS AND ESPECIALLY Boeing each gambled massively on two new airplanes that represent radically different approaches to the market. There is probably no precedent for such a divergence. The A380, because it can carry a huge number of passengers, is designed to fit within the hub-and-spoke pattern of air travel that the big airlines have favored. An A380 could take 550 passengers from Tokyo to, say, Los Angeles or New York, where many of them would then transfer to flights going to Denver, Phoenix, Cleveland, and so on. And, Airbus argues, this superjumbo airplane will be cheaper to operate than other aircraft, partly because it will burn less fuel per passenger. Its operating costs are expected to be 15 percent below those of Boeing's 747.

Boeing had the better strategy. Until recently, an airplane's range was equated with its size; the bigger it was, the farther it was expected to travel. But with today's more advanced technology, that needn't be the case. Boeing's 787 will carry half as many passengers as the A380 between cities set equally far apart, but will carry them *directly* from one point to another—from Tokyo, say, to Denver, Phoenix, or Cleveland—with no intermediate stop in a hub airport.

In arguing that its Dreamliner is more responsive to current market trends than the A380, Boeing is right. Flying on a double-aisle airplane eighty-five hundred miles point to point—rather than from one hub to another and then transferring, which lengthens travel time for passengers bound for smaller places—is certain to have a strong appeal for travelers, especially those who can afford to pay for that convenience. They can also avoid the risks of missing a connecting flight or losing a bag.

Boeing also feels that it can benefit from what seems to be a trend toward small airplanes. Jeff Shane, undersecretary of the U.S. Department of Transportation, notes the vast and growing array of regional aircraft, as well as business and private jets. "I see a sky darkened by dentists," he says half seriously.[4]

As for the leviathan, the A380, it may be too big for today's market, or may have come along too soon. The Airbus claim is that this new airplane and the thinking behind it will be fully vindicated over a period of five to twenty years. With airline traffic expected to triple over the next twenty years (also Boeing's estimate), Airbus argues that a super-jumbo-sized platform will be the only sensible way to move so many people. There probably won't be any new airports at the major hub cities or more room to expand existing facilities; the carriers will be unable to schedule more flights into the existing space, the reasoning goes, since airports can absorb only so many takeoffs and landings in one day; indeed, air traffic control is said to be saturated in most large airports.

Right now, one in every nine flights at Heathrow, for years the world's busiest international airport, is made by a 747 jumbo. But introduction of the bigger A380 will supposedly allow 10 million more passengers to fly to and from the airport with no increase in flights. Boeing disagrees, arguing that the A380 flights between major hubs won't reduce congestion because they will create large networks of connecting flights.

Another Airbus argument is that thanks to new technologies, the A380 will take up less landing and takeoff space than the 747 even though it is bigger. Not only was it designed to fit into all the same airports, it will fit into the eighty-meter box on runways that is a standard airport requirement.

The market for the A380 is believed to lie mainly in Asia. Singapore, Hong Kong, Shanghai, Taipei, Sydney, Seoul, and perhaps Tokyo are expected by Airbus to become hubs connecting fully loaded A380 flights to London and New York. Gradually, some of those cities will be served by A380 flights to other major cities, including Los Angeles.

Airbus people concede that the 787 should be a very successful airplane. And it will be if Boeing's radical business plan for the venture leads to deliveries of the plane close enough to contractually agreed specifications and close enough to contractually agreed delivery dates.

In the end, both new ventures may succeed, even if there have never been two such different airplanes competing in an airline market that is even more chaotic than usual.

IN DECIDING to build the 787, Boeing was behaving, in effect, as the company had in its braver days. Its calculation was that starting in 2008, when the 787 would be available, Airbus would be competing against it with the A330-200, the very airplane that had ousted Boeing from the middle market. But by then, that airplane would be middle-aged, offering less range and fewer technology-related sweeteners than the 787.

Boeing got Airbus's full attention. The 787's operating costs seemed certain to be lower than those of any other airplane, chiefly because a new state-of-the-art engine, along with the composites and the airframe's shape, would cut those costs substantially. And for the first time in fifteen years or so, Airbus reacted to Boeing. Competing against the 787 would oblige Airbus to fashion a better midsize airplane of its own. The question was, how much better? Would investing in an improved version of the A330-200 be enough? Or would the market snub a derivative and show a strong preference for two new look-alike airplanes, one of which might kill the other? Inevitably, there began to be talk of the fratricidal conflict that Lockheed and McDonnell Douglas had brought on with the L-1011 and the DC-10.

A simple derivative appeared to offer some advantages. It could be powered by new engines of the kind Boeing would be hanging on the 787 and thereby cut fuel costs. But with fewer of the 787's less basic refinements, a new Airbus could have been offered to airlines at a more attractive price, possibly for as much as $20 million or so less per copy. Also, this improved version of an existing airplane, the A330-200, would have had far less lead time than a wholly new model. It might have been available no more than a year later than the 787, or even around the same time if the 787's progress lagged, as seemed quite possible.

On December 10, 2004, Airbus made known its intention to begin offering the new Airbus, christened the A350, to launch customers. The announcement was made by Noel Forgeard, who was still CEO at the time. Among the points he could plausibly make was that the A350 "is in the unique position of being a full member of a comprehensive airliner family, hence benefiting from an unmatched level of commonalty." Forgeard was reminding potential customers that commonalty saves money all around, and in this case should further improve prospects for shortening the A350's lead time. It could also shorten the complex process of getting a new airplane certified by government agencies as airworthy. Airbus reckoned, or hoped, that a big part of its customer base would choose the A350 over the 787, both because of the commonalty issue and because sibling aircraft in the A320 and A330 families had given satisfaction.

Still, the case for a derivative was far from obvious. A choice that confronts suppliers relentlessly is whether to create a new airplane or build an improved version—a derivative—of an existing model. The clear preference among experienced Airbus and Boeing people is for the higher-cost option—new equipment. The biggest gain, they say, is made with "a clean sheet of paper," the industry's standard term for an airplane that isn't "backward compatible," a term used by aeroengineers. A new model normally offers better technology and improved fuel economy. It is likely to have more credibility but not to have an expensive heritage. And it can be harder to justify the costs of changing an existing production line.

Boeing had hoped to book two hundred or so firm orders for the 787 before the end of 2004. It sold just eighty-six, fifty to All Nippon Airways (ANA), the launch customer, and thirty to Japan Airlines, an order completed just before the end of the year. By then, however, Airbus was using the A350 to play with the heads of airlines. Exactly what sort of airplane would its A350 be? What Airbus was talking about appeared to be neither a clean sheet of paper nor an improved A330-200, but instead a blend of both. The blend, however, lacked definition. In what direction was Airbus tilting?

The cutting edge of the Boeing-Airbus competition had shifted to Asia several years before, and Boeing counted on various airlines in the Near East and Far East to buy the Dreamliner. They, unlike most of their European and American counterparts, could afford the airplane. And it was—is—a good fit for the route structures of several Asian carriers. But, they all wondered, might not the A350 be an equally good fit, or almost as good, and, given the Airbus family's commonalty, have fewer teething problems? And might not the A350 arrive with a better price?

Airbus wasn't dispensing much hard information, just enough to raise questions of that kind. "Guerrilla marketing" was a term used by some analysts to describe the tactic. But it caused airlines in Asia and elsewhere to hesitate. They wanted to be able to compare the pros and cons of buying Boeing's new midrange airplane with the features of the almost new Airbus.

As always, the airlines wanted two suppliers competing head-to-head. If one supplier, in this case Airbus, hadn't filled in the outline of its airplane, most of the carriers were willing to stand by until it did. So Airbus dribbled out the vital data, and the airlines on Boeing's wish list waited, although not very long in most cases. They began by making clear their aversion to a warmed-over A330. Next, they snubbed a better version that would have a new wing and a few other enhancements. What the carriers wanted was an airplane they could advertise as "newer than new," as "state of the art." Airbus was scrambling to create something—ideally, a new aircraft of a size and capability close to that of the 787 but with fewer costly refinements. The stakes could hardly be higher, especially for Airbus. It had begun to take too much for granted.

FOR MOST of the past twenty years, a tooth-and-claw battle for the single-aisle-airplane market has held center stage in the Airbus-Boeing saga. It set Airbus's A320 family against Boeing's 737's. The success of low-cost carriers such as Southwest and JetBlue in the States, along with easyJet and others in Europe, raised the stakes. For Boeing, an especially bad patch began in 1998, when British Airways, until then an unswervingly loyal Boeing customer, decided against the 737 and instead bought fifty-nine Airbus A320 and A319 aircraft, with options for fifty-nine more. (The A319 is a slightly smaller version of the A320.)

"There was a massive press," said Christopher Buckley, an Airbus executive who tracked the event from the start. "The announcement was the lead story on the front page of the *International Herald Tribune*, probably the only time in history that an aircraft order has been deemed the top news item of the day in a major worldwide newspaper."[5]

The most closely involved figure from British Airways was John Patterson, a senior vice president. "It was a strategic decision and more secondarily a customer services decision," he said. "There had been a dreadful breakdown in relations with Airbus in the early 1990s, and we were worried that if we didn't send a signal that we were prepared to bury the hatchet, we wouldn't be able to generate competition between the two companies—Boeing and Airbus."[6]

However, the senior management of British Airways, a group of eleven executives known as "the football team," regarded the choice as so important that it wanted a face-off of the two airplanes. Boeing and Airbus agreed. According to Buckley, the face-off occurred in the spring of 1998, with the team present. "The Airbus candidate," he said, "was an A319 flown into Heathrow by a Swiss charter carrier, and Boeing's was a 737-700 awaiting delivery to a German charter. The Airbus team withdrew and allowed the BA people to look over the cabin of the A319 with the Swiss flight attendants showing them the storage bins and describing the comfort factors from their point of view. This relaxed approach compared to the Boeing sales team's more aggressive approach seemed to work in Airbus's favor."[7]

That same year, JetBlue Airways also surprised all sides, especially Boeing, by choosing the A320 over the 737. In announcing the decision, David Neeleman, JetBlue's founder and CEO, said, "The A320 aircraft allows us to offer wider seats, more legroom, and more overhead storage space than any other aircraft in its class." JetBlue became the first low-cost carrier to begin life with a brand-new airplane.

Everyone, starting with Neeleman himself, had expected him to buy the 737, the airplane he knew best. His model was Southwest Airlines—the most successful airline, the biggest user of 737's, and his former employer. "John Owen, our CFO, had been at Southwest and bought their 737's," Neeleman says. "We knew nothing about the A320. Our business plan mentioned only the 737's.

"We went to Boeing. In Seattle, we offered a fair number. We didn't expect to get the same deal—as good a deal—as others [older customers], but we expected to be within shouting distance. We wanted to shake hands on it that day.

"They said our price was too low, not an aggressive price. We then began talking with Airbus. The Boeing people smirked and said, 'You will never buy those airplanes.' And the Airbus people thought we weren't serious and said we were using them as a foil [to drive down the price of the 737's].

"We sent operating teams to airlines that were using both aircraft—United, America West, and BA. None of them was buying more 737's. They were all moving toward A320's. We went back to Boeing, and they came down in their price—came down below our first price." It didn't matter. JetBlue had decided to buy Airbus.

Neeleman was influenced by the nose-to-nose face-off that BA had conducted. Relying on that and other reviews of the two airplanes, he says, JetBlue considered the A320 to have been ahead in all the ways that mattered to his airline. He cited the wider seats and generally higher comfort level. "We bought the airplane for no other reasons than because it was the right product," he says.

"Boeing," he continued, "should have started over with the 737, incorporated the good features of the 777 and various Airbus products. It might have cost a billion dollars, but that would have been better than dealing with a twenty-year-old fuselage."[8] (Actually, it was a thirty-year-old fuselage.)

Opinion within industry circles was that Airbus prevailed in this case only because Boeing's arrogance and tendency to take smaller players for granted alienated JetBlue's team, starting with Neeleman. That view is openly shared by several Boeing people.

Boeing usually attributed an Airbus victory to a capability made possible by government subsidies to underprice Boeing. And that, in some cases, was the reason. An example was the sale of A319's to the low-cost European carrier easyJet in October 2002. Christopher Walton, its finance director, says, "We began with the same view that other low-cost carriers had: Boeing's 737 was the workhorse. Our thinking drew on the Southwest experience with the airplane. We evaluated the 737 and the A319, and after nearly a year we decided they were equal—different operationally in some ways but for our purposes equal. Since our business relies heavily on quick turnarounds, we had to be sure the A319 would fit our business model. It did.

"We put out a blind tender. Boeing didn't seem serious until it realized that Airbus was a contender. [How could Boeing not have heard by then?] At that point, it was all about price, price, and price." Walton confirmed what Neeleman and other airline people said about the wider body cylinder of the A320 allowing more comfort and bigger cargo bins. "But," he said, "it was nonetheless about price."[9]

An Airbus executive, now retired, confirmed that version. "This easyJet sale was very important to us," he said. "We had to get over that hurdle—a low-cost operator that wanted to succeed like Southwest and fly Boeing 737's. So Airbus did whatever it took to make certain that its price would be lower than Boeing's."[10]

By that time, Airbus and Boeing were widely assumed to be cutting their catalog prices for these single-aisle airplanes by 40 percent or more. Beyond that, there might be further concessionary pricing, depending on how important a particular deal was judged by one of the companies.

In a brief period spanning the last two months of 2004 and the first two of 2005, Airbus and Boeing made a great deal of news. A succession of campaigns lost to Airbus in the low-cost airline market led to a shake-up of the Boeing sales force in early December 2004. Toby Bright, the senior sales executive, was replaced by Scott Carson, a well-regarded manager who had held various key jobs within Boeing Commercial Airplanes.

Carson's path, it seemed, would be uphill and strewn with obstacles, starting with Boeing's disordered corporate culture and a management that in recent years had become skittish about the commercial aircraft sector. The company's major operational problem had been too much bureaucracy, especially in its sales operations—one heard that in the United States, in Europe, and in Asian cities, including Beijing and Shanghai. "Boeing is too bureaucratic, much more so than Airbus," says the vice president for China of a major U.S. company. "The Boeing sales force here is American, not Chinese," he continued. "The Airbus sales force is Chinese. So is mine. The Boeing guys say they have to go to Seattle in order to push internally for the right decisions."[11]

"They fly in from Seattle," says a senior Boeing vice president. "We don't have nearly enough resident salesmen. And those we have in these places are more junior than they should be. If they are any good, the Seattle guys tend to cut them out."[12]

On December 23, 2004, the *Wall Street Journal* led the newspaper with an uncommonly long, uncommonly severe, and very well informed piece on Boeing's efforts to stay even with Airbus. It cited several of Boeing's deficiencies, starting with its sales force and a deeply flawed approach to selling airplanes.[13]

The article created a huge buzz in industry circles and throughout the wider world of industry watchers. Harry Stonecipher, who was Boeing's CEO and is now retired, reacted defensively, but he also told some senior Boeing people that the piece was mostly accurate—"about ninety-eight percent accurate," he told members of his entourage.[14]

Several at Boeing joined in endorsing the *Journal* article. "It partially lifted the curtain on the company's stunning incompetence in selling and marketing airplanes," said one executive.

An airline that wants to buy just three or four airplanes is in the enviable position of pitting Airbus against Boeing in what can resemble a life-or-death struggle. How, then, given the stakes, could Boeing's management tolerate such weakness and disarray in its sales operations? If Harry Stonecipher could acknowledge the validity of the *Journal* article, why hadn't he done something about the problems it described?

Or, more to the point, why hadn't Alan Mulally fixed some of these problems? He had been president and chief executive of Boeing Commercial Airplanes since 1998, and before that had been a senior vice president of the company for many years. Starting in 1999, Airbus overtook Boeing in annual orders; it booked more orders in 2001, and beginning in 2003 has delivered more aircraft.

Asked if he had considered firing Mulally, Stonecipher said, "Yes. Sometimes it's hard to get Alan's attention. We had a come to Jesus session. I got his attention."[15]

The article had quoted the aircraft industry's preeminent buyer of airplanes as saying, "Boeing's senior management is going to have to roll up their sleeves and really get competitive or they will be strengthening the perception they are conceding the market leadership to Airbus." The voice was that of Steven Udvar-Hazy, founder and boss of the International Lease Finance Corporation (ILFC), the biggest buyer of both Boeing and Airbus aircraft.

Those Boeing executives who applauded the *Journal* piece deplore their company's insistence on referring decisions to committees. "It's not that way at Airbus," one of them complained. "An Airbus guy can get an answer immediately and rarely has to bring in one of the top guns. Also, the Airbus people have more authority because they are higher-level guys. Customers can raise a question with Airbus and get an answer immediately. Its people have easy access to the top management. The Boeing process is very complicated."[16]

THEN CAME THE LOSS of another "all-Boeing airline" to Airbus. It was Air Berlin, also a low-cost operator, and Germany's number-two airline; it had built its business around Boeing's 737. Air Berlin's CEO, Joachim Hunold, spent eleven months negotiating with Boeing in an effort to get some flexibility in the price. "Boeing," he says, "never thought we would go to the competition and they took us for granted. That's a dangerous thing to do when your competitor is so strong."[17]

Commenting on the lost deal, Stonecipher said, "The long and short of it is we are not engaging with the customers. We don't seem to have a strategy." He also noted that Boeing had done "a couple of stupid things and treated the airline's CEO in such a way that it headed him in the wrong direction."[18]

The list of deals won by Airbus and lost by Boeing was an impressive and lengthening one. Boeing was losing, in part at least, because the airlines' management in many, possibly most, cases felt as if it had been taken for granted. The company suffers from what one of its executives calls "residual arrogance."[19] An equally appropriate term for this tendency would be "persistent denial."

In a competition involving two airplanes with little to choose between them, winning is likely to depend on strict adherence to first principles, one of which is paying unstinting attention to the customer's interests, large and small. Another is finding the right moment in the campaign to cut the price of your airplane. In the Air Berlin campaign, as in so many others in recent years, Boeing neglected both these principles.

According to the *Journal* article, Joachim Hunold, "fed up" with Boeing, "flew to Airbus's headquarters in Toulouse . . . [and] after a 90-minute meeting over lunch with top executives . . . shook hands on a $7 billion deal for up to 110 single-aisle planes."[20] (They were A320's.) One also heard this version of events from disaffected Boeing people.

However, it doesn't square with Airbus's better-informed account, one that comes much closer to portraying the ups and downs in a not untypical sales campaign. An executive in Toulouse who was directly involved in the Air Berlin deal says, "Sadly, I have never known a deal just to 'fall into our lap.' The *Journal* article missed out on the eighteen-plus months that we had spent marketing the A320 family at Air Berlin. Back in early 2003, we began to sense that Boeing was treating Air Berlin as a captive customer who wouldn't even dream of ever changing from their 737-800's. We steadily worked on our relationships with the airline's management, and also on convincing them that the A320 could be a very real alternative.

"We made a fairly aggressive proposal in late 2003, which we then improved early the next year. Quite simply, I think Boeing misjudged the timing of when to make the right counterproposal—they just weren't convinced that Air Berlin would go for Airbus under any circumstances. Air Berlin became exasperated with Boeing's belief that there was no urgency to make any significant changes to their proposals.

"With much of our marketing and technical work completed, I strongly urged Joachim Hunold of Air Berlin . . . to come to Toulouse to meet Noel Forgeard and see if we could finalize an opportunistic deal. This is exactly what we did last May. We shook hands on a preliminary agreement.

"Knowing no definitive contract was signed, Boeing—completely caught by surprise—then did everything possible to win back Air Berlin. By October, their unit price for the [larger] 737-800 had actually become cheaper than our agreed terms for the A320. We had a very tough time hanging on to our deal and finally signing the contract [in November], but Hunold was a man of his word—he had shaken hands with us back in May, and despite some difficult negotiations, kept his side of the bargain."[21]

For Boeing, this painful event virtually coincided with another, similar one. In mid-December, AirAsia, Malaysia's low-cost airline and one that had been an all-Boeing carrier, announced that it was buying eighty Airbus aircraft. AirAsia is the leading low-cost operator in the Asia-Pacific region and is expanding rapidly. Airbus, explained Tony Fernandes, its chief executive, "ran a fantastic campaign, really proactive: they had to go out and win because we were a Boeing operator."[22]

A month later, Boeing announced that it would take a $615 million pretax write-off, amounting to forty-eight cents a share. Nearly half of the losses arose from efforts to win a major military contract, while the rest involved various costs of closing the production line of the 717, Boeing's smallest airliner.

In Toulouse on January 18, Airbus formally rolled out its A380. It was a major media event, which the French rather breathlessly characterized as the "Reveal." Among the five thousand attendees who gathered before a football-field-sized hangar at the unveiling were France's president, Jacques Chirac; British prime minister Tony Blair; German chancellor Gerhard Schroeder; and José Luis Zapatero, Spain's prime minister. Chirac called the Reveal a milestone "on the path of European integration."

Ten days later, China Southern, the country's largest carrier, announced that it was buying five A380's, a long-awaited deal and one that Airbus saw as opening the huge Chinese market for its flagship. The deal was valued at $1.4 billion before discounts. Orders from other Chinese carriers were expected to follow. Nearly lost sight of was more good news—that China Southern was also buying twenty A330's, bringing sales to Chinese carriers of this popular workhorse to fifty-six.

But Airbus's news was obscured that day, at least in the United States, by another Reveal in the form of some even better, eagerly awaited news for Boeing: six Chinese airlines would be buying sixty 787's, another deal that had been hanging fire for several months and one worth $7.2 billion, again before the heavy discounts that the Chinese are able to insist on. The importance of this announcement could hardly be overstated. The success of the 787 program was judged to depend partly on how many would be sold in the Chinese market, for which the airplane was always judged an ideal fit.

The strategic thinking of both Airbus and Boeing is driven by the Asian market, starting with China; most industry watchers assume that sooner rather than later China will become the largest market for both long-haul aircraft and those designed for domestic use. It is currently ranked number four. Apropos, Boeing's good news became the occasion for the company to redesignate the 7E7 as the 787. But Boeing seems to have had another, possibly stronger motive for making the change and making it then. "Incorporating the eight at the time of the China order is . . . significant because in many Asian cultures the number eight represents good luck and prosperity," said Alan Mulally.[23]

The good news from China didn't altogether dispel doubts about Boeing's business plan for the 787. On the very day that the big Chinese purchase of the airplane was announced, Boeing was still unable to declare that it had a signed an industrial contract with its various risk-sharing partners, the three Japanese "heavies" plus Alenia and Vought. Mitsubishi Heavy, the presumed prime contractor for the airplane's wing, had not yet broken ground on the new plant in which the work would be done.

Still, within a few months of those end-of-the-year defections to Airbus by Boeing carriers, the notorious *Journal* piece, and related blows to Boeing's self-esteem, fortune pivoted abruptly in Boeing's direction. Bitterly hard fought campaigns that pitted the 787 against Airbus's A350 were won by Boeing, mainly because it was selling the best airplane and doing so very aggressively. In those spring months, Airbus was saying that Boeing's commercial operations were once again being sharply run. And the 787 had a useful effect on the company's entire product line, because it told the industry and the airlines that Boeing was still in the game.

The outset of the 787-A350 duel coincided with the worst of the strife and bitterness unleashed by bitter struggle between Boeing and Airbus and their governments over the subsidies Airbus got from its official patrons. All of this was happening at a time when both Boeing and Airbus were operating without chief executives. Boeing had cashiered Stonecipher, and Noel Forgeard was supposedly in transition from Toulouse to Paris—from Airbus to its parent company, EADS.

In winning the various campaigns, Boeing was now tearing a page from the Airbus playbook by making what are sometimes called "bad sales," a term for selective transactions that cause pain because the seller earns little, if any, return. However, a bad sale that snares one of the other party's customer airlines is usually seen as a strategic move and well worth the sacrifice. In losing sequential battles to Airbus for sales to low-cost carriers, some of them expected to buy its 737, Boeing had suffered a heavy blow. Then, Airbus experienced a similarly hard blow when Boeing began selling sizable numbers of 787's to carriers that had been flying A330's in the middle market and had been counted on by Airbus to buy its newer version, the A350.

In short, Boeing started turning itself around by not just building a better mousetrap but selling it at concessionary prices to airlines of possibly pivotal importance that might instead have bought the other party's paper airplane. Boeing had altered its strategy, and apparently put behind it at least some of the problems that had been the talk of the industry. Some of the credit goes to Scott Carson, who took charge of the sales force and wasted no time in changing its attitude and lack of edge. "I told them," he said, " 'We are now number two in sales,' and I made clear that the company was number two in other ways." The *Wall Street Journal* article, he said, "was right."[24] Carson is now in a position to impose still broader changes. In September 2006, he was selected to replace Alan Mulally and take charge of Boeing Commercial Airplanes. After thirty-seven years with Boeing, Mulally left to become chief executive and president of the ailing Ford Motor Company.

NOT VERY LONG AGO, Boeing had thought of itself—justly—as the greatest aerospace company the world had ever seen. Boeing's operations were driven by an internal logic and a rugged integrity built on respect for itself and its product. Then Boeing began behaving as if it had lost those attributes, whereas Airbus behaved as it if had taken possession of some or all of them.

As noted earlier, things in this business are often not what they seem. For many years, Airbus had the advantage of being the underdog. It did not have the heavy legacy of product obsolescence—the legacy of a successful past. Boeing had a family of good airplanes built with dated methods and 1960s technologies. The new arrival could afford to be innovative and bold; and Airbus was all of that. As the 1990s wore on and Boeing's troubles grew, the two companies seemed to have traded places. Boeing became the underdog, enough so that as recently as April 2004 a Seattle-based reporter could ask, "How did Boeing go from being 'plane maker to the world' to fighting for scraps?"[25]

However, Boeing's Commercial Airplanes group has survived a procession of mistakes, predictably, and appears to be all the way back and then some in the business it turned away from in the early to mid-1990s. Moreover, those mistakes and the company's eccentric management style tended to camouflage its strength. Sales of its new airplane in the early months of 2004 pointed up one asset that Boeing hadn't squandered: its rich talent pool. Boeing's aerodynamicists are as good as any. They were able to design a new and promising state-of-the-art LCA once their deeply risk-averse management and board made the seemingly counterintuitive decision to go ahead with the project.

Chances are that the two companies will continue to trade places over periods of uncertain duration. The product line of one may seem to dominate, or come close to dominating, the other's product line for a time before the market changes direction and shows a preference for some of what the underdog has begun to offer.

As for what may dictate the impermanence of advantage, it can be changes in one party's corporate culture; these occur over a period of years and are not reversible overnight. It may be the greater willingness of one party to exploit a technology that is available to both. It may be just good luck, as one party accidentally hits on a product that is percisely what the market decides it must have. With its 787, Boeing showed a greater willingness than Airbus to exploit some advanced technology, and was then able to design a product that looked right to several airlines and later to the financial markets.

CHAPTER THREE

Folly and Hypocrisy

EVEN BEFORE AIRBUS lifted the curtain on the A350, Boeing had begun reacting to it, mainly by mounting a full court press against the launch aid for new airplanes that Airbus had received from governments in the form of subsidies. This meant trying to undo an agreement between the United States and the European Union (EU) that was reached in 1992. At the time, the administration of President George H. W. Bush had begun to worry about the American makers of large commercial aircraft. McDonnell Douglas's fortunes were heading straight down, and even Boeing looked to be less robust and more vulnerable than in the past. Something, it seemed, might have to be done about insulating the country's top export and the people who produced it from still greater adversity.

And that argued for clipping the wings of Airbus—setting a limit on the benevolence of member governments. There ensued an uphill and drawn-out negotiation between the Washington and EU bureaucracies that led to an agreement on subsidies in 1992. It provided that no more than 33 percent of the development costs of a new airplane could be covered by governments. Although Boeing wanted a lower percentage, its leadership privately described the outcome as a step in the right direction and supported it. Agreement to ban production subsidies also cheered Boeing's leadership.

As seen at the time in Seattle, the agreement did cap the Airbus subsidies. And it defined them as loans repayable with interest provided that the airplanes were actually built and made some money. If not, the loans would be regarded as outright subsidies. Airbus would be required to repay the first 25 percent of development costs at "government rates," the rest at commercial rates.

McDonnell Douglas went along with this odd brew, although reluctantly. It had pushed for an agreement that would have all but removed Airbus's unique advantage. Instead, it got one that confirmed the right of European governments to continue to subsidize Airbus and thereby squeeze McDac. The agreement seems to have reflected Washington's judgment that McDac was finished as a serious player in the airliner game. In any case, its net effect was to solemnize Airbus's position as number two after Boeing. And it may have been the first time that the U.S. government had accorded other governments the right to subsidize their industries. In that sense, the agreement carried huge implications for U.S. trade policy.

A few weeks after becoming president, Bill Clinton traveled to Seattle. During a brief stopover in Detroit, he was asked about Airbus at a town meeting. "The Europeans are going to have to quit subsidizing Airbus," he said. "I am not going to roll over and play dead." Clinton was referring to the governments of France, Germany, and Britain.

Clinton was strongly drawn to this subject. Starting on day one of his presidency, he discussed it endlessly with staff, took any opportunity to bring it up with people who might have had some involvement with it, and collected relevant articles from newspapers and magazines. He not only carefully read but even underlined pieces from the *Financial Times* and the *Economist*. When the issue under discussion was Airbus subsidies, he pounded the table. For him, it didn't seem complicated: Boeing required protection; it was America's number-one earner of hard currency and number-one aerospace company. Airbus impressed him as a major threat to American competitiveness. He even talked about going to Congress to get the same subsidies for American companies competing with Airbus, but didn't follow through; he doubtless assumed that Congress wouldn't go along with any such move.

On February 22, Clinton visited Boeing facilities in and around Seattle. The company had just issued a startling announcement that it was laying off twenty-eight thousand people, or 20 percent of its workforce; Boeing was also slashing production of its 737, 757, 767, and jumbo 747 models by 47 percent over the next two years because of a dramatic falloff in demand from the enfeebled airline industry.

Page one belonged to Clinton after a speech that he delivered to workers in the plant where Boeing makes its wide-body airplanes and where it was then developing the 777, the company's first new airplane in twelve years; the plant itself was the world's largest enclosed space and still growing. "I think you and I know, deep in our hearts," the cheering audience was told, "that most of these layoffs, maybe not all because the airline industry itself has problems which are bleeding back on to you . . . but a lot of these layoffs would not have been announced had it not been for $26 billion that the United States sat by and let Europe plow into Airbus over the last several years. So we're going to try to change the rules of the game."

Apropos, the assemblage was told that Mickey Kantor, "my trade ambassador, will be closely monitoring the agreement which was finally made last year with regard to limiting European subsidies to Airbus to allow a level playing field." Clinton also pledged $8 billion of investment in aeronautics research and development over the following five years.

Seattle's economy, as Clinton judged it, was the most export-dependent in the country and the model for operating in a global economy. After the speech, he met privately with twenty or so notables from the intersecting worlds of the aircraft makers and the airlines. The main purpose of the meeting was to give him direct exposure to the plight of the airlines. No notes were taken. Frank Schrontz (then Boeing's chief executive) and two of his colleagues, along with John McDonnell of McDonnell Douglas, represented the manufacturers; also on hand were the heads of most of the major carriers.

The Boeing position was that it didn't want help from Washington, except in removing barriers to trade. Unlike the elated workers on the factory floor, management people weren't cheering; they took what they heard at face value and didn't fancy it. Boeing wanted no part of a trade war with Europe or any other part of the world. At the time, Boeing was selling more airplanes in Europe than Airbus was selling in America, or would be likely to sell in that market, which was still the biggest despite the weaknesses of the U.S. airline industry.

"He invited himself here, and he made two strong statements," said one Boeing executive. "Our strategy was to get him back off the limb he was on. He was heading for strong action."[1]

A few weeks later, Schrontz said that he had been "impressed with Clinton's openness, his general understanding and willingness to do something about the problem. He went around the table, with everyone invited to make two- or three-minute comments. They were all over the map. He listened patiently. He asked good questions and seemed relatively knowledgeable on the issues. It was a useful discussion—a good start from my point of view. The key will be whether he can deliver."

Asked about the Airbus subsidies, Schrontz said that he told Clinton during the meeting that matching subsidies was not the answer. "We will oppose that," he said. "We don't like subsidies. Also, we are in an awkward position. We still have sixty percent of the market. To say we need financial help rings hollow to a lot of people."[2] By then, Boeing was willing to concede a 30 percent market share to Airbus.

The 1992 agreement on limiting subsidies to airplane makers—the one that Clinton had seemingly threatened to undo—amounted to a truce between Washington and the European Union. For years, the Americans had railed against the putative $26 billion in subsidies that Airbus was thought to receive. What's sauce for the goose is sauce for the gander, said the Europeans. They meant that the spin-off from the heavy American investment in military aircraft benefited the commercial programs of Boeing and McDonnell Douglas.

Each side exaggerated. The real number of subsidies that had paid most of the development and production costs of the Airbus family couldn't be pinned down, but was thought to lie closer to $13 billion, leaving aside interest, than $26 billion.

If Clinton ever did contemplate changing the rules of the game, he thought twice about it. When Britain's prime minister, John Major, and Germany's chancellor, Helmut Kohl, paid their respective get-acquainted calls on the new president, they were told that he approved of the subsidies agreement. François Mitterand, France's president, who came a bit later on a similar errand, probably heard the same thing. In a joint news conference that followed their meeting, Clinton was asked about his supposed hostility to the subsidies agreement. His problem, he said, lay not with the agreement but with the previous lack of federal support for America's aircraft industry.

TWELVE YEARS LATER, in the spring of 2004, Boeing decided to pick a fight over the subsidies agreement. Airbus had moved ahead of Boeing and had to be regarded as fully capable of financing its products without governmental assistance. The U.S. government threatened to withdraw from the 1992 agreement and file a complaint against Airbus in the World Trade Organization (WTO). Then it did withdraw.

Spokespersons on one side tended to caricature the other, describing the competition as joined at the hip with government, with treasury doors wide open. Each side tended to inflate those of its arguments that had core elements of validity. The level of humbug rose.

As in 1992, Airbus argued that Boeing, too, drew on government support in launching or improving its airplanes, but did so more indirectly. Airbus people, along with bureaucrats in various European capitals, somewhat overstate their case. They persist in declaring that U.S. military technology literally flows back and forth between one side of the house, defense, and the other side, commercial. Technology is fungible.

Europeans watch the U.S. military establishment deploy state-of-the-art military platforms that they cannot or will not try to match. And they take careful note of NASA's research in aerodynamics and the benefits it can offer America's aerospace industry. But Boeing can say correctly that the product of some of this work may become available to *all* sides, including Airbus. Indeed, Airbus has at times turned NASA-based research into innovative improvements in its aircraft, while Boeing stood by and watched. (Its mind-set stubbornly cautious then, Boeing appeared to be telling itself that if it isn't broken, don't fix it.)

Airbus can also draw on the military programs of its parent company, EADS, although this base is much smaller than that of its American counterpart. Spending on military hardware in the European Union probably equals a third of the Pentagon's equipment budget. More important, the U.S. military spends roughly five times more on research and development than the Europeans.

In May 2005, the *Chicago Tribune,* Boeing management's hometown newspaper, published a heavily researched article under a banked headline that read "Arming for Trade War: Boeing Sleuths Seek Proof of Improper Subsidies to Airbus Series."[3] The headline notwithstanding, the piece was a balanced account of how the parties draw support from official entities, both national and regional. "Boeing," it said, "developed evidence of billions of dollars more in infrastructure projects and other public support that the company contends give Airbus a competitive advantage." That argument is credible.

The article argued that "the EU could find that its case [for receiving launch aid] is tough to make. . . . Airbus has jumped from a 30 percent market share in 1992 to 50 percent of commercial-aircraft deliveries today, so Airbus would be hard-pressed to prove any harm." The piece didn't note that what actually helps Airbus more than subsidies is the infusions of capital from member states to the EADS ownership.

However, the piece sided with Airbus on one of its major contentions: "Airbus claims of U.S. research subsidies will not be easy for Boeing to shake. A visit to NASA's research center in Langley, Va., illuminates how Boeing directs and carries out NASA research and also benefits from the findings. [The research center is actually in Hampton, not Langley.] Boeing has used Langley virtually as a proprietary research laboratory. At Boeing's urging, scientists there have researched lightweight composite materials, high speed—aircraft wing design and other subjects. Much of that technology made its way into the 787, a highly efficient plane made mostly from carbon-fiber composites."

Actually, only about half of the 787 will consist of composites, and a great deal of Boeing's knowledge of composites derives from its experience with the B-2 stealth bomber program. Moreover, Boeing does on occasion pay for the use of one of NASA's wind tunnels and understandably regards the data gained as proprietary.

On June 7, 2005, just a week before the Paris Air Show began, the Pentagon's inspector general released a 256-page report that appeared to support the argument that Boeing's influence within the U.S. military establishment lay somewhere between remarkable and excessive. The report's focus was the proposal to lease modified Boeing 767's to the air force as refueling tankers. "We all know that this is a bailout for Boeing," wrote Ronald G. Garant, an official of the Pentagon comptroller's office, and then deputy undersecretary of defense Wayne A. Schroeder. According to the *Washington Post,* the IG's report provided "an extraordinary glimpse of how the Air Force worked hand-in-glove with one of its chief contractors . . . to help it try to obtain the most costly government lease ever."

The report concluded that "four top Air Force officials and one of Defense Secretary Donald Rumsfeld's former top aides, Undersecretary of Defense Edward C. 'Pete' Aldridge, violated Pentagon and government-wide procurement rules, failed to use 'best business practices,' ignored a legal requirement for weapons testing and failed to ensure that the tankers would meet the military's requirements." It also connected Rumsfeld to the affair, citing a statement by former air force secretary James G. Roche that Rumsfeld had told him "he did not want me to budge on the tanker lease proposal."[4]

Surprisingly little notice was paid to a very different Airbus argument—that a large part of Boeing's development costs for the 787 were being underwritten by the Japanese government in the form of direct support to the companies engaged in building the wing and various other parts of that airplane. There then developed a kind of

Who Struck John argument over which of the two disputing companies was engaged, or most deeply engaged, in questionable financial arrangements.

Washington complained that Airbus had been able to overtake Boeing in sales of commercial airplanes partly because of $15 billion in government loans that Airbus had received on less-than-commercial terms. The EU countered, charging that Boeing had gotten $23 billion of support since 1992 in the form of federal research grants and Japanese government backing of suppliers, along with a tax credit for exporters, a subsidy that was ruled illegal by the WTO and is known in trading circles as "extraterritorial income." The WTO authorized the EU to retaliate by imposing up to $4 billion worth of sanctions, the biggest award in the WTO's history.

Still, in *Business Week,* Stanley Holmes, who has in the past come down hard on Boeing's mistakes and misdeeds, said, "If sales of Boeing's 787's flop, Boeing loses billions and faces the risk of going out of business. If A380 sales falter, Airbus doesn't have to repay the $3 billion in loans."[5] He had a point. Airbus is not required to repay the loans it has received for an aircraft program that loses money.

The reality is that each side will find ways of helping its commercial aircraft industry. And each deploys arguments against the other's methods that are less ambiguous than the truth. Governments have diverse but comparably effective ways of supporting companies that are surpassing earners of foreign exchange, or that have unequaled reservoirs of advanced technology, or that must be relied on to convey people and freight within and beyond national boundaries. Europe's political culture favors munificent safety nets and industrial policies that help to sustain them. The U.S. approach to protecting the tough, capital-intensive aerospace industry is less direct, more complicated, and perhaps less effective, but not by much.

Many, if not most, of the arguments on either side of the subsidies issue were complex, more than a little contrived, and unconvincing in several cases. Boeing's were marginally more persuasive or less unpersuasive, but it didn't really matter. The mistake was revisiting the issue.

53

It was made by Boeing, or more accurately by Harry Stonecipher, the company's former chairman and CEO.

The decision to start a fight was Stonecipher's, although his reasons were not obvious, even to most Boeing people. Many, probably most, executives felt that Boeing's management had put the company out on a limb. But why? A part of the Boeing team calculated that interfering with Airbus's finances could divert, or retard, its efforts to weaken the 787's prospects by creating a competitor airplane.

Another reason was that Airbus seemed to have gotten itself out on a limb with the A380, and that the limb might topple and the big airplane with it if Airbus could be denied big infusions of money from its governments. A comment by Boeing's chairman, Lewis Platt, connected these reasons for having a fight. "It should not be easy for them to launch the A350 program, as they're choking on trying to finish the A380," he said.[6]

A very different theory was ventured by Henri Courpron, who was then president and CEO of Airbus North America. After noting that he was speaking only for himself, not for the company, he said, "The fight is not about commerce, it's about politics. And it isn't about the A380 or protecting the 787. Boeing was trying to build political sympathy because it was on a losing streak and steadily losing market share to Airbus. Then came the tanker fiasco. So Boeing said to itself, 'We can't win, so let's turn to the government.' The line was: 'We are losing because Airbus is cheating.'"[7]

He could have added, plausibly, that Boeing's assault on launch aid had in effect maneuvered Washington away from investigating the company's misbehavior on various defense-related matters and toward protecting it. By a vote of 98 to 0, the U.S. Senate passed a resolution urging the government to do exactly that.

Whatever the motives that lay behind the Boeing move, it surprised most industry people, especially veteran Stonecipher watchers. "Harry," one of them said, "is well known to feel strongly that companies that know what they are doing do not play the trade card, and that a company that goes down that road shouldn't be in the business."[8]

THE REACTION to Boeing's move against the 1992 agreement was mixed. Within the United States, there was considerable editorial support; Airbus was seen as exploiting an unfair advantage over its American competitor, the ex-champ. "Boeing's frustration is kind of understandable," wrote a prominent American aviation analyst. "If A380 development depended on commercial paper or company cash flow, the program wouldn't have gotten past the flying bowling alley demo phase. It must really tax Boeing's patience to watch its prize 747 legacy driven to an early grave by some bloated airborne welfare queen."[9]

Elsewhere, the reaction ranged from negative to hostile. The concern was that Boeing's pressure on subsidies and the 1992 agreement could and probably would have a serious ripple effect, depending on how far it went. Most of the aviation world's tightly interconnected key players wanted to head off a trade war between Boeing and Airbus. The airlines, always easily rattled, had to worry about having to pay higher prices for new aircraft if government support for suppliers were to fall off thanks to a WTO ruling.

America's two major engine companies—GE and United Technologies—worried about being drawn in. They feel as if they make the key part of any airplane but do need one to hang their engines on. So they affected neutral positions vis-à-vis Boeing and Airbus. And they have another, even larger reason to be hands-off, one that points up the muddled quality of the entire dispute: the engine groups receive more financial help from governments, as well as from NASA, than do the airframe companies.

For example, France's government owns Snecma, an engine company, and over the years has poured huge sums into engines for which Snecma is a subcontractor of GE. All the development for GE's most successful engine, the CFM-56, came from Snecma. In effect, the French government has been subsidizing a piece of the American aircraft industry as well as its own.

"We think Harry is way off on the subsidies issue," said a senior vice president of GE Aircraft Engines at the time. "We think he has been led astray by Rudy deLeon and that big Washington bureaucracy Boeing has in Arlington."[10] (DeLeon was then a senior vice president and a member of the Boeing executive council. He directed all federal, state, and local government operations for the company. The large Washington staff he directed is housed in a twelve-story building located in Arlington, Virginia.)

"Retaliatory measures do not help Boeing," said one lawyer, most of whose experience has been with cases involving international law, much of that on behalf of Boeing. "WTO cases are an art form," he continued. "They can only offer leverage. It's not a matter of winning, but filing the case. You file in order to improve your position, not remove a problem. Lawyers who work on trade issues tell clients, 'Avoid doing things you can't control.' "[11]

A number of people with comparable experience agree and would add that (1) WTO cases are fraught with risk and have uncertain outcomes; (2) governments can help on issues such as these mainly by exercising discretion—so that in this case the U.S. government should have used whatever leverage it had by exchanging back-channel messages with other involved governments. Moreover, a widely held opinion was that even if Boeing won the trade fight, it would be doing itself at least as much harm as good. "You can win the fight but lose the village" was a comment often heard.

The betting among the lawyers was that this dispute would not go the distance—not reach the WTO, which would be very unhappy if it did. The WTO would shrink from ruling on a large and high-profile dispute between its two strongest members.

In August 2004, President George W. Bush and Senator John Kerry, his opponent in the presidential campaign, made similar noises, but Bush drew the most attention. In mid-August he attacked European government subsidies for Airbus and revived the prospect of bringing the issue to the WTO.[12]

Two weeks later, with the issue gaining heft, Harry Stonecipher traveled to Brussels and London. He alternated between pleading his case in reasonable and measured terms and, in effect, going over the top. Naturally, it was the shrill language that got attention, as, for example, the put-down of Airbus's new airplane. "I think the A380 is the dumbest thing anyone has ever done," said Stonecipher.

The comment was noted in a well-balanced account of the visit to London by John Gapper, the widely read chief business commentator of the *Financial Times.* "Boeing's complaints about Airbus have some merit," he said, explaining that Airbus "would have been unable to develop a range of aircraft as rapidly without backing from governments that wanted to create a European rival to Boeing."[13]

Gapper also noted, first, that "Airbus may well be overestimating the potential market for very large aircraft"; and second, that "most passengers would probably prefer to fly direct routes on smaller aircraft such as the 787, given the choice." But Gapper argued that Boeing's way of complaining "is counterproductive. Instead of damaging Airbus, it makes itself look like a sore loser, a once-powerful company that cannot cope with being overtaken by a rival it used to dominate." He concluded by citing the financial perks that Boeing gets. "Boeing," he said, "insists that this is wholly different, but you could have fooled me." The article appeared under the headline "Boeing Has Not Mastered the Art of Griping."[14]

Some broader, more muted considerations were outlined by Jeffrey Garten, who was undersecretary of commerce for international trade in the first Clinton administration and is now dean of the Yale School of Management. "Should a case be filed," he wrote, "transatlantic relations will be further poisoned, just when there is a critical need for cooperation on Iraq, Iran and other explosive political issues. Cooperation between Washington and Brussels, so essential to successful global trade talks, could be undermined.

"The judicial outcome is already clear," wrote Garten. "Both . . . companies have taken considerable government handouts. The court will declare both guilty, creating a political stalemate in which both sides will probably ignore the penalties the WTO wants to impose."[15]

As 2004 wound down, the chief trade negotiators for the European Union and the United States—Pascal Lamy and Robert Zoellick—were both moving on to other jobs, Zoellick less immediately. They would be missed, not least because it had always been clear that the best outcome would be an agreement worked out in confidential talks between them, as opposed to an angry, litigious process, one that was likely to be the ugliest, most destructive of WTO battles and last several years.

The issue had been greatly inflated. Of course, subsidies do matter, but less than this disorderly quarrel seemed to suggest. What matters most is getting the product right and selling it. The divergent fortunes of Airbus and Boeing since the 1980s had far less to do with government support than with how the two companies competed in an unforgiving business. Boeing thinks, doubtless correctly, that government support precludes a failure of Airbus. But Boeing should have focused less on failure than on building the new products that would have responded most effectively to trends in the marketplace.

Boeing took an extended recess from its core business. The 777 was the last airplane it had built. Lamy called Boeing's loss of market share a "self-inflicted decline,"[16] a sentiment echoed by most of the aviation industry, including numerous Boeing people.

FOR A BRIEF TIME, reason was allowed to prevail. In early January, Zoellick and Peter Mandelson, Lamy's British successor, reached a provisional agreement designed to freeze all new subsidies and litigation for three months. Mandelson said then, "If pursued the whole distance, this gladiatorial clash would have succeeded in giving a Pyrrhic victory to both sides. The poison spread by this conflict would have spilled into other aspects of the trans-Atlantic relationship."[17]

Within three days of the moratorium, however, the companies were putting down markers. Airbus applied to the four member governments for roughly $1.3 billion to help finance the development of the A350. Airbus officials talked of continuing to expect "repayable" launch aid to be available, albeit at a lower level, even after the two sides had completed talks on what both described as massive and illegal subsidies. An Airbus official added: "We are preparing everything in good faith on the basis we would get launch aid." A spokesman for Zoellick objected strongly, saying, "The objective on which we agreed is to secure a comprehensive agreement to end subsidies, and I repeat, end."[18]

Noel Forgeard, then Airbus's CEO, said that his company's application for launch aid would be allowed to "quietly sleep" while the talks between U.S. and EU negotiators proceeded. The United States warned that unless an agreement was reached within three months, or was well in hand by then, Washington would be ready to litigate.

The hard issue turned on whether the contesting parties could agree on some rules of the road for financing their new airplanes: Airbus's A350 and Boeing's 787. Would or could Airbus acquiesce in the various devices by which Boeing was financing development of the 787 unless Boeing withdrew its objections to launch aid for the A350?

The truce was not likely to head off the clash, and it didn't. Zoellick and Mandelson are alike in various ways, including some that matter. Each is highly intelligent, highly skilled, and impelled by a powerful ego. Lamy, Mandelson's predecessor, was equally intelligent, equally skilled, and more experienced in these matters than Mandelson. Also, his ego wasn't a problem. As rival negotiators, he and Zoellick were fine. However, Mandelson and Zoellick were an accident waiting to happen.

It did happen in late March, about eight weeks after the truce was reached. With the deadline agreed under the truce little more than a month away and the parties still far apart, each negotiator was becoming vexed and running out of patience with the other. They spoke on the telephone, and after some harsh words were exchanged, the call ended abruptly.

Then they worsened matters by going public. On the first of April, an op-ed piece by Mandelson appeared in the *Washington Post* in which he compared the American approach to supporting Boeing very unfavorably to Europe's method of supporting Airbus.[19]

Five days later, an angry response came from Zoellick. In what the *Financial Times* described as an "unusually personal attack," Zoellick accused his opposite number of using "spin" in the dispute "and compar[ed] him unfavorably with his predecessor, Pascal Lamy." The fallout of all this, the article said, "could also damage trans-Atlantic cooperation on other trade issues."[20] It then appeared that the truce was a dead letter and that the dispute could be en route to the WTO, where each party stood a reasonable chance of being ruled against. There also appeared a possibility that Washington and Brussels might go to war over the Airbus-Boeing dispute and other trade issues. It should have been clear from the first that personally uninvolved negotiators operating in a back channel should have managed the affair. Instead, it had been personalized, with only the lawyers likely to prosper.

In May, the office of the U.S. Trade Representative filed a complaint with the WTO about European subsidies to Airbus, and the European Union then filed a countercomplaint about federal and state subsidies to Boeing. But by then negotiators and lawyers alike had to compete with major distractions. The war in Iraq and an increasingly vulnerable domestic program were consuming the attention of President Bush's administration. The rejection of a newly minted constitution for the European Union, notably by France and the Netherlands, produced a political crisis that deeply affected all of its members. It also pointed up the absence of leadership and focus in major European countries, and the anemic performance of their economies.

The largely self-induced problems in the United States and the European Union could cause each side to turn inward and further complicate shared problems. On the subsidies issue, they both misplayed their hands, especially the Europeans, because they had the most to lose but also the most to gain. Airbus in particular had the most to lose, because it has relied heavily on the launch aid, a highly visible crutch but one increasingly hard to defend. Airbus also had the most to gain, provided that those who were pulling the strings were willing to allow a change in direction.

Instead of announcing that member governments of Airbus would be asked to provide $1.3 billion for the A350, the Europeans should have stated a willingness to give up launch aid for the new airplane provided Boeing agreed to take a comparable step. The quid pro quo, if agreed to, could have required Boeing to forgo arrangements with the three Japanese heavies, the companies that would be building 35 percent of the 787, including the wing, unless they, too, commercialized their roles (gave up government subsidies) and, in effect, allowed a standard for so-called launch aid to be created. Any such standard would appear to be compatible with the best interests of the various parties.

According to published reports, the Japanese suppliers would receive $1.6 billion of direct assistance from their government in return for their work on the 787—an amount at least equivalent to the launch aid Airbus was intending to request from its official patrons. The idea of commercializing launch aid had appealed for some time to various politically shrewd Airbus executives who wanted their Paris-based management to give up launch aid altogether and to rely solely on commercial paper. They were aware of pockets of support within each of the member governments—stronger in some than in others—for proceeding without this kind of help.

Rightly or wrongly, however, various British and German advocates of commercializing the aid have worried that if they didn't provide it, the French would, and then insist on locating all the work on a new aircraft program in France. (It's known, tongue in cheek, as the "Franco-French" scenario.) So the issue was partly about jobs and about making certain that key pieces of Europe's aerospace industry remained in each partner country.

For example, although the British have talked a good game in private about giving up launch aid, some parts of their system like what they see as a decent return on the money under current arrangements. Also, on the A350 program, Britain would acquire much the largest share of launch aid because its industry would be responsible for the wing, the most innovative part of the new airplane and the one that would hence absorb most of the engineering.

Airbus was being victimized or was victimizing itself by the warfare among its various patrons. The member governments that supplied the launch aid were mad at one another and at the European Commission, which they thought wasn't much help. In turn, the Commission resented their encroachment on its turf. And all sides were mad at Airbus, because the company didn't seem to know what it wanted but did resent their interference.

The problem, or mess, was circular: Airbus couldn't say what it wanted because these same governments—French, British, and German—were the ones that could dictate the decisions that mattered. And these governments, especially the French, were internally divided over what to do. "It's like trying to herd cats," said one disgruntled Airbus official. "My hope," he said, "is that Jim McNerney [Boeing's new leader] will decide that his first big task is to fix Boeing and then say to himself, Why should I screw around with this trade issue? Let's make a deal."[21]

As Airbus saw it, the foolishness was compounded by its own corporate manager, EADS, which aspires to replace Boeing as the supplier of aerial tankers to the U.S. Air Force, and hence has wanted to end the fight over subsidies. The company's hierarchy worried that continuing to accept launch aid for Airbus would allow elements in the U.S. government and Congress to block efforts by EADS to break into the high-margin U.S. defense business. The steady decline in Europe's spending on defense pointed up EADS's concern, and also the gap between its priorities and those of Airbus, which has no interest in trading launch aid for military aircraft sales.

During the Paris Air Show, a biennial event held outside Paris at Le Bourget Airport, the Europeans tried belatedly to clear the air on the dicey question of a trade on subsidies. But their position was largely rhetorical. Airbus would give up launch aid for the A350 provided Boeing surrendered most of what the Europeans were complaining about—indirect subsidies from the Pentagon, plus the help from Japan on the 787, plus a subsidy from the state of Washington, where the 787 will be assembled.

Boeing swatted that back. Even though the company's declaratory position was "Everything is on the table," its chairman, Lewis E. Platt, argued that the only issue was the $15 billion in launch aid that Airbus had received over the previous thirty years. "It's very hard to imagine a quid pro quo," he said. "To me, their position seems to be, 'We'll give up launch aid if you give up something.' We think we've made our position clear that we have no launch aid to give up."[22]

Instead of asking for so much, Airbus could have proposed zero launch aid for both the A350 and the 787, or a different sort of arrangement whereby each party would receive up to $1.5 billion in subsidies for its new airplane. Either approach would have amounted to a step toward a level playing field.

Airbus has some talking points. What it gets in launch aid is limited to one-third of a new product's development costs, and how much that works out to per program is a matter of record. But the details of the Japanese government's financial involvement with the three heavies are often described as murky. What is known is that the terms of this assistance are more generous than what Airbus receives from its patrons and that the amounts are larger.

Boeing would probably have said no to any proposal that equated launch aid in Japan with launch aid in Europe, if only because the 787 program already harbored several risks and uncertainties. The company is depending heavily on this new airplane because its portfolio of products is aging.

The importance that Boeing attributes to the 787 resonates in its company rhetoric. "It will be the mother and father for whatever we build for probably the rest of this century," a Boeing spokesperson said grandly at the Paris Air Show,[23] which made more news than usual. Possibly. For now, it seems to be the most interesting, advanced, and potentially successful new airplane that the world airline market has seen in recent years. But it has still to be built.

Boeing would recoil from having to redesign its complex relationships with key suppliers and thereby slow down its development of the 787. However, a proposal from Airbus linking launch aid for the A350 with comparable Japanese government support for the 787 would have been fully compatible with the WTO and have put the ball in Boeing's court. Airbus could have said to Boeing, "This is what we will do. What will you do in return?" And Airbus could have started talking with the Japanese about launch aid.

That sort of conversation would not have been possible so long as Airbus continued to accept launch aid. The Japanese had already said that much and more about their unwillingness to become a party to the dispute. But by aligning its position with WTO rules, Airbus would have been better positioned to nudge the Japanese toward serious talks.

However, the Europeans were split on whether to play the Japanese card. "We don't want to upset the Japanese," Henri Courpron said with little conviction. "Airbus would love to do business in Japan. We have a one or one and a half percent market share there on a good day," he added sardonically, "and this would make it more difficult to sell the A380 in Japan."[24] Japan Airlines is on a short list of Asian carriers that are judged likely to buy the A380. Incidentally, the European Union, in filing its countercomplaint against Boeing, did not mention Japan.

The importance to Boeing of its Japanese connection cannot be overstated. Boeing has been a presence in Japan for more than half a century. Japan's government and its aircraft industry are deeply involved with Boeing. The informal arrangement amounts, in effect, to what is characterized as offset: in return for Japanese industry having acquired a privileged-supplier relationship with Boeing, Japan's airline market—the world's second strongest (after the United States) until the Chinese market matures—has become a Boeing preserve. The two principal airlines, Japan Airlines (JAL) and All Nippon Airways (ANA), have fleets composed almost entirely of Boeing aircraft. Offset, it's worth noting, is in direct conflict with WTO rules.

In return, Japan's three heavies built about 15 percent of the Boeing 767 and 20 percent of the 777. Now the three are designing and building a substantial part of the 787, including the wing, the clever part of any airframe; it is Boeing's first new airplane since the 777 entered service in 1994.

Boeing draws on low-cost financing from the world's second-largest economy to pay a major share of its airplane's development costs. Why else build major parts of it four thousand miles away from Puget Sound? Clearly, this is about having access to cheap money and, again, to what remains the world's prize airliner export market. Briefly, Boeing can use Japanese money to carry a big part of the 787's development costs and worry later about fine-tuning the financial arrangements with the three heavies.

Still, while the relationship is of vast importance to both sides, it does remain one between a principal and three suppliers who have acquired a demanding and exacting role that Boeing no longer wants to play. These three do have leverage. They know—and so does Airbus—that the attraction to Boeing of the Japanese suppliers lies mainly in the strong financial support they receive from their government.

The three companies do have differences with Boeing over how to operate, and there have been contentious issues concerning money, some of which won't go away. These were reflected in the prolonged absence of formal agreements between Boeing and the three heavies, which felt that the 787 posed huge risks for them, including an all-composite fuselage and other novel features and uncertainties. Boeing, they felt, was expecting too much from them in return for their taking on these risks. At one point, they judged that the deal on offer from Boeing would cover just 70 percent of their costs. Boeing had asked one of them, Mitsubishi Heavy Industries, to accept an even larger role, but MHI refused.

Another of the large uncertainties has involved the market price of the 787, more exactly, the size of the discounts offered to various customers. The issue is who feels the pain—the airframe maker or its suppliers—that is caused by selling airplanes at concessionary prices. "There are always discounts on any airplane," says Larry Clarkson, who in the 1990s was Boeing's senior vice president of planning and international development and managed negotiations with the Japanese. "The 747 may have been the only one that has sold somewhere close to its list price. On the 787, some of the pain will be shared, but

Boeing will absorb most of it, because the company won't allow any of the parties, even its risk-sharing partners, to know the size of the discounts. Although the biggest customer for the 747 was Japan Airlines, the discounts it got on price were among the smallest given in the 1980s and '90s."[25] If the three heavies knew that, JAL would presumably also find out—and very quickly.

The contractual arrangements on the 787 were not agreed to until May 26, 2005, eighteen months after the decision to go forward with the airplane. Boeing's relationship with Japanese industry harbors vulnerabilities. A less confused, opaque, and divided European leadership might have probed them to advantage. As for who exactly decided to downplay the Japanese issue, Henri Courpron said, "No one can find the fingerprints of whoever made the decision."[26] It's hard to see how this messy dispute can be settled unless the parties dispose of the Japanese issue in one way or another.

In October of that year, the EU proposed restarting negotiations over launch aid, after EADS announced that it would postpone taking launch aid in the meantime. Within hours, the U.S. Trade Representative's office replied that it would continue legal action against the EU at the WTO.

In the spring of 2006, these same official parties were in control, and not much was happening other than talks about talks. At the Farnborough Air Show, James McNerney, Boeing's chief, said, "I am optimistic that we will get a negotiated settlement, but I believe it will take time. This is a goverment-to-goverment issue. I don't want to get out in front of my government."[27] The companies, seemingly weary of the stalemate, could do little about it.

CHAPTER FOUR

Market Share—the Airlines' Enemy

THE MAJOR U.S. AIRLINES are floundering. In little more than three years after September 11, 2001, the industry worldwide lost more money than it had earned since the start of powered flight. Rising oil prices enlarged the difficulties, as did the SARS epidemic. The heaviest losses were incurred by American carriers.

Although the impact of 9/11 on airlines everywhere was substantial, their problem was not and is not passenger traffic. Over the years, demand for air travel has shown itself to be reliably resilient. It normally falls off in periods of turbulence and then bounces back quickly. Boeing estimates that air travel worldwide has tripled since 1980. Boeing and Airbus are both forecasting 5 percent annual growth in airline travel over the next twenty years.[1]

The woes of America's airlines were largely self-inflicted, decades in the making, and are worsening. Much of what has gone wrong can be traced to 1978, when the Airline Deregulation Act was adopted. It liberated the airlines by allowing them, instead of a government agency, to decide which routes they could fly and at what cost to the passenger. Government supervision of what had been judged a public utility gave way to free market economics.

Predictably, the industry's irrational tendencies took over, and it quickly outgrew itself. By the late 1980s, the legacy carriers—the half-dozen major carriers that have been around longer than most of the others and operate both nationally and internationally—had embarked on a feeding frenzy, adding new airplanes to their fleets without retiring older ones. (These are hardy, long-lived vehicles.) Credit wasn't a problem—there was a great deal of money chasing airplanes; airlines were borrowing 120 percent of the net purchase of their new aircraft. And they were busily expanding their hub airports.

Airline deregulation, a useful step in principle, was never about building a strong industry; it was about lowering ticket prices by creating competition. And it did give rise to a commodity marketplace, hence competition. But most airlines either didn't favor deregulation or, like Delta Airlines, openly opposed it.

United Airlines, the nation's largest carrier at the time, was the only strenuous advocate. The other big airlines had been reluctant to give up a regulated environment, which had offered an unstable industry protection against its prodigal tendencies. The new freedom to choose the routes they flew *might* enhance profitability, but it also meant that they would live or die in the marketplace. With the arrival of marketplace economics, the carriers all responded to the pressure to expand service and invade routes flown by competitors.

Some of them expected to see a Darwinian logic that would gradually work to the advantage of both the industry and the public by strengthening some airlines and pushing the less fit toward mergers or oblivion. Or, as various industry people felt, deregulation might breed chaos and, sooner or later, some form of regulation.[2]

The carriers had invited a perfect storm. Having foolishly overextended themselves, they became largely oblivious to the harmful effects on earnings of rampant competition, much of it mindless. Their new equipment not only allowed but dictated expanded service—more airlines battling one another on more routes.

Richard Ferris, for a time United's CEO and chairman, was asked in 1981 about the tendency of the liberated industry toward self-destructive behavior. "Watch the blood on the floor," he said. "It will get so deep that the carriers will become rational."[3] They didn't.

A decade or so later, three of them—Trans World Airlines (TWA), Continental Airlines, and America West—were in Chapter 11 bankruptcy proceedings. The industry's big three—United, American, and Delta—were themselves under serious financial pressure and complaining bitterly about the protection from creditors afforded carriers in Chapter 11 and the fare wars to which they were addicted. In turn, the all-but-bankrupt airlines blamed their problems on the big three, especially American, for their extravagant overbuying of equipment, a behavior pattern that weakened the industry's financial base.

But the larger problem was the battle for market share. Most of the carriers were losing their shirts chasing it. Then as now, their mantra seemed to be: HE WHO DIES WITH THE BIGGEST MARKET SHARE WINS. "Deregulation gave them all a chance to die," recalls Edward Colodny, a former CEO and chairman of US Airways who spent most of his career in the airline industry.[4]

Herb Kelleher is sometimes described as having reinvented air travel some years before deregulation was enacted. Kelleher has made a massive success of Southwest Airlines, the carrier he founded, by doing the opposite of just about everything the bigger airlines have done and continue to do. From the time Southwest began operating in June 1971, his priority was keeping costs down, not building market share. "Market share has nothing to do with profitability," he said. "Market share says we just want to be big; we don't care if we make money doing it." Some companies, he said, increased their costs by 25 percent in order to get an additional 5 percent share of the market.[5]

In 1990 and 1991, the embattled airline industry lost $7 billion and was astride $75 billion of debt. The debt-equity ratio within the industry was about 75 percent. Net cash flows were covering just 25–35 percent of capital expenditures, and financial leverage on some carriers was so strong that they couldn't cover fixed costs.

Around this time, calls for imposing re-regulation on the industry began to be heard. The deregulated environment had fallen far short of the claims that had been made by its advocates. In the main, it had allowed the carriers to enfeeble themselves and leave the United States with the oldest fleet of airliners of any industrialized country.

Within aviation and congressional circles opinion was divided. Some voices that carried were heard expressing "philosophical opposition" to regulation. But many such people would add that if the carriers couldn't discipline themselves, perhaps some way of imposing a code of sensible behavior on them should be found. That sort of talk never came to anything, largely because the argument that deregulation was, in principle, a good idea was generally acknowledged.

Nor did the talk reflect reality—that the industry was still tightly regulated. Aside from broadcasting, probably no other industry has comparably narrow restrictions on where companies can operate or on foreign ownership. This restrictive attitude stems from outdated notions about airlines as instruments of national security—ferrying troops to combat zones, for instance.

Failed efforts by British Airways (BA) to acquire an American base offer a vivid example of the kind of mischief that these restrictions can cause and have. In July 1992, BA and USAir (as it was called then) announced their intention to join forces. BA intended to invest $750 million in a major American carrier on the verge of financial collapse. Shortly thereafter, the big three—American, United, and Delta—banded together to block the bailout of USAir. They were joined by Federal Express, with the group then becoming known as the "fat four."[6]

Their case, a politically potent one as it turned out, was that allowing BA to absorb USAir would lead to the creation of a preeminent domestic carrier, one whose global reach would give it heavy and unique advantages. The issue for the administration of President George H. W. Bush was whether USAir might have to join the lengthening list of airline fatalities or be allowed to merge with BA and thereby threaten the well-being of the big three, the backbone of America's airline industry. Where did the consumer's interest lie? Where did the national interest lie?

U.S. carriers were losing big money at the time and selling off airplanes at very low prices so as to generate enough cash to avoid bankruptcy. Their bonds were no longer investment grade. They were shunned by banks, insurance companies, and pension funds, and were having to pay heavily for what they could borrow. Foreign carriers, most of them government-owned, were becoming lenders of last resort, although not, of course, disinterested lenders. For example, they wanted permission to fly between U.S. cities, picking up and unloading passengers. And in an increasingly globalized economy, it was hard to see why they should be denied this right, which is called cabotage.

But what every big foreign airline really craved was the freedom to buy a major U.S. carrier. This right of "inward investment," as foreign control is euphemistically known, would provide far greater and more reliable access to the lush American market than cabotage. But the law provides that three-fourths of a carrier's voting stock must be U.S.-owned and three-fourths of its senior officers and directors must be U.S. citizens. Non-Americans can own up to 40 percent of the equity.

However, dropping the protectionist rules would require changes in domestic law, and Congress, if asked, was certain to refuse amending existing law unless other countries—notably Britain, France, Germany, and Japan—extended reciprocal benefits to the United States.[7]

To no one's surprise, BA's proposed merger with USAir churned up political turmoil. Two strong multistate lobbies formed up. One, belonging to BA-USAir, fought hard and resourcefully to maneuver approval of the deal. The other fought just as hard on behalf of the big three/fat four, and it held better cards.

The man in the middle was Andrew Card, then secretary of transportation and until recently President George W. Bush's chief of staff. Given the prohibition on foreign ownership, Card would have had to veto the deal if it appeared to transfer control of USAir to BA. However, BA was proposing to acquire 21 percent of the voting stock and one-fourth of the board membership. That degree of control would have provided a blocking minority, one that could have enabled BA to approve or disapprove major aircraft purchases and capital outlays.

BA's proposal didn't stray beyond the letter of the statute, but did present Card and his department with a politically loaded question of how to interpret the statute and its intent. The decision went against BA—unfortunately. The deal, had it gone through, would have produced concessions on the British side and, in turn, promoted competition on domestic and international routes. It would have brightened prospects for a more liberalized air travel environment.[8]

The reality is that America's airline industry remains more strongly protected than most. BA, for example, had wanted the right to fly passengers nonstop from continental Europe, notably Paris, to New York without touching down at any of its British terminals. This would have allowed BA to become a multihub carrier in Europe, just as its American competitors were at home.

But here again BA would lose the argument. Paris was the biggest European gateway for TWA, at the time one of America's major carriers. TWA did not want to compete against BA in Paris—and, as it turned out, would not have to. Then as now, neither the freedom nor inward investment nor cabotage nor any of the other liberalizations that fall under the deceptive rubric "open skies" would be allowed to unbind air services agreements.

CARRIERS in the United States and around the world are having an easier time leasing airplanes than buying them. Leasing is a financial tool, one that Airbus and Boeing use as a distribution channel, especially for airlines that lack access to capital.

The bankruptcies of some airlines at the start of the 1990s and the flirtation with bankruptcy of others had a lot to do with the rapid growth of leasing companies. They have been the fastest growing segment in the trade.

The purchase of a new airplane typically means paying a third of the cost in the two years prior to delivery. The plane may cost $45 million, meaning a progress payment of $15 million. That is a lot of cash for many airlines. But with a lease, the pressure is greatly reduced. A cash payment covering the first three months of the lease may be all that is required. And that might be no more than, say, $900,000, or about $300,000 per month.

Airlines lease equipment for the same reason that people lease cars. The off-balance-sheet financing is very attractive. A carrier records the rental expense, whereas an aircraft purchase is recorded as a liability on the balance sheet. Leasing is probably the key component of aircraft acquisition, partly because it offers considerable flexibility. A lease may run for three or four years, and then be extended. Or the aircraft may be returned and replaced with one that is more immediately useful. Leasing allows carriers to mix their fleets more productively by taking aircraft in and out of leasing. It allows a lessor to hold an airplane for three to five years, then to flip it at the depreciated price and take a tax advantage.

In December 2004, a piece in the *New York Times* by Micheline Maynard showed the extent to which U.S. carriers are "flying on borrowed wings." The fleets of the two biggest—American and United—were shown to be about 45 percent and 41 percent leased, respectively. US Airways stood at 76 percent, Continental at 65 percent. Among the low-cost carriers, Southwest leases about 23 percent of its airplanes, JetBlue 37 percent. Altogether, nearly half the aircraft used by U.S. airlines are leased.[9]

The leasing business has its roots in the 1970s. It began with a Hungarian immigrant named Steven Udvar-Hazy, an airplane buff since childhood. Upon graduating from UCLA in 1972, Udvar-Hazy solved a problem for Alaska Airlines by arranging to lease to another airline a Boeing 727 on which the carrier couldn't make payments. A year later, Udvar-Hazy and two fellow Hungarian immigrants, a father-and-son team named Gondas, started a company designed to lease airplanes. With just $50,000 in capital, this company set in motion the process that rearranged the airline industry's pattern of acquiring planes.

A decade or so later, Udvar-Hazy and his partners discovered that thanks to deregulation, a new airline market was emerging; the start-up carriers it begot needed just the sort of help that an alert and resourceful lessor could provide. Lenders were avoiding the start-ups and also avoiding the carriers in Chapter 11. The self-destructive tendencies of other large airlines also created opportunities for the lessors.

Udvar-Hazy's company, known by then as the International Lease Finance Corporation (ILFC), prospered and grew rapidly. Udvar-Hazy himself has since been described as the aviation industry's megastar, even though he is little known beyond that world. He became somewhat less anonymous when his donation of $66 million to the Smithsonian Institution created a second facility for the Air and Space Museum; the Udvar-Hazy Center, located at Dulles International Airport near Washington, opened in 2003.

A few years after ILFC began spreading its wings in the 1980s, a small Irish company began buying airplanes, especially Airbus products, and leasing them. The company had blended two Irish symbols by calling itself Guinness Peat Aviation. It was a good name, but the company's reach exceeded its grasp. After buying more airplanes than it could dispose of, Guinness Peat collapsed. General Electric collected the pieces, which became GE Commercial Aviation Services, known for short as GECAS.

GECAS became the largest leasing company. Next is Udvar-Hazy's ILFC. And they operate very differently. GECAS deploys a bigger fleet, but ILFC buys the most new airplanes. GECAS purchases very few wide-bodies. ILFC is the largest buyer of the wide-bodied aircraft produced by both Boeing and Airbus. ILFC is not a lender, GECAS is. ILFC does the larger part of its business outside the United States, while GECAS does more of its business within. GECAS is a major piece of the GE toolbox. GE, for example, can guarantee a purchase by GECAS of, say, several new Boeing airplanes, provided Boeing is mating them with a GE engine.

GECAS has had exceptional growth since 9/11, becoming virtually the only major lender to most American carriers. Some of them resent GECAS, however, arguing that its financial support of strapped legacy airlines gives some of them a second life under Chapter 11 that they don't deserve. Allowing nature to take its course would strengthen the industry, the critics of GECAS contend. Southwest Airlines is being harmed "by the capital coming into the market to keep some of the weaker players afloat," according to Laura Wright, chief financial officer of Southwest.[10] But GECAS has a lot to lose if carriers it is propping up go under. It would be left with a great many distressed assets—homeless airplanes.

By 1994, the financial crisis afflicting U.S. airlines had begun to subside and was followed by a benign period of five or so years in which they got well. The rising tide created by a strong bond market and resurgent economic growth lifted all boats, even the airline industry. Between 1995 and 1999 it generated a net profit of more than $20 billion. The profit margins of legacy carriers were ranging between 7 percent and 10 percent.

But cautionary sounds began to be heard. In 1996, Michael Levine, executive vice president of Northwest Airlines, said: "I think historically, the airline business has not been run as a real business. That is, a business designed to achieve a return on capital that is then passed on to the shareholders. It has . . . been run as an extremely elaborate version of a model railroad, that is, one in which you try to make enough money to buy more equipment."[11]

Predictably, the better times of the late 1990s led U.S. carriers back toward their old ways and the start of another cycle of misery. With a patched-up resource base and credit becoming available, they yet again began acquiring too many new airplanes. They also negotiated labor contracts that might not have cramped their style in good times but in hard times would be barely sustainable, if at all. And they started steadily hiking the fares of the business-class trade, their largest source of revenue. Business-class travelers were seen then by most airlines as "price insensitive" customers who wanted to get there fast and be on time for a meeting. Their tickets were a tax write-off, and what they cost didn't seem to matter much.

But then, as the dot-com bubble vented, the economy's hyper-growth phase shut down. For the legacy carriers, the timing could not have been worse. Raising business-class and other fares coincided with the growth of low-cost airlines and the greater transparency that became available via the Internet; in steadily greater numbers, air travelers were surfing the net for the best prices. Internet travel sites, such as Expedia, Travelocity, and Orbitz, took hold.

Also acquiring greater transparency were the encrusted problems of the airlines. The financial pressure got heavy. Lenders who had helped the industry by softening loans after the events of 9/11 restored the stiffer terms. Over the next four years U.S. airlines cut capital spending by 62 percent while taking on $16 billion of new debt to cover losses.[12] Since 2000, the legacy carriers have eliminated more than one hundred cities from their schedules, although regional airlines now operate many of the routes.

The ripple effect of serious and concurrent adversity cut a wide swath. According to Louis Miller, executive director of the Tampa International Airport (which is probably as well organized and designed as any airport anywhere), "The financial instability of the six legacy carriers represents the single biggest problem for airports. The airports get no public money and are fully self-supporting. Tampa Airport takes in $170 million per year in revenue. Thirty percent of that comes from airlines, the rest is from parking, car rentals, food, and beverages." (A rule of thumb is that any commercial airport that handles 2 million or so passengers won't need public assistance.) Troubled airlines, Miller said, "are using airport assets, or pending assets, to shed debt." US Airways, he noted, rejected a new hangar worth $27 million to the airport and its bondholders.[13]

Indianapolis International Airport has had a similar problem with United Airlines. As part of its bankruptcy deal, the carrier was allowed to cancel the lease with the airport on what was to be its second major maintenance center. The airport was then obliged to begin leasing out the facility to other users.

The price of fuel, which management can't control, is a major part of the punitive cost structure that airlines wrestle with. Another large component, of course, is labor, notably the costs of keeping pilots in the air.

Among the ills blamed on deregulation is the surfeit of airline pilots. Besides being overabundant, they are widely regarded as the world's most overpaid high-end technicians. During the worst downturn in the U.S. airline industry's history, legacy carriers were pressed hard by pilots to award or sustain contracts that were probably not sustainable. These contracts could hasten the collapse of some carriers, and the jobs from which so many of their pilots have prospered.

Relations between the senior management of legacy carriers and the pilots' union—the Air Line Pilots Association (known as ALPA)—have worsened since deregulation. Some industry analysts argue that the pilots are largely to blame. Oddly, the salaries of those who fly for the legacy carriers, besides being too high, are based on the size—actually, the weight—of the aircraft they fly. Hence, a pilot who normally flies a four-engine wide-bodied airplane nonstop between two cities set far apart is better paid than one who has the more demanding responsibility of taking off and landing a smaller airplane at sundry airports on a given day or evening.

Of course, the pilots do have plenty of leverage. For the airline, a strike means watching its revenue stream dry up as heavily mortgaged aircraft sit idly on the ground. And pilots have other weapons. They can burn high-cost fuel by letting engines idle overlong. They can slow down operations. For example, United Airlines pilots staged a slowdown in the summer of 2000, when weather and air traffic congestion already had put the carrier under heavy pressure. The slowdown enabled these pilots to win one of their richest contracts ever.[14] That contract is held up as having badly injured the industry's second-largest carrier, which two years later entered Chapter 11.

A long article in the *Financial Times* portrayed the widening scope of the union-management row in detail, with blunt examples and quotes. Rick Dubinski, a former head of ALPA, apparently told United management in the palmy late 1990s, "We don't want to kill the golden goose. We just want to choke it by the neck until it gives us every last egg."[15]

And Robert Crandall, the irreverent former chief of American Airlines, scolded both sides, saying, "Airline employees were compensated at a level nearly twice the average for all U.S. industries. The two highest paid professions were doctors and airline pilots. However, doctors averaged 41 hours of work per week, while pilots averaged 22 hours per week."[16] He is probably right, but it's equally true that among airline chiefs Crandall led the way in buying too many airplanes during cyclical upturns.

Entering Chapter 11 bankruptcy proceedings does offer enfeebled legacy carriers a weapon of sorts with which they can even the playing field. Section 113 of the bankruptcy code gives executives the power to tear up labor contracts and abridge the unions' leverage. Delta and American have secured concessions from the unions after invoking the threat of bankruptcy. US Airways has been steadily cutting costs with this tactic. The salaries of some of its pilots have fallen from $150,000 in 2002 to $70,000.[17] Their pension plans, along with those of flight attendants and other groups, are at some risk.

United Airlines warned that it might terminate some of its pension plans, adding that unless various contracts with unions could be renegotiated some aircraft would probably be repossessed. That warning got some attention; most travelers are not reluctant to fly a bankrupt airline, but one that has airplanes being repossessed is a different matter.

In November 2004, United announced that it would no longer support its pension scheme. It had a gap of $6.3 billion between the cost of retirement benefits and the assets available to pay for them. The costs are insured by a government-sponsored safety net, the Pension Benefit Guaranty Corporation (PBGC). However, the PBGC was and is also running a serious deficit. It reported a deficit for the year ending September 30, 2004, of $23.3 billion, more than twice that of the year before.[18]

A few weeks later, United announced a tentative deal with its pilots' union. The members agreed to forgo their pensions in return for more than half a billion dollars in convertible notes, which would compensate them for a significant part of their pension loss. However, the deal was contingent on every other union at United giving up its pension plan, willingly or unwillingly. But the other groups, starting with the flight attendants, refused to give way. And United continued to tread water, as did the other legacies.

In early February 2005, the *Financial Times* began a long article on the airline industry by noting, "After a year in which airlines cut jobs, trumpeted cost-cutting initiatives and reported record traffic, fourth quarter earning should have marked a turn-round. Instead, net losses for the six biggest U.S. airlines were seven times higher than a year ago, at $4.1 billion."[19]

Delta's CEO, Gerald Grinstein, elected to do more than talk about changing the pilots' pension plans unless they agreed to concessionary steps. Like other legacy chiefs, he did that, too, but then, early in 2005, he took a radically different and, indeed, astonishing step, one possibly born of desperation. In effect, he broke away from the legacy airlines and more or less aligned Delta with the low-cost carriers (LCCs) by capping and simplifying fares, plus cutting domestic fares by as much as 50 percent. Various restrictions, including the requirement for overnight stays on Saturday, were scrapped; that move had been aimed at discouraging business-class travelers from using discount tickets. In announcing his U-turn on revenue, Grinstein said, "Following years of confusing fare complexity, many customers no longer believed they were receiving a quality product at a competitive price."[20]

Within the industry, Delta was seen as forced to act because of the invasion of its markets by LCCs. They were competing with Delta at its Atlanta hub, on the East Coast, and in Florida. And three of them—JetBlue, Southwest, and AirTran—were limiting ticket prices to $299 one way, much less than the new cap of $499 that Delta had just placed on its fares. "Maybe they will get more real," said JetBlue's David Neeleman.[21]

Getting more real, however, would mean matching Delta's much lower, much simpler fare structure with an equally radical new approach to paring costs; but even with their survival at stake, the legacy carriers probably won't shrink their cost structure enough—enough, that is, to allow them to adopt the low-cost model and compete on even terms with LCCs. Within three years or so of 9/11, airline load factors had reached an all-time high and yet these companies were in a financial free fall.

It's probably only a matter of time before some or all of the six legacy carriers make their exit. Whether any of them can survive will depend on events. One or more of them might find solid ground by upgrading service, improving on-time performance, and, in the bargain, gaining major concessions from the unions. Two of the six— Continental and American—appear to be in somewhat better shape, or less vulnerable, than the others.

Suppose, some airline watchers wonder, this less wobbly twosome was to sponge up the best routes and the choice equipment of the ones actually walking the plank. Would the investment promote their chances of survival? Probably not. JetBlue and other LCCs could and probably would pick up such assets themselves, probably for fifty cents or so on the dollar, and thereby become an even stronger and more erosive force.

THE SKIRMISHING between pilots and management over salaries and pensions obscures a large hidden cost to legacy carriers in the form of union work rules that prevent people from doing jobs that they are not specifically authorized to perform. A pilot may not touch luggage. A flight attendant isn't allowed to change a blown lightbulb.

The low-cost carriers are not afflicted with these austere work rules because, for the most part, they have managed to dodge or contain the unions. Some of them pay wages that begin further down the scale than those paid by the major carriers. Some of them make their own arrangements with pilots, of whom there continues to be a surplus. Southwest Airlines, the senior and most successful LCC, has over time been able to make its pilots among the industry's highest paid, yet without harming the company's balance sheet, the best in the airline sector.

In the airline industry's time of deepest woe, the more successful LCCs have injected their people with a team spirit built on pride and a sense of connecting with growth organizations that will make it and possibly flourish. The absence of rigid work rules gives the LCCs a big advantage over the legacy carriers. Flight attendants working for some LCCs routinely clean the airplanes between flights so that turnaround time can be shortened and the expense of using cabin service crews avoided. Similarly, baggage handlers are often seen helping with the tugs that push back the airplanes.

Moreover, at Southwest and JetBlue, management people do not hesitate to help clean up the airplane or assist with luggage on the ramp. Herb Kelleher does too when he is aboard a Southwest flight, and he also talks to passengers. David Neeleman, the highly original and inventive founder and leader of JetBlue, sent a message that got his company's attention when he started assisting his crews while traveling. He may help the flight attendants or, during a stopover, pick up luggage, and even at times grab a handheld vac to help police the airplane and shorten ground time.

Shortening ground time is for these two carriers both a first principle and a cause. From the start, JetBlue's management expected the first bag to arrive on the carousel within ten minutes of its plane's arrival at the gate, the last one in twenty. Southwest negotiated labor contracts that allowed flexibility in operations of the system. According to a book on the airline, "When a Southwest plane pulls into the gate, employees in ground operations run for the aircraft like a pit crew scrambling to get an Indy car back on the track. . . . When a flight is running late, because of weather, it's not uncommon to see pilots helping customers in wheelchairs board the plane, helping the operations agents take boarding passes, or helping the flight attendants clean up the cabin between flights."[22]

Southwest is fully unionized, JetBlue not at all. JetBlue's management is known to feel that the arrival of a union would mean that the company had somehow failed the workforce. Southwest was always open to the presence of unions, partly because of the congenial environment it had created. One or more persons employed by a legacy carrier might have a complaint that would oblige their union to file a grievance. A union involved with Southwest could do that, too, but thus far wouldn't have had to. The difference is attitude.

The LCCs are not saddled with the traditional defined benefit plans that oppress the legacy carriers. Instead they offer 401(k)'s with company matches and profit sharing. Southwest provides stock option plans that at first were available only to management and pilots. Now they are available to flight attendants as well. Employees can also buy company stock at discounted prices. Few stocks have outperformed Southwest over the past twenty-five years.

Among the reasons for the success of Southwest and JetBlue has been the simplicity of operating one kind of airplane. That business model keeps maintenance and training costs low. The legacy carriers fly mixed fleets, and some of them even operate different engine types on the same airplane. Southwest operates only Boeing 737's, and JetBlue uses the Airbus equivalent, the A320 (although it will be adding one other, shorter-range aircraft to its fleet).

In recent years, the most intense struggle between Boeing and Airbus has matched the 737 against the A320 for supremacy in the low-cost market. Over time, the A320 gradually gained the advantage because it is a newer airplane and, for various reasons, increasingly in favor with low-cost carriers. That is important, because those carriers, plus various leasing companies, are buying the new airplanes. The strapped legacy carriers are buying very little new equipment. Instead, some of them are cutting back. Well before reforming its fare structure, Delta decided to delay the delivery of 10 new Boeing aircraft and cancel options for 113 others.

Some of the low-cost carriers are more austere than others. There is a spectrum of passenger comfort and services. JetBlue, with reserved seating and seats with monitors showing twenty-four channels of direct satellite TV, lies at the gentler end. David Neeleman refers to his company as a services company (not as an airline). He removed a row of seats in the rear of his aircraft so that passengers seated there have more legroom. In distinguishing his approach from Southwest's, he says, "We wanted to spare people the stress of getting to the airport in time to get seats with family. Otherwise you feel you are fighting your way into the airplane."[23]

In the middle of the comfort spectrum are Southwest and Britain's easyJet, among others. At the harsher end is Ireland's highly successful Ryanair, often called a Greyhound bus; its CEO, Michael O'Leary, describes his business plan as "piling 'em high and selling 'em cheap."

What actually defines Southwest and JetBlue is the coherence of their business plans; the various pieces fit together and complement one another. Apart from keeping costs in line with a low-cost structure, this means training people to be friendly and, in turn, keeping them happy by communicating—explaining the steps that management is taking and why these will serve employee interest. And there is little sense of hierarchy in either place.

It began with Southwest, almost the only low-cost carrier to survive the hurly-burly of the immediate post-deregulation years. Fifty-eight airlines began life after deregulation, and only one—Southwest— stayed the course. If Kelleher, its leader, is the industry's most successful figure, he is probably the most flamboyant as well. By one account, Southwest "was propelled by the outrageous antics of its chain-smoking, bourbon-swigging chief executive ... who cultivated an outlaw image by riding a Harley-Davidson and dressing up in Elvis Presley costumes at company events."[24]

David Neeleman is very different. He is a seventh-generation Mormon who was born in 1959 in São Paulo, Brazil, where his father did missionary work for a time. But the family had its roots in Salt Lake City, where Neeleman grew up and also began his professional life. He now lives simply with his wife and nine children in Connecticut, and commutes to the airline's main office in Queens. (Neeleman and a few of his colleagues also work out of an office in Darien, Connecticut.)

Rather intuitively, it seems, Neeleman began edging into the role of airline entrepreneur while still in his mid-twenties. By 1985, he was maneuvering a minuscule airline, called Morris Air, into existence. He openly imitated Southwest by flying Boeing 737's, serving peanuts-only snacks, and demanding swift turnarounds, with crews offloading the arriving aircraft, cleaning and refueling it, and taking it off again in just twenty minutes.[25]

Neeleman based Morris Air in Salt Lake City, and concentrated on flying between there and Los Angeles, a route he had studied and knew well. Morris Air got off to a good start and before long was growing and outperforming other airlines on that route.

Although fiercely determined to create a smaller version of Southwest, Neeleman had ideas of his own. One of them, as described in a book about JetBlue by Barbara S. Peterson, "would help usher in one of the most far-reaching changes in the way airlines do business: electronic ticketing." An airline passenger, Neeleman decided, didn't need to get a ticket—only a reservation number and a boarding pass. The more elaborate and costly ticketing process would be bypassed, and a great deal of money would thereby be saved. Also, the airline would be paid up front by customers with credit cards arriving at the airport. Neeleman was one of a very few airline bosses who was prepared then to reject an entrenched system that was relied upon by most of the other players, not least travel agents.[26]

Neeleman became rich when he sold Morris Air to Kelleher, who felt a need to beef up Southwest because United Airlines had Southwest in its sights. The deal included bringing Neeleman to Southwest in a senior role. His association with Kelleher didn't last long, however. Neeleman's innovative ideas, persistently advanced, strained the tolerances of older and more experienced members of the Kelleher team.

Later, however, Neeleman would infuse his start-up, JetBlue, with the larger part of the Southwest culture.

The two business models have remained similar in ways that matter, but each has characteristics that set it apart from the other. Both fly their customers point-to-point, not to big hub airports from which many travelers must change planes so as to reach their actual destinations. Southwest's route structure is built around short hauls. Its marketing and growth strategy was built around stealing these high-volume short-distance markets from the majors.

JetBlue has been flying longer routes, including many transcontinental routes that Neeleman's start-up plan had targeted. His assumption, since borne out, was that JetBlue could sell lots of $129 tickets to people who would otherwise be paying $899 to United or American for the same trip. But first he had to find the right airport location, one that would accommodate his purpose: to create an airline built around high-frequency, low-cost service. For that, he would need a major airport located in a major metropolitan area.

He wanted to be in New York, but Newark Airport and La Guardia were at full capacity. That left John F. Kennedy Airport. He chose it, thereby surprising many industry people. JFK, they thought, was in a serious and well-deserved decline, partly because people found it overly hard to reach. Also, it was seen as having "a growing crime problem, a sizable homeless population and, in popular lore at least, its cargo hangars functioned as a sort of ATM for organized crime." And by this account, many other airline managements had decided against using JFK "after the Port Authority of New York and New Jersey had failed to get support for a one-billion-dollar plan to rebuild the airport around a central terminal."[27]

However, JFK appealed to Neeleman and his team in part because it served mainly international carriers whose operations were concentrated in the late afternoon and early evening hours. The earlier part of the day offered a lot of dead time. "You know most of the time Kennedy is so quiet that you could go bowling on the runways," observed one of Neeleman's colleagues.[28]

Neeleman wanted JetBlue to start big and expand quickly. That part of his plan would depend on the availability of slots at the airport he chose and the willingness of the Department of Transportation to award them to JetBlue. ("Slots" is shorthand for rights to take off and land at specific times.) In Neeleman's case, this was especially tricky, since he was asking for seventy-five slots, many more than are normally assigned. Airlines generally do not ask for more than a few slots at any one time, just enough to accommodate some modest expansion of service. But Neeleman was requesting a bushel basket of them, saying, in effect, "Our plan requires predictability. Give us seventy-five now, and over the next couple of years we will ramp up operations and use them all."

Neeleman got the slots, partly (perhaps mainly) because his business plan impressed the Department of Transportation as bold but credible. It impressed other parties as well, starting with the financial community. "I'm initiating coverage of JetBlue Airways with a '1' rating," wrote the chief airline analyst at a major investment bank on April 9, 2002.

> This company is doing an IPO of 5.5 million shares of common stock that was expected to price . . . with a range of $22–24. In that range, the stock would price in a market cap of approximately $1 billion. However, the retail demand is cult-like (think Krispy Kreme) and most analysts would not be surprised to see a first trade of up to $2 billion in market cap. . . . It's been a long time since we've put the words "hot" and "deal" (not to mention "airline") in the same sentence, so I'm not sure whether the overall market is ready for more. If history's any indication, though, I do know that the underlying fundamentals . . . should justify some pretty extraordinary valuations . . . in the intermediate term.
>
> JetBlue is a low-fare, low-cost passenger airline that has differentiated itself in a commodity business with customer service and live TV. With both short-haul and long-haul routes, it

focuses on underserved markets and large metropolitan areas that have high average fares. It is the first start-up carrier to use all new A320 aircraft—it has 24 now and will have another 59 by 2007. *So, shiny new planes, low fare, friendly service and live TV are its marketing schtick.*

Equally impressed, it seems, were senior Airbus people in Toulouse. "First of all, Neeleman was impressive," says Benoit Debain, senior vice president for finance. "He had sold Morris Air to Southwest, and he had $130 million equity. That is a lot for a start-up. We had at first been skeptical about a plan that included taking out some seats and putting TV in the rest of them. The banks in the U.S. would say, 'You can't make money that way.' "[29]

At first, however, JetBlue was to have been a joint venture with Richard Branson, Britain's remarkably successful creator of Virgin this and Virgin that. But the joint business plan immediately collided with the statute that limits (as noted) a foreign entity's ownership of an American venture to 25 percent of voting shares and 49 percent of total equity.

Branson had wanted the partnership with Neeleman to enlarge his standing in the American market. He was not content with being a passive voice and withdrew from it, a step he now deeply regrets. "In retrospect," Branson says, "I should have taken a forty-nine percent minority share and called it VirginBlue instead of JetBlue."[30] Had he done so, he would have made yet another fortune. He and Neeleman parted amicably.

Like most airline watchers, Neeleman has been awaiting the demise of US Airways. When and if that actually comes about, JetBlue would move into the ultrahigh-fare short-haul market in the Northeast. But planning for the step has led JetBlue away from one of the first principles of the Southwest model: keep things simple and cover the entire route structure with just one airplane. Instead, Neeleman will penetrate the new short-haul markets not with his fleet of A320's but with another airplane—a hundred-seater made by Embraer, a Brazilian company that specializes (very successfully) in regional aircraft and is now the world's fourth-largest airplane maker.

Whether Neeleman is fated to regret his divergence from the Southwest model won't be clear for some time. In May 2005, US Airways drew a reprieve from near-term disaster by merging with America West, another seriously sick carrier, in a deal creating the sixth-largest U.S. airline. Moreover, Airbus is loaning the partners $250 million that will be largely devoted to buying up to twenty A350's.[31] With US Airways a little less close to the edge of the cliff, the question for JetBlue is whether its new Embraer airplanes can be aligned with its route planning or will become a problem.

These planes, although obviously smaller than the A320's, are a bit wider, hence more comfortable, and they have full-size overhead bins. They would be a good fit for JetBlue, provided a chunk of existing capacity—that is, the US Airways route structure—disappeared. That could still happen. But the merger buys time; roughly how much defies prediction.

JetBlue's use of reserved seating was a major divergence from Southwest. Southwest, as always in full compliance with its low-cost model, was reluctant to shoulder the added expense of arranging for passengers to reserve their seats. Curiously, Herb Kelleher, unlike Neeleman, saw no reason to include this feature in what he himself insists on describing as "a customer-service business," not an airline. That is expected to change, and it will. There is no indication that Southwest will emulate JetBlue's added attraction—the twenty-four channels of DIRECTV.

Meanwhile, Southwest, without dispensing seat assignments or providing in-flight entertainment, has continued to outperform all other U.S. airlines in the ways that matter. In 2002, its market capitalization was $4 billion—more than all of the legacies put together. Three years later, the Southwest number had climbed to $11 billion, and the combined total for the legacies had slipped and was closer to $3 billion.

Legacy airline stocks are ignored by long-term investors. Day traders are the only ones speculating on the paper that has been out there for years.

Adding insult to injury, the low-cost segment of the industry has experienced its biggest growth since 9/11. While the major carriers cut back, Southwest, JetBlue, and other low-cost carriers were boosting capacity. In March 2005, Southwest announced its intention to expand capacity by 10 percent without adding further employee head count.[32] The announcement coincided with news that, because of rising fuel prices, four of the six legacy carriers were planning to freeze or reduce the number of seats on domestic flights, even though the planes were generally flying full.[33]

Some of the major carriers, notably United and Delta, have created smaller siblings built on the low-cost model. United's is called Ted; Delta's was Song, a short-lived match. It's unlikely that a low-cost affiliate can mate profitably with any of the major airlines, given their bad habits and high cost structures.

The question arises: If Delta and United managed to bring down their costs, would either of them choose to create a low-cost affiliate? There is a long history of "low-cost airlines *within* an airline," not one of which has stayed aloft for very long. Although JetBlue appeared to be Song's role model, its revenue per passenger seat mile remained well below JetBlue's. Its cost structure resembled Delta's. Legacy carriers seem unwilling to accept that the cost advantage of JetBlue and Southwest is based on much more than not serving hot meals.

Hubert Horan, an experienced airline analyst, notes "the growing ability, across the economy, for new business models to rapidly overwhelm long-standing traditional models. Common examples include Home Depot [which rendered the local hardware store obsolete] and Wal-Mart [which overpowered department stores and other traditional retailers].

"Imagine Nordstrom feeling threatened and deciding to start a no-frills, low-price store across from Wal-Mart," says Horan. "It would be a disaster. These things [the airline within the airline] are strictly the product of desperate CEOs who don't know the first thing about the industry and who hire McKinzie to produce some type of magic solution."[34] According to Horan, Gordon McKinzie sold the Song and Ted projects to Delta and United even after other similar experiments, also inspired by McKinzie, had been tried unsuccessfully.

The legacy carriers hope, and some of them seem to believe, that the leaner cost structures of the LCCs will over time mature and level the playing field. That might happen, but if and when it does, some of those older airlines will have been done in by their costs, as well as by a severe capacity glut, punitive fuel prices that could go higher, and a thin revenue stream. Increasingly, they are being seen not as legacies, but as dinosaurs that will have to rediscover the evolutionary path or become extinct.

CHAPTER FIVE

Playing the Game

THE ROUGH-AND-TUMBLE BUSINESS in which Airbus and Boeing battle for every sale is strewn with traps. Nothing is certain until the contracts are signed. Often a senior Boeing or Airbus executive will reach what seems to be agreement with an airline customer. The chemistry is good, and there may even be a handshake. The winner retires later in the evening—usually much later, since the bargaining can take most of the night. He may then discover the next day or a day or two later that his company actually had lost. The customer might then say, "I liked the deal, but I was overruled by my board." Chances are he wasn't overruled, but instead used the deal that Party A thought had been reached to squeeze an even better one from Party B.

When Jean Pierson's tenure in Toulouse began, about 40 percent of the airline market lay in North America. As Airbus was then—a new, foreign, and untested player—it wasn't likely to make much of a dent in that market, although it had created a separate organization in New York. Its chairman was Alan Boyd, an accomplished and universally respected figure. In every job Boyd had held, whether chairing the Civil Aeronautics Board or becoming the first U.S. secretary of transportation (to name just two), he left behind a vast circle of admirers and well-wishers. People liked working for him and with him. And he knew the aircraft industry's rough terrain better than most.

Boyd and Pierson were a good fit, although stylistically very different. Boyd, who is now retired and living in northern Florida, was low-key, unflappable, and analytical. Pierson was a dynamic and, indeed, vivid figure. It would be hard to find a chief executive in his or any other business with more expressive body language. And it would be hard to find one who exuded a more acute mastery of the details of this endlessly demanding trade. Like most European aerospace executives, past and present, Pierson has a strong command of English, although richly accented.

In April 1985, shortly after taking over, Pierson visited the New York office. "It was on the twenty-first floor of a building in Rockefeller Center," he recalls. "This was a tower. I'm a factory-floor guy. There were no Americans there, except for Alan. There were just Germans and French there.

"This was my first visit, but it was clear to me we were going nowhere. I said to Alan at dinner, 'Either we end this operation now or we become aggressive. First, we have to get out of this tower and go somewhere else. We need a product support center. Let's build an integrated U.S. operation and hire one hundred people—all Americans—and give this operation an American face.'"[1]

He says now that he had wanted "an authentic American presence, not some transplanted Gauloise-smoking Frenchmen" (that is, people very like himself). "We looked at Miami and someplace near Atlanta," he continued. "Finally, we chose a location around Washington, near Dulles Airport. We would have good air service there and plenty of land. There were lots of subcontractors nearby. It was a good compromise, although we did locate our pilot training center in Miami. Yes, it's a world market, but each village has its own character. I decided to put sales and marketing people in a place who had the color of the village. That was priority one in the U.S."[2]

Alan Boyd then recruited seven young Americans whom he and Pierson hoped would be able to sell Airbuses. Each was given an airline to pursue. One of the seven was John Leahy, a former Piper Cub salesman, who rose quickly—"like a rocket," says Pierson. Leahy soon became vice president for sales in North America, and, as noted, Pierson brought him to Toulouse in 1996 as vice president for sales. Leahy, too, may be en route to becoming a legendary figure. "John Leahy is the most formidable aircraft salesman I've ever met," says Richard Branson, of Virgin Atlantic, who has bought several planes from him.[3]

"He is the best airplane salesman in memory," says John Rose, chairman of Rolls-Royce aeroengines. "Boeing has no one like him—no one with the talent and obsessive drive to sell airplanes."[4]

Alan Boyd, who hired Leahy, says, "He is a great salesman. He will not take no for an answer. He has an excellent mind but is not tolerant of those who are less acute than he."[5]

Within the company, Leahy is widely described as friendless but much admired and relied upon. Some of the people who like him least feel that his contribution to Airbus nearly matches Pierson's. Although his rapport with Pierson was never strong, they were a formidable team. Pierson says, "I might tell him, 'We can't sell the airplane beneath that price, but do everything else you have to [that is, make concessions], and I will take care of the board.' "[6]

They became known as "big John and little John," and they are configured accordingly. In selecting Leahy for the top job in sales, Pierson knew he would upset an Airbus partner, British Aerospace. However, BAe, as it's known, had not been a great success in running the sales operations. What it was very good at was building wings.

"Only he [Pierson] would have put an American who spoke no French in that job," Leahy now says. "He saw it as a chance to change the politics of the organization. And he did. The company now runs itself in English. And we got the market share in Europe up to the market share we had developed in the U.S."[7] (This was an allusion to the remarkable spurt in sales to U.S. airlines after Leahy took control of the American operation.)

Holding on to market share in either sector would not be easy. Airbus first had to show that it could support its products reliably. "No one thought Airbus could build a competent and comprehensive product support system," Pierson recalled. "So we had that to overcome. It is the unglamorous, nuts-and-bolts part of the business."[8]

Before Pierson took over, product support was a less than consuming affair for Airbus. According to Clyde Kizer, who was then Airbus's executive vice president for product support in North America, "there was no twenty-four/seven in France, or Britain, or Germany. Airline customers who complained were told at least once by senior management in Paris that if they 'operated equipment the way we told you to operate it, you wouldn't have these problems.'"

In 1992, Kizer ran a survey of U.S. airlines aimed at showing which manufacturer had the best product support. "Boeing," he said, "came out first, GE second, Pratt third, and Douglas fourth. There was no number five. Airbus was judged so bad we were listed sixth."[9]

In Toulouse, Pierson put Gerard Blanc, who became executive vice president for operations, in charge of product support. "We were not well rated," said Blanc. "I had no experience. We were being hit on the head by the airlines. There was skepticism about our professionalism and the promptness of our reactions.

"We had to change the mind-set of our people. 'A problem will have to become an opportunity,' I said. 'I will be happy only when five airlines which I select give us an unsolicited vote of confidence.' It took a while, but we got them."

Blanc talked about the difficulties. "We Europeans," he said, "do not have this sense of service that the Americans and Asians have. It is a service mind-set that we lack. Maybe it is cultural. Maybe it is education. We didn't seem to have a natural talent for it."[10]

The advent of Pierson at Airbus coincided with a transfer of power at Boeing. T. Wilson, who had steered the company for sixteen years, was succeeded by Frank Schrontz, a capable and widely respected figure whose background and style bore little resemblance to his. Wilson was plainspoken, often earthy, and throughout his forty-two-year career with Boeing lived in the same house that he had purchased in the late 1940s while employed as a junior engineer.[11]

Wilson had succeeded another towering figure, William Allen, who spent forty-seven years with Boeing and is probably best remembered for his decision to build the 747. Making that move amounted literally to betting the company, and indeed, building the 747 very nearly did kill Boeing. Many years later, Boeing executives still spoke of the awesome but excruciating experience of creating what seemed an outrageously large airplane, one that none of the airlines needed or that very few were interested in buying; an airplane whose principal requirement— an engine strong enough to power it—didn't exist and might not become available, at least not in time to meet Boeing's delivery schedules with customer airlines.

As the weight of the new airplane grew steadily, so did the thrust requirements, so much so that Pratt & Whitney, the engine maker, couldn't keep up. Wings will break if they don't have the weight of the engines to hold them down. So Boeing had to put blocks of concrete on the wings in lieu of the engines that should have been there. In short, for a time Boeing confronted the prospect of rolling out the world's biggest gliders instead of the first jumbo airliners.

In trade talk, Bill Allen was "being sporty"—risking a lot in order to keep his company ahead of market trends and the competition. His successor, T. Wilson, was a kindred spirit. Boeing's performance during the Allen-Wilson years was a primer on how to succeed in this exigent business.

Frank Schrontz was selected to succeed Wilson by Wilson himself, not by a committee. He was a lawyer and had spent part of his career in the Pentagon, first as an assistant secretary of the air force and then as assistant secretary of defense. In these jobs he drew high praise. His interests were always wide-ranging; he was active in a variety of civic and charitable organizations.

As Wilson's heir apparent and then his successor, Schrontz might have been described as better suited to a subtly changing and more worldly environment, one in which a seat-of-the-pants decision by the leader on a complex issue could be frowned on by the board. Partly because of his Washington experience, Schrontz was judged capable of giving his somewhat insular company a more international outlook, which in turn might help in the global marketplace. (He demonstrated his feel for that and more by helping the Clinton administration bring about APEC—Asia-Pacific Economic Cooperation.) Moreover, he was well liked, within and beyond his company: "a real gent" was a phrase often used to describe Schrontz. And he injected some discipline into various company operations that lacked it.

But Wilson would have been a very hard act for anyone to follow. Most of the senior people whom Schrontz inherited had judged Wilson the complete leader, their polar star. Perhaps inevitably, some of these retired "Boeing heritage" people—those who had been with the company in smoother times—now recall the start of their company's decline as having coincided with the end of the Wilson era.

The company didn't change overnight, however. The shift in leadership had a lot to do with personal style. Schrontz was considerably more cautious than Wilson. He was also a more formal and distant figure.

The Boeing Commercial Airplanes group regarded itself—and described itself—as a company of engineers; most of the people who mattered at that time were engineers. Schrontz was not an engineer, but it was often said of him that he could think like one. According to John Hayhurst, a former senior vice president and member of the executive council, "He could get excited by the hardware, and he had a command of details. And he was courageous. It was Frank who stepped up and launched the 777."[12]

It was also Schrontz who stood accused by some colleagues of waiting too long to launch this minijumbo. But Schrontz's timing on the 777 launch was vindicated by events. Although Airbus's own minijumbo, the A340, began life first, Boeing leapfrogged its rival by investing enough time, energy, and resources in the longer-range and more profitable version of its 777, thereby allowing the airplane to enter service well in advance of Airbus's counterpart.

Schrontz worked very closely with Dean Thornton, who became president of the commercial airplanes group in February 1985, at the same time Schrontz was appointed the chief executive. Both were from Idaho, and they had attended its state university at the same time. Thornton was an accountant by formation, but he too could think like an engineer, was very comfortable with the patois of engineering, and was highly regarded at all levels of a company that had exacting standards. Thornton, like Wilson, was blunt and direct, and he probably resembled Wilson more closely than any other contemporary.

Among various demanding jobs that Wilson gave him was serving as vice president and general manager of the 767 division when the airplane was developed and brought to the market. In that role, Thornton dealt directly with the Japanese heavies, the first time the three were subcontractors on a Boeing program. (In 1969, Mitsubishi Heavy Industries contracted with Boeing to build carriage kits for the 747.)

It was, of course, Schrontz who became the focus of complaints about steps that seemed to stray from standard Boeing practice. "Frank did things in a new way," says Stanley Little, who for many years was vice president for industrial and public relations. "It was a new style, more cautious. Things would be on hold. And lots of questions were asked about why we were doing what we were doing instead of having us just doing it. Things got proceduralized."[13]

Some operations became more proceduralized, probably because they had to be. Schrontz and Thornton had to start coping with the effects of airline deregulation that were beginning to take hold. The regulated environment had been easier on all parties, except for the air traveler. An airframe maker knew that a portion of his costs could be passed on to the airline, which in turn could pass on its higher costs to the passenger, provided the Civil Aeronautics Board approved the increase in price of a given fare.

The industry model was changing. At some point not far off, the airlines would have considerably less money to spend on acquiring new equipment. It would take another five years or so before that point was reached, but the handwriting was on the wall.

Boeing's new leadership, like Airbus's, was focused on the changes under way in the airline market. Boeing was telling itself, "This is going to be a commodities marketplace now. We've got a full product line, which will let us concentrate on revamping the factory floor and cutting costs." Briefly, the focus in Seattle began to switch from products to process. It wasn't that way in Toulouse. Airbus didn't have a product line, and Pierson and a few of his colleagues were thinking about new airplanes, less about process. Pierson and Roger Beteille—who, as noted, was regarded as a founding father of Airbus and, for quite a while, Europe's foremost aerodynamicist—wanted to build a new single-aisle airplane. "Beteille was convinced we should do it," Pierson recalls, "provided the airplane brought with it a lot of new things. He wanted a clean break with Boeing's 737 and Douglas's DC-9 in aerodynamics. He wanted some carbon fiber [hence, less weight] and a new flight management system.

"Since 1976, we had been working on a new cockpit—flight management system—in the lab. It was fly by wire. It was being tested on the Concorde [the Anglo-French supersonic transport], where I was production manager. But only in 1982 did we decide that we were ready for fly by wire."[14]

Fly by wire is a system for moving an airplane's control surfaces with electrical impulses transmitted by wire. It replaced the heavier standard system that did the job with cables and pulleys. The new electronic system, assuming it took hold, would allow computer-driven controls to handle an airplane and direct its course. The yoke, or joystick, would go.

This was Airbus chutzpah. Fly by wire, although by then being used in combat aircraft, was wholly alien to the culture of airline pilots. The system would give them little to do aside from putting navigational points into the computer and pushing buttons on a small side stick that transmitted impulses to the aircraft's flaps and ailerons.

The decision to adopt such a radically different, if simpler, system was, to put it mildly, controversial. Bob Crandall, boss of American Airlines, told Pierson that because his pilots were opposed to the new cockpit, American couldn't buy the A320, the new airplane's designation.

As for Beteille, he was not just fully committed to fly by wire; he wouldn't support going forward with the A320 without building a new flight management system around it. "The fly by wire was all Beteille," says Bob Alizart, Pierson's former executive assistant and his friend.

"He held up the decision on the A320 until there was something new and remarkable with which to challenge Boeing."[15] That would be the new cockpit.

The bold venture was then held up for nearly three years, partly because none of the engine makers had a power plant that closely fitted the A320's requirements. Beteille, according to Pierson, had to persuade GE to improve its CFM56 engine, which was to become one of the two most widely used engines for single-aisle airplanes, especially Boeing's 737. But this improved version of the engine was made available to Airbus for the A320 at a time when Boeing 737's were still being equipped with an earlier version.

"We then inspired an engine that would compete [with the CFM56]," says Pierson. "It was a partnership arrangement between Rolls-Royce and Pratt [& Whitney]. So the fly by wire brought with it a lot of other new stuff."[16] In fact, the partnership Pierson cites included German, Italian, and Japanese companies. The consortium was christened International Aero Engines (IAE). And its first new engine, the V2500, would compete on roughly even terms with the vastly successful CFM56, the product of a partnership between GE and the French engine maker Snecma.

But the more serious and intractable difficulty confronting Pierson and Beteille was about money—more exactly, about convincing the British and German governments to provide the launch aid that the project needed. The Germans gradually fell into line, but a few key members of Prime Minister Margaret Thatcher's government were strenuously opposed to further enlarging this partnership with what they saw as European socialism. In the end, though, she ruled against them. Ruling the other way, she knew, would probably cost Britain its place in the Airbus consortium.

The delays hurt. Pierson and especially Beteille had been counting on their new airplane, because it was state-of-the-art, to outperform Boeing's 737 in the marketplace. It would—but years later, and only after the longest-lasting, most episodic and evenly balanced competition the industry has seen.

The advent of the A320 was a turning point. Its importance to what has become of Airbus and Boeing can't be overstated. A truly pivotal mistake lay in Boeing's reluctance to replace the 737 with a new airplane. "Boeing should have killed this upstart," says Alizart. "If Boeing had produced a clean sheet of paper the A320 would never have become Airbus's bread and butter."[17]

The A320 embodied an array of technological advances that became common to the Airbus models that were to come. Just the fly by wire should have been a wake-up call for Boeing.

Gradually, Airbus converted major users of the 737, some of whom had bought only Boeing aircraft, to the A320. It became Airbus's stalking horse. By the late 1980s the A320 was giving Airbus market share, credibility, and cash, all of which Airbus leveraged and used to create the A330 and A340. And the A330-200, which entered service in 1998, killed a Boeing workhorse, the 767.

"All of our big turning points were in the U.S. market," said Gerard Blanc, Airbus's executive vice president for operations.[18]

THE PERIOD between 1985 and 1998 was one in which Airbus rose and Boeing held steady. Together they killed McDonnell Douglas. For most of that time, Boeing chose to regard Airbus as an annoyance but not a serious threat. But Airbus, unlike Boeing, was telling itself that technology matters, and so do new products. In a book about Airbus, Stephen Aris wrote: "What impressed companies like Northwest Airlines, who placed a $3.2 billion order for the A320 in 1986, was not the number of computers on board, but the numbers the technology could deliver in terms of operating and seat mile costs."[19]

The battle for the single-aisle market had been launched a year earlier. Besides the fifteen A320's that American Airlines had bought, Pan American had bought sixteen, with an option for another thirty-four. But the Northwest order is worth pausing over because it showed how the game between airframe makers is played—how it is never over until it is definitively over. The order was notable, first, because the key fig-ure was Franz Josef Strauss, who was then chairman of the Airbus executive committee. Strauss, who was among the consortium's strong and formative figures, had been West Germany's minister of defense and had served for many years as the leader of the Bavarian wing of the country's Christian Democratic political coalition. Like Pierson, Strauss was a vivid and dominant personality, and they got on very well.

Recalling the Northwest buy of A320's in 1986, Pierson says, "I was in my office and Strauss called. That was an event. 'Come to Munich tomorrow,' he said. 'Steve Rothmeyer,' he said, who is a good friend of mine, is going to be there. [Rothmeyer was the chief executive of Northwest.] He'd been invited to come for hunting. I checked with [Alan] Boyd, who said the A320 was of interest to Northwest.

"There had not yet been any negotiation, and we started the talks. And there were other talks. In the end, we shook hands on one hundred Northwest options for the A320. There were difficulties then with the British, who said our price was not high enough. I then called the chair-man of BAe. 'This is the first strategic deal in the U.S.,' I said. 'You have convinced Mrs. Thatcher to give you money [the launch aid that France and Germany were also providing], now you can tell her about this.' So BAe came along. I'd have resigned if anyone had blocked this deal."[20]

"The Northwest deal was of enormous strategic importance for us," recalls Alan Boyd. "Northwest had been a Boeing customer. Boe-ing had provided Northwest with all kinds of credits."[21] Northwest became Airbus's first big American customer, and was also the first of John Leahy's major conquests; it was he who did the heavy-duty nego-tiations on the deal.

No one expected Boeing to yield this home turf without reacting, and according to Leahy, Frank Schrontz reacted by sending an order form to Steve Rothmeyer that left blank the price being sought. Roth-meyer, again according to Leahy, told him that it was all over; he had made his decision.

Rothmeyer's version differed in the details. "Yes," he said, "I did make the deal with Airbus, and yes, Boeing did come back after the deal had been made, saying, in effect, let us try again. We weren't being competitive. They wanted to offer a better price. But the call was not made by Frank. And it wasn't made to me, but to one of my executives."[22] Clearly, the level at which the call was made hardly mattered.

Rothmeyer chose the A320, he said, because he was "buying a clean sheet of paper. The fly by wire appealed to me a lot. It was very attractive. And there were a lot of other things in the airplane—the galleys, the lavs suited the configuration Northwest wanted. It performed very well with either of the two engines, and we were offered a very good price on those. But the commonalty was a special feature. We were intending to buy A330's and A340's, so the commonalty was important."[23] These larger and a bit younger siblings of the A320 shared many of its features, including the cockpit. This commonalty in the Airbus family is known to have tilted a number of sales campaigns toward Airbus.

The febrile overspending by airlines no longer bound by federally imposed restraints reached a peak in the late 1980s. Would it last? In late September 1990, Frank Schrontz and Philip Condit, executive vice president and general manager of Boeing's commercial airplane group, told the editorial board of the *Seattle Post-Intelligencer* that the cascade of new orders had slowed but that the company's order book looked solid for the next two years.[24]

Within those two years, each of the big three carriers—American, United, and Delta—scaled back orders of Boeing aircraft. And all three announced that they were reducing capacity—a step without precedent for any one of them. Europe's airline market was soft, too, mainly because the costs associated with Germany's unification had weakened all of Western Europe economically. In that woeful market, not even Boeing could shrug off a customer's decision to stretch out orders for new equipment, cancel orders, or elect to buy equipment from the competition if the price was right.

In July 1992, Boeing was shocked when United—its biggest and most reliable customer over the years—bought fifty narrow-bodied airplanes, said to be worth roughly $3 billion, from Airbus. United was choosing between Boeing 737's and Airbus's newer A320's.

Conversations between Airbus and United about the A320 had been going on for three years. "We were flying it in Toulouse in 1988," recalls Gordon McKinzie, who was manager of United's new technology division. "It was competing against the early versions of the 737—the 200 and 300." The idea of choosing Airbus over Boeing was a sobering question for United. "We spent a lot more time looking at the A320 than we did the 737, because that was a known quantity," says McKinzie. "We had to look at the likely maintenance costs, the costs of spares, the infrastructure we'd have to build around a fleet of those airplanes. It would mean getting new parts and adjusting to suppliers we hadn't dealt with."[25]

In talks with United, a delegation of twenty or so Airbus people was closeted for twenty days in a motel outside Chicago. They represented the marketing, finance, engineering, and sales divisions. John Leahy was probably the key figure. The sessions lasted most of the night, with the back-and-forth usually recessing at about 2 or 3 a.m., at which point some of the Airbus people would work through the rest of the night preparing talking points for the next day. The talks would resume at 7 a.m. "It was all about what they wanted and we were willing to give them," recalled Clyde Kizer, who was then president of Airbus Product Support. "It wasn't complicated but was very tough."[26]

Airbus had often competed for United's business, but had never before won an order. "We had grown weary of being used to drive down the price of Boeing airplanes," said Alan Boyd. "And we said as much to Steve Wolf [who was then United's chairman]. 'What do you want?' we asked him. 'Fifty airplanes,' he said. The terms were agreed on. Boeing then made a bad situation worse by deploying heavy guns—United board members—against the management's decision. But Wolf told Boeing it was all over. It was a huge precedent and a blow to Boeing's vanity."[27]

Frank Schrontz demurred. "For a customer like United, that would have been a very desperate activity for Boeing," he said. "If asked by a board member, I might tell him what I think, but no board member asked me."[28]

A fine fuzz obscures many details of this episode. Airbus and Boeing offered conflicting versions of what happened, and United's management was reluctant to talk frankly about the tactics it employed to drive down the cost of the new airplanes. And drive them down it did. Just how far down and how many sweeteners the winning side—Airbus—provided wasn't clear. What actually goes on between airframe suppliers and their all but financially prostrate customers is the stuff of legends and sets their business apart from any other.

Probably no one has figured in more crucial transactions than Pierson, not least Airbus's breakthrough with United. Although the terms of that deal were reached in Chicago, it had to be approved by United's Wolf and Airbus's Pierson; they had agreed to do so in Toulouse.

But, Pierson says, Boeing and, more interestingly, GE had other ideas. "Steve Wolf was on his way to Toulouse via Paris and was passing the night at the Crillon hotel," Pierson recalls. "Frank Schrontz and Jack Welch called him there separately and proposed selling him the 737 with the CFM56 engine [the GE engine], with an additional discount of $500 million, provided Steve canceled his trip to Toulouse. Steve told me about the phone call. He came to Toulouse, and we closed the A320 deal after lunch."[29] Pierson says that Welch called him and denied ever making the offer to Wolf, or even calling him. But Steve Wolf confirmed Pierson's account of this affair in every detail.

"They made a strong tactical mistake, knowing Steve Wolf," said Pierson. "I was determined and so was United. Schrontz was just doing his job, but I was furious with Welch because his engine, the CFM56, was also an A320 engine." So why, then, did Welch try to help Boeing? "Welch's motivation was as simple as Jack is," said Pierson.[30] He meant that with the 737, GE had a monopoly—it was flown only with the CFM56 engine, whereas A320 customers had a choice of that engine or the V2500, which had been jointly developed by GE's main competitors, Pratt & Whitney and Rolls-Royce. Airlines relish having options; engine companies relish exclusivity, although they don't often get it.

"There were several incidents when GE gave larger concessions on their engines for Boeing airplanes than for Airbus's," says Alan Boyd. "Airbus got that information from airlines, even though GE always denied it. Jack Welch was running the show then."[31]

The purchase by US Airways of 130 aircraft in the A320 family, with options for nearly 300 more, is a legend of another sort, although it, too, centered on Pierson and on Steve Wolf, who had moved there from United. It happened in October 1997, a year or so before Pierson's retirement. The final moments of a typically laborious process occurred in Wolf's office, which was located in Arlington, Virginia, adjacent to what is now the Reagan National Airport. Pierson was accompanied by Jack Schofield, who was then chairman and CEO of Airbus North America. "We were close to the deal," says Pierson, "close enough so that it seemed ceremonial." But Wolf wasn't ready to sign, and he imposed new conditions, says Pierson. First was accelerating the delivery schedule of the airplanes. Next, Wolf wanted an additional 5 percent discount on aircraft, spare parts, pilot training, and everything else associated with the purchase.

On the first condition, Pierson recalls saying, "We will argue." They then reached a compromise on the issue. Discussion then turned to the discount, at which point Pierson began slowly lowering his trousers and saying, "I have nothing more to give." He then allowed the trousers to fall around his ankles. He had picked his moment carefully. The door to Wolf's office was open, and, Pierson says, "Not only Steve but people in his outer office could see what was happening." Wolf, he says, "took the point, and I said to him, 'Now you can tell those people that Pierson never said no to your chairman.'"[32]

Schofield says, "Pierson had lost a lot of weight. Doctor's orders. His bulky outline had narrowed. When he said, 'I have nothing more to give,' Wolf said, 'Pull up your pants. I don't need any more money.'"[33]

If Airbus hadn't gotten Boeing's full attention before, it did so now with the sale to United, an airline that hadn't bought a non-Boeing airplane since 1978. Clearly Boeing wouldn't remain competitive at the low end of the market, a key segment, unless it did something about the 737, an older, less comfortable, less technologically advanced airplane than the A320. Replacing the 737 with a clean sheet of paper impressed most Boeing people, senior and junior, as the obvious answer to the A320.

However, the company was then engaged in building the 777, possibly the best of the jet era's passenger aircraft to date. It was a highly innovative and, as it turned out, very expensive airplane, more so than it had to be. The cost overruns were not only high but higher than anyone in the company imagined they could reach, partly because of mistakes and partly because Boeing was doing some things differently. It adopted Airbus's computerized fly-by-wire system but with a mechanical backup. It offered optional folding wings that, by reducing the wingspan, would allow the 777 to use existing airport gates and taxiways. (None of the airlines took Boeing up on the folding wings version.) Boeing used more composites in the 777's structure than it had done in the past.[34]

Boeing estimated the development costs for the 777 at $4 billion, although the real number was probably close to $14 billion. It then read, or misread, what seemed to be the handwriting on the wall: the cost of developing new products—at least in Boeing's case—argued for a recess from the company's core business, competing in the market with state-of-the-art aircraft. It would be an extended recess, lasting until the decision was taken late in 2003 to build the 787.

So it came to pass that a self-anointed "company of engineers" provoked and exasperated precisely its best aircraft makers, along with numerous senior executives, by building derivatives of the 737 instead of a new airplane. Boyd E. Givan, who was senior vice president and chief financial officer throughout most of the 1990s, says, "Once the 777 was certified and delivered in 1995, it became clear we wouldn't have any new products. Instead, we did derivatives of the 737—the 700, 800, and 900. 'Derivatives Are Us,' as in Toys 'R' Us," he said bitingly.[35]

Boeing called the improved models the 737NG, for "Next Generation." In many, if not most, of the ways that affect an aircraft's operating costs, this improved 737 was a new airplane, one that has done very well in the market, at times as well as the A320, and at moments better. (Actually, the 737 has outsold all other passenger jet aircraft by a wide margin. As of the start of 2006, it had logged more than 6,000 orders, whereas the second-place aircraft—Boeing's 727—booked 1,831 orders in its day. Still, the 737 is a 1960s design and has gradually conveyed a sense of being old wine in new bottles.)

Airbus had dodged a bullet. Given Boeing's dominance at the time in every segment of the airline market, a newly minted 737 could have all but buried the A320, as Airbus people like to point out. Instead, the two companies treated the airline market to the sort of competition it craves. The airlines have since grown accustomed to the contesting claims of Airbus and Boeing about the operating costs of the A320 and the 737. The validity of these claims lies in the eye of the beholder. They can be used to prove whatever case the parties want to make to the airlines. One airplane may be portrayed as having lower operating costs at six-hundred-mile stage lengths, whereas the other may appear to do better at fifteen-hundred-mile segments in the same airline's route structure.

Deciding whether to build or not to build new aircraft is always confusing, rarely more so than in the early 1990s. At that time Airbus still lay deep in Boeing's shadow. McDonnell Douglas was still in play. The U.S. airline industry was unavailingly trying to cope with the worst financial crisis of the post-deregulation era.

Fifteen or so years later, John Leahy would say, "This industry operates in ten-year cycles. It found the bottom in the early 1980s. It reached a peak in the later 1980s, and it fell off a cliff in the early 1990s. It was reacting to the cyclical effects in the world economy."[36]

Dean Thornton took a simpler view: "It's all traceable to a time when we made and they bought too many airplanes," he said.[37]

THE HIGH-STAKES affair between Boeing and Airbus has had no more interested audience than the big three engine makers: GE, Pratt &

Whitney, and Rolls-Royce. The struggle for the engine business matches the intensity of the Boeing-Airbus jousting. And like Boeing and Airbus, the big engine makers have been trading places. A short history of their ups and downs over the past thirty-five or so years would go like this:

First, Pratt & Whitney, a division of United Technologies, began taking for granted its tight grip on the airline engine business. In 1970, Pratt had a 90 percent market share of this trade and a corporate ego to match. Like Boeing, Pratt made reliable, top-of-the-line products; and as with Boeing, a mix of arrogance and a series of misjudgments by management allowed the competition to close the gap and then forge far ahead. In 1970, Pratt had one president and four vice presidents. By the late 1980s, it had five presidents and fifty-seven vice presidents, and the company's market share had fallen to roughly 15 percent.

Back in the 1970s and 1980s, when the first wide-bodied aircraft were developed, Rolls-Royce ran a poor third to Pratt and GE. Gradually, Rolls-Royce closed the gap and, in the mid-1990s, could match or even outperform the other two in various big markets. Good products, hardheaded management, and aggressive price discounts had to be there, but Rolls-Royce also got a strong assist from HMG (Her Majesty's Government) in the form of launch aid that between 1998 and 2003 amounted to £450 million.*

Its competitors—GE and Pratt—contend that this assistance enables Rolls to spend far less of its own funds on research and development and, in effect, to "buy" market share.[38] Probably more important, however, is the golden share in Rolls-Royce held by HMG, in theory to prevent some foreign company from buying this crown jewel. Actually, the golden share serves to assure the financial community that Rolls-Royce is a reasonably secure investment and protected against financial failure. And then, Prime Minister Tony Blair provides another strong assist. He was seen by GE and Pratt as a supersalesman for Rolls-

---

*Washington hasn't lodged objections to this subsidy, partly because of Rolls-Royce's special importance to Britain and, more important, because of the special relationship between Washington and London; the war in Iraq, of course, has tightened that link.

Royce engines. Blair attached as much—and probably even more—importance to the commercial aircraft industry as Bill Clinton did.

Pratt has seen itself becoming less able to compete, thanks in part to Rolls-Royce's privileged relationship with its government and, at least as important, to what could be called GE's larger toolbox. "We don't have to go to the U.S. embassy somewhere to arrange a meeting with the top people there with one of our senior guys," says a GE executive. "Our top guy in that country can arrange those meetings. Also, we have a banking operation, and that can do a lot for a country."[39] He could also have mentioned GECAS, the GE leasing company and one of the world's two largest buyers of passenger airplanes.

And he could have noted some very large advantages that GE brought to the engine competition: they all involved the CFM56, which is not just the company's most successful engine but the most successful commercial engine of the jet era. First, although the CFM56 involves a fifty-fifty partnership, the French company, Snecma, contributed most of the research and development funds for it. Second, under the terms of the GE-Snecma deal, the revenue stream from the engine is divided fifty-fifty, but the costs are split in a way that favors GE. Third, GE was able to contribute the high-technology, high-value part of the engine—the "hot section"—which originally powered the B-1 bomber. (This is an example of the flow of technology between the U.S. defense and commercial sectors that Airbus grumbles about.)

Like Boeing and Airbus, the engine makers must take seat-of-the-pants decisions on where the airline market may be headed within the life of any new product. Between the 1970s and the early 1990s, Pratt badly misread the tea leaves. In its procession of mistakes, Pratt's biggest was betting on the wrong Boeing airplane. The company saw little future for Boeing's improved 737, even though it supplied an engine for the early version. Pratt tried instead to sell engines to airlines that had ordered the 757, an airplane the market never warmed to and one for which for which Pratt lacked an engine of the right size.

The 737NG, although not the best of breed, did, as noted, become a vastly successful airplane. Pratt had the right engine for it. So did

GE—the CFM56. But with Pratt not stepping up, Boeing granted GE exclusivity on the 737NG; the airplane with that engine would be sold as a package. GE and Snecma have since delivered more than fifteen thousand CFM56 engines, of which roughly two-thirds were for 737's.

This was an unusual move on all sides. Engines are normally sold separately, and there is normally a choice of two, sometimes three engines. As with the airframes, the carriers want to be able to play the suppliers off against one another. The 737's rival, the A320, is sold with two engines: the CFM56 and the V2500, the latter of which is widely judged a somewhat better engine because it has more advanced technology. The V2500 is referred to as the "company engine," because an alliance of seven companies, of which Pratt and Rolls-Royce are the main members, sponsored it. That engine and its success have kept Pratt's commercial division alive. (Pratt currently relies mainly on its large and prosperous military business.)

Each of the three engine companies has made serious mistakes, although none perhaps as serious as Pratt's rejection of the 737. GE, for example, refused a tempting offer from Jean Pierson in 1997 to put an engine on the extended-range version of Airbus's A340. The decision was made by Jack Welch, GE's supreme boss, who insisted on having no competitors for that airplane's engines. Pierson recalls him saying, "I put money on the table, and I want exclusivity. But I said, 'I will never put myself in yours or anyone's hands.' "[40] (In fact, Pierson later granted Rolls-Royce exclusivity on that airplane.)

"Airbus was very angry," says one GE executive. He added that James McNerney, Boeing's new chief, had just taken over GE's engine group. "Jim's first big job with us," he said, "was to rebuild our relations with Airbus. And he did."[41]

It is a media event when a major airline orders new airplanes and the engines for them. The size of the purchases assures prominent coverage. But the exact details of a given transaction—the contractual arrangements that can mean the difference between winning or losing the deal—are normally treated by the seller and the buyer as proprietary information. The seller usually tries to conceal or at least obscure them from other potential customers, the more so since many airlines attempt to obtain, often successfully, what the industry calls "most favored nations" clauses. These have the same meaning—what is available to one is available to others—in the commercial aircraft business as in trading arrangements between nations.[42]

The engine side is a confusing business—as tricky as selling the airframes but a little less risky and less straightforward. What an airline pays for an engine doesn't affect the price it may be paying to Boeing or Airbus for a new airplane, even though engines are 25 to 30 percent of the total value. The process begins with the purchase by Boeing or Airbus of an engine that it has selected for one of its airplanes. That engine is then sold to an airline. But the engine company will already have steered matters in its direction by offering discounts directly to the airline, along with other incentives.

Engine makers can be even more creative than the airframe manufacturers in finding ways for financially strapped airlines to purchase their wares. "We don't sell engines, we make concessions," says a key figure at GE. "We say, 'Here is the price, and if you pick us we'll pay some of your development costs.' We might also say, 'Here is what we can do for you—provide you with ten years of spare parts and some extra engines.'"[43]

Engines are normally the chief source of tension between the airlines and their suppliers. They are expensive, complex, and vulnerable. The frequency-of-repair rate on engines is much higher than on other parts; they require a far greater degree of after-sales service. Engines burn at very high temperatures and consume two or three times their value in spare parts over their lifetime. Engine suppliers earn much more money from sales of spare parts than the airframe companies do.[44] That allows the engine makers to offer huge discounts to their airline customers. The airframe, by comparison, generates less than 10 percent of its value in spare parts.

Some engine company people describe what they do as selling "at a measured loss." They can, they know, more than make up for their loss through maintenance and sales of spare parts. "It's a razor/razor-blade industry," they like to say. "We give the razors away and make money on the blades." More than half of what an airline spends on equipment goes to the engine suppliers.

The three companies operate in much the same way, although for a time—during the mid-1980s and early 1990s—Pratt did so more aggressively than its competitors. In the early 1980s, engine discounts averaged about 30 percent of selling price. But by 1991, with Pratt allegedly showing the way, the companies were giving up to 80 percent, and average discounts were hovering at about 50 percent. In effect, all three players were losing money—certainly not making any—on the engines they were sending out the door, but recovering it on sales of spare parts.

By 1995, Rolls-Royce apparently decided to hike its market share sharply by becoming at least as aggressive as the competition and, indeed, even more so. In 1997, for example, Rolls offered a remarkably high discount on engines purchased by Singapore Airlines (SIA) for the first extended-range version of Boeing's 777. Over the years, SIA bought eighty-three of them, all with Rolls-Royce engines, although Pratt had been the airline's regular engine supplier. Pratt was told by SIA that Rolls had "offered a deal we could not refuse," according to a former Pratt executive who was closely involved. "It had to be close to a hundred percent," he says, "because we lost and we were north of eighty-five percent."[45]

More recently, GE had a similar experience. All Nippon Airways (ANA), the launch customer for Boeing's 787, was a reliable GE customer and expected to remain one. Instead, ANA surprised all sides—shocked GE—by selecting a Rolls engine for its 787's. No one doubts that this transaction also involved an offer that couldn't be refused. According to a GE executive, "ANA came to us and said, 'This is what Rolls is offering. What can you do?' We walked away."[46]

Rolls had begun selling an approach called "total care," offering to include within the engine price several years of free maintenance. GE and Pratt proposed similar deals. However, Rolls, unlike its competitors, was also capitalizing research and development costs instead of expensing them. The costs would not show up on the profit-and-loss statement, only on the balance sheet.

In recent years, some airlines started buying new equipment not because they may have needed it but strictly in order to receive the huge checks reflecting the discounts on offer. More often than not, these airlines use the money to pay operating expenses.

AN AIRLINE'S CONTRACT with Boeing or Airbus guarantees certain performance characteristics of the engines, such as the amount of fuel they consume. The airline and the engine supplier sign a separate agreement that covers such matters as the cost of spare parts and the period of time, typically three thousand hours, during which the engines must perform reliably.

"You are pushing the envelope with each engine," says a very experienced Pratt executive. "You never know whether it will work until you begin testing—whether, for example, the EPA [Environmental Protection Agency] will frown on the emissions. There are two key emissions. One is nitrous oxide, known as NOX. The other is CO_2. But as you push one of them down in order to comply with standards, you push the other one up. It's very tough to get around that trade-off. There is also the problem of noise level going up as you keep emissions down. You have to operate in accordance with the internationally agreed standards on noise."[47]

The interplay of the engine and airframe makers lacks rules and predictability; it can be chaotic. Boeing or Airbus will present a new airplane that is intended to carry, say, three hundred passengers for seven thousand miles. The company will guarantee a fuel consumption—fuel burn, as it's known—of no more than X. An engine company will see no difficulty in meeting the thrust requirement, but meeting a fuel-burn guaranty is always tough. Boeing and Airbus normally offer the airframe and engine guaranties to airlines as a single package, along with penalties to be imposed if the guaranties are not fulfilled.

If an engine falls short of its guaranteed specifications, the airframe maker—Boeing or Airbus—will inform the airline that its new plane will be able to go the full seven-thousand-mile distance but will be burning more than the agreed-upon amount of fuel. What will have happened is that the airplane just got heavier, as new planes usually do. And the additional weight dictates more engine thrust, hence a bigger fuel burn.

The ensuing penalties to be paid to airlines cost both engine and airframe makers, heavily in most cases. To avoid being burned with penalties, engine makers tend to hedge by adding margins to the specifications. But if the airframe doesn't stray from its specifications, the engine designed to carry 300 people 7,000 miles will be able to do that much and a bit more. Actually, the designers determined long ago that their engines always need another 10–15 percent more thrust. In short, engines are designed for aircraft growth. One GE executive says, "If you are dealing with a one-million-pound airplane and the airframe guys miss the specified weight by one percent, the engine will need a lot more thrust to carry that weight."[48]

THIS SYSTEM PROMOTES continuing strife between the airline and engine companies, who tend to blame each other when problems develop. Occasionally, the strife triangulates to include the airframe maker, as it did in July 1989, when a United Airlines DC-10 lost its center engine about an hour after taking off from Denver. The failure was caused by a crack in the front fan disc, which holds the fan blades. The aircraft's hydraulic lines ruptured, and the plane lost hydraulic power; it was not controllable. It crashed near Sioux City, Iowa. Some inspired maneuvering by the flight crew allowed a crash landing, causing 111 deaths. However, 172 of the passengers, although injured, survived, and 12 were uninjured.

Three months later, an engine part found in a field showed that the failure was caused by a crack in the disc's titanium. Investigators then learned that as part of United's inspection procedure the crack had been coated with a fluorescent dye. A fluorescent light is used to scan such parts and look for flaws that ought to show up. United had followed this procedure four months earlier, but had not detected the crack.

GE was sued for the disc failure and United for failing to discover the crack. McDonnell Douglas was sued for "faulty" placement of its hydraulic lines. The cases were all settled with "contributions" from each of the three parties—United, GE, and McDonnell Douglas. The level of acrimony ran very high. United has not bought an engine from GE since the event.

Although passenger aircraft and their engines are constantly improving and becoming more reliable, the companies still find plenty to quarrel about. Most often it is a carrier complaining that the costs of flying an airplane are unreasonably high. Its manufacturer then censures the engine for having too little thrust or consuming too much fuel. But the engine supplier almost certainly will blame the aircraft's designers for having allowed too much drag. Engine makers see the aircraft as just a great quantity of aluminum wrapped around the vehicle's only technological marvel, its propulsion system.[49] (And there is something to that, although a little less than contended.) Over the years, these disputes, although routine, have become steadily more hard-edged, as the importance of restricting fuel consumption drives the entire industry.

CHAPTER SIX

Meltdown and Merger

By THE EARLY 1990S the effects of airline deregulation were taking hold. Air travel pricing had become increasingly irrational. The carriers were selling tickets below cost, and except for Southwest Airlines, all of them were operating in the red. Still, Boeing's share of the ailing aircraft market held steady at 60 percent, and the company continued to make profits despite the serious downturn within the industry.

Although Frank Schrontz and Dean Thornton were still in charge in the early 1990s, generational change was in the air. A gifted engineer named Philip Condit was second only to Schrontz in authority and was on track to become his successor; the question was when, not whether. Although Boeing had a pool of brilliant engineers, few were as creative as Condit, who also possessed other attributes, notably a glossy education and a wide culture, that had impressed various senior players who mattered, including T. Wilson. A well-honed operational skill helped.

Condit was born in 1941 and graduated from the University of California, Berkeley. He obtained a master's degree from Princeton in aeronautical engineering and another, in management, from the Massachusetts Institute of Technology. In 1997, he became the first Westerner to be awarded a doctorate from Science University of Tokyo. After joining Boeing in 1965, he went from strength to strength. Among Condit's several distinctions was leading the team that launched the 777 and, in the process, finding a solution to a major design problem.

Thornton, president of Boeing's Commercial Airplanes group, retired in January 1994 and, as expected, was replaced by Ronald B. (Ron) Woodard, who had been executive vice president of that division. Woodard and Condit represented a new order at Boeing— a group of people in their middle years who were poised to take charge.

A retired Boeing executive who worked closely with all of them says, "With Wilson, Schrontz, and Thornton, people understood that what the company did or did not do wasn't about them, whereas in the case of their successors it was all about them."[1] By and large, the new top-tier people impressed some of their older contemporaries as arrogant and complacent—as having grown up in a company that had a 65 percent market share, which they considered a birthright. Hard lessons for them and the company lay ahead.

It's worth pausing over Condit and Woodard. Of all the personalities in the Boeing Company's procession of senior managers, they may have been as omnicompetent as any who preceded or followed them. But they did the company more damage than any of the others, mainly because, whatever their attainments, both lacked judgment and perspective.

Condit, the more consequential of the two, was very indecisive, whereas Woodard was often too quick to make a decision. A composite view of Condit by several colleagues would read: "a brilliant and innovative engineer who froze before managerial decisions and could only see fifty shades of gray."

Woodard, like most of the company's senior executives then, was an engineer by formation, but was more generally seen as a high-energy, highly capable, hard-charging airplane salesman. He was described by some of his peers as "tomorrow's leader." Others, including at least one senior figure on Wall Street, described his operational style as "testosterone based." In any case, he, like Condit, seemed certain to have a preeminent role, and he, too, would become deeply controversial.

The movement of senior executives occurred while the 777, then under way, was creating the huge cost overruns noted before. Many years later, Alan Mulally, who succeeded Condit as program manager, acknowledged that the 777 cost $6 billion more than he first estimated.[2] (The real number is thought to have been higher still.)

The launch customer for the 777 was United Airlines. Its program manager for the airplane was Gordon McKinzie, who led a team of six to work with Boeing on design and related matters. "We were followed," he says, "by an ANA team, then JAL [Japan Airlines]. We were involved in all the design reviews, and we did steer some of the decisions. We often met to try to take a common position.

"We were always mystified by Boeing's program costs. They might have spent $10 or $12 billion on the 777. Huge amounts were devoted to facilities. They built two bays for the assembly lines. The first bay still houses the active assembly line, but they never opened the second line. They use the second bay for storage."[3]

The 777 would be Boeing's last new airplane for quite a long time. Innovation in the factory would become more important than product innovation. Curiously, the process of modernizing the factory floor would lag, too, despite the rising concern within the company about itself.

Boeing's corporate arrogance had begun to coexist with a recognition that it was no longer as good at manufacturing as it had been. Its production methods were anachronistic, just slightly updated from those that were used to build B-17 and B-29 bombers during the Second World War.

The recession that followed the Gulf War in 1990–91 seemed to be an opportune moment to fix the production system. By 1993, the trendy phrase chez Boeing was "world-class." Senior executives were in curious disagreement over whether the company had ceased being world-class in its various parts or only in its manufacturing techniques. Schrontz and Thornton found the self-flagellation and autocritique that was under way lower down exaggerated. "I reject the notion that we are not a world-class company," said Schrontz. "On manufacturing, though, we have a long way to go."[4]

Various colleagues took a darker view. R. Michael (Mike) Little, who supervised quality control of wide-body airplanes, took issue directly with Schrontz. "I do not think we're world-class," he said. "We are a marvelous company and have been for a long time. But we haven't changed much in forty years. We are still using techniques that were refined after World War Two. Condit says if we don't do a lot better, we are doomed. We want to stay in the phone book."[5]

Condit had been telling colleagues that "Boeing wouldn't be in the phone book" for very long if it didn't change its ways. The company, Condit said, "would have to slash its costs dramatically, a goal that would dictate halving cycle time—the period in which airplanes are built and delivered to customers."[6] Bob Crandall, the blunt leader of American Airlines, had gotten Boeing's attention by telling Schrontz and Thornton that their airplanes "cost too goddamned much money."

Then, as orders fell off in the early 1990s, the pressure to change became stronger. "We thought airplanes were different," Woodard said. "We had a romantic notion. But we are a manufacturing company like everybody else. We have to build a product that meets customer needs more cheaply than anyone. Our system was inflexible and complex. We've had databases doing back to 1958."[7]

A reinvention of Boeing was under way. Delta Point, a small consulting firm in Bellevue (a high-tech suburb of Seattle) that specializes in showing companies, including very successful ones, how to change with the times, was retained. For more than a year, the hundred top Boeing people, including Schrontz, Thornton, Condit, and Woodard, went through Delta Point's program in teams of eight.

Phase one was a seven-day seminar in which team members read large books about Japanese production methods, along with selective Harvard Business School literature. The executives had to take written tests to see if they were absorbing the stuff. The second and even more intensive phase involved two-week visits to Japan—specifically to companies there that were judged "world-class" by Delta Point; they included Toyota, Nippon Steel, Canon, NEC (Nippon Electric Company), and Mitsubishi. Each team visited eight to ten companies over a two-week period.

A typical day began at 6 a.m.—on a bus that was actually a moving conference room with tables and video systems. Mornings consisted of presentations by the host company's senior management. Informal discussions were held over lunch. Afternoons and evenings were taken up by factory tours and question-and-answer sessions. Notes were compared on the bus trip back to the hotel and then over dinner. The typical day ended at about 10:30 p.m.

"Most of us were profoundly affected by the experience," said Mike Little. "Some of us came away angry, others frightened. We were angry at ourselves. There was nothing wrong with our products. It was our procedures that had to change."[8]

The hundred revisionists—the company hierarchy—had been imbued with a spirit of apostolic reform. They set about imparting what they had learned in Japan to the second tier—a pool of fourteen hundred or so executives who were responsible for making the airplanes. A four-day course called WCC, for "World-Class Competitiveness," was designed and taught by those who had been through the full Delta Point program. Next came the labor force. Management decided to teach the same course to the factory floor to reinforce the lessons it had learned. An instructor's manual was put together, and it cascaded down through the company.

The major lesson drawn from the Japanese experience concerned how to manage inventory. Boeing's leadership abruptly discovered that inventory is a cost; that on any given day the plant in Renton, where the narrow-bodied aircraft are built, would have $3.5 billion in inventory lying about. Doing something about it meant replacing the old system of storing items on the factory floor with the so-called just-in-time procedure, under which a supplier arranges for just the right quantity of an item to arrive at the plant within minutes of the time it is scheduled for use.

The model for how to do that, along with various ways of streamlining the assembly line, was Toyota. It drew unqualified raves from all the visitors. "The most refined concepts, the sharpest edge," said Little. "Truly world-class in everything they do," said James Johnson, an executive vice president who was running the wide-body division then.[9]

Boeing people saw two Toyota models—the Camry and the Lexus—going down the same assembly line. At some fairly advanced stage, the various units became one thing or the other. The visitors were impressed, so much so that they began to feel an offstage presence—Toyota. During the visit, they heard Eiji Toyoda, CEO of the Toyota Motor Corporation, say: "We're in the transportation business. It's our destiny to be in the airplane business."

A comment in the instructor's guide for a "World-Class Competitiveness" course developed by Boeing read: "Their [Toyota's] long-term goal includes not only cars, but all forms of transportation. Also, their long-term goal is not to be the best transportation company in the world. It is to be the only one." (As recently as August 2004, a senior Boeing VP said, "Boeing is still sending people to look at Toyota. And it has empowered teams to redesign workplaces. They openly call it 'the Toyotaization of Boeing.' ")[10]

Boeing's exact goal then—cutting its costs by at least 30 percent—lay well ahead. "We are not even close to completing this reform," said Condit. "If we cut the cycle time in half, we'll cut it again."[11]

Woodard concurred. "We are still grabbing low-hanging fruit," he said. "But we are on our way to amazing things." None of those things would be an appreciable reduction in cycle time; that lay well ahead. But Woodard and others were giving a different tone to what had recently been a self-styled "engineers' company." Anticipating and satisfying customer needs had become the focus of a company that once upon a time designed an airplane (like the 747), sold it to one customer (like Pan American World Airways), and then persuaded that airline's competitors that they needed it, too.

In designing the 777, Boeing brought in engineers from eight customer airlines: American, United, Delta, ANA, JAL, Cathay Pacific, Singapore Airlines, and Thai Airlines. "They all wanted the inside of the airplane to be different," said Little. "The differences turned on the size and shape of the seats and on the location of the galleys and lavatories."[12]

"The lavs and galleys are designing the airplane," said Alan Mulally, who was then a vice president and one of the company's other highly regarded and upwardly mobile engineers. He had succeed Condit as manager of the 777 program.[13]

"ANA," he continued, "contributed 215 ideas, of which 160 were incorporated. Inevitably, one involved the lavatory, in this case the toilet seat. ANA worried about the 'problem hit sound'—the falling seat. A rubber bumper on the seat, they felt, wasn't good enough, and they recommended a mechanical bumper." Boeing agreed, but designing one that did the job and satisfied all requirements was a massive problem and required a lot of engineering and testing before the task was completed. "In other days," said Mulally, "the conversation would have been about flutter, drag, and takeoff. Now it's about this kind of thing."[14]

Mulally was echoed by Woodard, who cited the long lead time for designing the lavatories—longer than for other components—mainly because they were being designed by the customers, clearly a sore point. Completing them, he said, could take as much as eighteen and a half months; just moving the Kleenex box a few inches, he added, means reengineering the entire unit. He favored switching to modular standardized lavatories. Airbus, too, was customizing airplanes at that time. Its catalog of options was about as thick as Boeing's.

Boeing, Woodard said, "had done a lot of technology for the sake of technology. Technology fascinates engineers. We would custom design airplanes for carriers. We are through custom designing the product line for each carrier," he declared.[15] Woodard was determined to streamline procedures. It was, of course, the right goal, but he would break a lot of crockery trying to reach it.

ALTHOUGH AIRBUS was still being described in Seattle as mainly a jobs program, it was drawing more of Boeing's attention. According to an article in *Business Week* in 1992, Airbus had begun to threaten Boeing. Airbus had some advantages. "It didn't have Boeing's long history of doing things one way," said Boyd Givan, who, as noted, was the company's chief financial officer for most of the 1990s. "It was more adaptable and was doing the thing better. Boeing liked the snap-in-place assembly technique."[16]

Airbus, too, was streamlining procedures, reducing costs, and watching the Japanese carefully. It adopted seamless laser welding of fuselage assembly, instead of using rivets, and that helped with weight. Competing against Boeing was seen in Toulouse as being partly about improving technology and partly about lowering costs. "We can reduce our costs by a certain measure every year," said Airbus executive Gerard Blanc. "That is how you stay competitive. It is all about mind-set. We employ fifty-five thousand people, who, along with our suppliers, must share a vision. That is the strength of the Japanese. They are so good at convincing themselves and then being followed."[17]

"The Airbus factories and manufacturing processes are more modern than Boeing's," said James Womack, a management analyst and the founder and CEO of a nonprofit corporation called the Lean Enterprise Institute, in Brookline, Massachusetts. "Airbus," he said, "uses more automation than Boeing. . . . It uses more robots than people to build fuselage shells at its plant."[18]

Womack wrote a book with Daniel Jones called *Lean Thinking* for the Massachusetts Institute of Technology; it sold six hundred thousand copies. The book is based on the Toyota model and describes a business system for the twenty-first century. Among the companies examined by the authors was Pratt & Whitney. "If you could fix Pratt, you could fix anything," they said.

Between 1995 and 1997, Womack spent eighteen months as a day-rate consultant to Boeing, under an arrangement made by Ron Woodard. His efforts, he said, "were aimed at halving production time, halving costs, and eliminating many of the mistakes." He favored getting rid of half of the company's vice presidents and a vast amount of factory space. How much, he wondered, would it cost to reconfigure the company? He discussed Boeing's problems with Woodard shortly after arriving in Seattle. "I tried to get a sense of Boeing's numbers," he said. "But I couldn't. Instead, I got engineering metrics—lift weight, lift drag, et cetera. But no cost data. I became the first guy to tell them the sky is falling. That's hard."[19]

The arrangement never came close to working, partly because Woodard and others were being told things they didn't want to hear and partly because Womack is described as having exercised little restraint or discretion in saying what he had to say. One basically sympathetic executive characterized some of it as close to "inflammatory." In any case, Womack failed to dent management's thinking about its problems, and Woodard ended the arrangement. As for the Toyotaization of Boeing, nothing much was happening, and there would be no discernible progress for another five or so years.

Dean Thornton's departure in 1993 turned out to be more of an event than it may have seemed at the time. Thornton had been a so-called T. Wilson man, and under his leadership, the line was held at Boeing on business economics. "He balanced revenue and costs," said a colleague and admirer. "He was respected by sales and production people alike. He had self-control and resisted temptation to cut prices if that meant cutting production costs."[20] Thornton's focus was broad. Woodard's focus was sales.

"In the old days, there was a checks-and-balances system," said Larry Clarkson, a versatile former senior vice president. "Corporate had to bless production rates and other key decisions. But Phil, when he became chairman, did away with checks and balances. And he put a salesman in charge of the commercial side."[21]

Thornton's legacy included a strong product order base, more than strong enough to convince the Condit-Woodard tandem that all was well with Boeing. Woodard began to live off this order base, which stretched three to four years. Then, after riding it for a while, he created his own base. In doing so, however, he got the cost-price equation upside down. First, he decided, as he put it, "to reach the point of having the product in the configuration the customer wants in six months. I believe our competition can't do it. We will sell more airplanes if we can bring orders closer to the customers."[22] At the time, according to Woodard, it took fifteen months to produce a 757, seventeen months for a 767.

Then, not long after Woodard took over as president of commercial operations, Boeing began a price war with Airbus. Discounts on aircraft sales that had averaged 10 percent under Thornton rose to 18 percent and 20 percent, at times even reaching 30 percent. The Woodard strategy was to outproduce Airbus, sponge up market share in the discount war, and in effect bury Airbus, a stated goal of his. He would be remembered for having cut the budgets for producing airplanes while ramping up production with no apparent concern for the costs.

Woodard's explicit contempt for Airbus was also made clear. Airbus, he would say, has no product line and is finished. "Ron Woodard was more arrogant than anyone I've ever known," said Jean Pierson. "He had a simple message: We'll take prices down twenty to twenty-five percent, and Airbus will be unable to follow. We will flood the market with a lot of aircraft. Airbus will be dead. But we did follow Boeing."[23]

Woodard had chosen a bad moment to go to the mat with Airbus. First, Boeing's 737 line wasn't selling well. Second, a cluster of people within the company had begun to worry seriously not just about the costs of making Boeing airplanes but about how these costs compared to Airbus's. They knew that Airbus had adopted lean manufacturing techniques much earlier. They saw Airbus winning numerous competitions. They doubted that government launch aid to Airbus programs explained what was happening. They concluded that lower production costs were allowing Airbus to price its airplanes beneath Boeing's prices. And they sensed what one of them later called "a cost crisis."

The in-house skeptics organized two studies (by outsiders)—one in the latter part of 1995, the other in early 1996—of Airbus's cost structure. Airbus plants were visited. The results were closely held but shocking. They showed that Airbus and Boeing each had the capacity to supply one half of the world's aircraft needs. However, Airbus was using 22–23 million square feet of production space. Boeing was using 55 million square feet. And by any measurement, Airbus was shown to have a 12–15 percent cost advantage over Boeing in production and tooling. Boeing's production costs were shown to be abusively high.

If taken seriously, the studies argued for a restructuring of Boeing operations and the closure of several of its large operating sites. The corporate executive council—which, of course, included Condit and Woodard—was briefed, and a handful of other senior executives got a similar briefing.

Curiously, it was on Phil Condit's first day as CEO, in April 1996, that the results of the first of the two studies were presented to the corporate executive council. The meeting lasted two and a half hours. It was agreed that a major consolidation would have to be undertaken. It was further agreed that 1997 would be a bad year for Boeing.

"Phil said, 'Let's not shoot the messenger,'" according to one closely involved Boeing figure. "That was a courageous act. But he then said that we must keep this information secret from everyone. The top eighteen guys in the company heard it, but not the others. It's unlikely that the board was exposed to it."[24]

The leadership then began a vigorous campaign aimed at showing that Boeing would make $3 billion in 1997. But the skeptics had information that clearly pointed in the other direction, indicating that the company would be lucky to finish at zero in that year. The data were about $4 billion apart. An idea to close some plants and redesign the company was spiked.

Some Boeing people felt that Condit was at the bottom of their problems, in large part because he had chosen what one of them called "a one-dimensional salesman, Ron Woodard," to replace Thornton. The discount rates had gone up, along with the backlog of orders and production. But the high discounts created expectations that they would become industry standards. In that sense, they did long-term damage.

More immediately, the conflict between higher production rates and reduced spending for production appeared to harbor major trouble. However, Woodard insisted that the operations divisions produce budgets that one of his colleagues said "understated their actual costs. They were being forced to produce unrealistic budgets. Then, in 1997–98, they found themselves having to live within them. Woodard then said he'd been given budget commitments and the divisions didn't meet these commitments."[25]

Several people in and around Boeing worried that a tsunami-like event lay ahead. In May 1997, a special team formed to review the problem issued a report that concluded, "Our production system is broken."[26] The company had worked through Thornton's order base and now would somehow have to produce and deliver the aircraft that Woodard had ordered. The problem, big enough by itself, was enlarged by a series of events and mistakes that started in 1995 when many more employees than expected accepted an offer of early retirement. Several of them were engineers whose absence created a delay in the preparation and delivery of blueprints for various aircraft programs. Others were among Boeing's most highly skilled mechanics.

Next came a sixty-three-day strike that began late in 1996, coinciding with the production buildup, which in turn led to the hiring of thousands of new workers. But there remained a shortage. Also, the workers who had been on strike had to be resettled in their jobs.

Finally, in the fall of 1997, the industrial equivalent of a tsunami struck Boeing. The production line couldn't keep pace with what were being called "the steepest production increases since the dawn of the jet age." The airline market was coming back from the downturn, and Boeing's heavily discounted products sold briskly—too briskly. The factories seized up under the strain. Airplanes got out of sequence. Some were being painted before they had been fully built and assembled.

Boeing's suppliers were also unequal to the pressure; they couldn't deliver enough parts, or even the right parts, to the factory floors in Everett, where the 747's are assembled, and in Renton, where the 737's are made. The other lines, including the 777, were similarly affected.

The plants were running out of aluminum and a broad range of small items such as fasteners used to attach parts to fuselages.

The largest number of orders involved the 737NG, of which derivatives were being developed and sold. "The 737 had the fastest ramp-up ever," said John Hayhurst, a highly regarded former Boeing vice president who had at one time been general manager of 737 programs, with responsibility for design and production of that family. However, in the disorder that was under way in Renton, derivatives were being launched before deliveries of the base airplane had been completed. Several Boeing customers whose deliveries were delayed or postponed probably became better targets for Airbus.

A reporter who covered this string of events recalls seeing "chaos and even panic. There were uncompleted planes parked everywhere—in Renton, around Lake Washington—more parked airplanes than anyone could remember seeing. There were special teams of top mechanics working around the clock, but the workers at every station were way behind. All the lines were out of control. Angry mechanics and machinists were calling the press, saying they were working triple shifts and still behind. But the factory bosses, when called, would say, 'Everything is fine.' "[27]

On October 3, 1997, the company was obliged to announce that it was halting production of both its 737's and its 747's for about three weeks. Halting the lines was a radical step. Nothing comparable had occurred in twenty years. And the company would have to pay heavy penalties caused by late deliveries of aircraft.

A few days later, Harry C. Stonecipher, who had run McDonnell Douglas before the merger with Boeing and was now Boeing's president and chief operating officer, sent Condit a terse e-mail: "We do know for certain that there is a big surprise coming, and I think we owe the Street a heads-up." On October 22, Condit did come clean. Boeing's production meltdown would force the company to write off $2.6 billion, the largest such charge in its history. Overnight, shares fell 8 percent, wiping out about $4.3 billion in value.[28]

Condit's announcement was followed nine days later by a federal lawsuit filed on behalf of shareholders against Boeing's senior management, specifically Condit, Woodard, and Boyd Givan. The suit charged them with knowing the previous spring that sharply hiking production was risky and would cost the company money. "Boeing," the suit noted, "should have recognized much of [the] known production inefficiencies in the June 30 quarterly financial statements. No such recognition was made due to Boeing's . . . desire to maintain [the] stock price until the merger with McDonnell Douglas was complete." For that reason, ran the argument, "Boeing had to keep the price of its stock increasing, or at least be certain that the price did not decrease, in order to ensure that the merger would be approved by McDonnell Douglas's shareholders."[29]

In September 2001, four years later, Boeing reached a $92.5 million settlement in the shareholder lawsuit. In an investigation lasting three months, *Business Week* reported that

> the company did not admit guilt. Although some of the evidence uncovered by the plaintiffs' lawyers was revealed in court documents, the vast majority was locked under seal at Boeing's request.
>
> . . . Several inside witnesses indicate that Boeing did more than simply fail to tell investors about its production disaster. It also engaged in a wide variety of aggressive accounting techniques that papered over the mess. . . . Critics say the company should have taken charges for the assembly-line disaster in 1997, even if it meant jeopardizing the McDonnell Douglas merger. They also claim that Boeing took advantage of the unusual flexibility provided by program accounting—a system that allows the huge upfront expense of building a plane to be spread out over several years—to cover up cost overruns and to book savings from efficiency initiatives that never panned out. . . . None of the outside watchdogs ever barked. The board never forced Condit to come clean about the company's production problems. Stock analysts and business journalists underestimated them.[30]

The events on which the dispute turned occurred in 1997–98, a time when Boeing won a major battle with Airbus for market share, but lost the war. Boeing lost money in 1997 even though it was a peak year for airplane sales. Ron Woodard disappeared, along with profitability. One Saturday in September 1998, Condit summoned Woodard and fired him, according to a cover piece in *Business Week*. "He told me he had a real close brush with the board, and he was almost dumped two months before," Woodard told the magazine.[31] "In its more than eighty-year history, Boeing has rarely removed one of its top executives," commented *Aviation Week*.[32]

"One of the most dangerous places to be is first place," Condit told a visitor late in 2005. "You tell yourself, 'Our technology is better, our costs are better, and the other guy is cheating.' You have to be brutally honest with yourself. We should have said what we knew—that Airbus is doing a lot of things superbly. That was not a great lightbulb going off in our heads."[33]

THE FIASCO on the production lines overshadowed, at least for a time, the merger between Boeing and McDonnell Douglas, a far more pivotal and historic event. The merger struck Boeing heritage people—many and probably most of those who were in Seattle—as calamitous; it was, they thought, a marriage of polarized business cultures. It would cost Boeing its equilibrium, they feared.

Others, notably several major stockholders and various parts of the banking community, were happy to see Boeing join forces with the second largest of the defense and space companies and thereby be able to hedge against the large uncertainties and risks inherent in its core business. Also, the Department of Defense was very glad to see McDac—a preeminent but mismanaged supplier of advanced weaponry—paired with a better and stronger company.

The merger was never predictable, certainly not in the way that it came about. A few people, including Phil Condit, tried to make it happen, and events played into their hands, as did the steady decline of McDonnell Douglas. In the summer of 1992, it posted a 51 percent plunge in earnings and a 62 percent fall for the Douglas Aircraft division. Wall Street began to wonder whether McDac could or would remain committed to the commercial side of the business. In 1996, Douglas Aircraft obtained only 40 orders for new airplanes, compared to 435 for Boeing and 269 for Airbus.

Politics at their loftiest inadvertently played a role in the merger. French presidents and British prime ministers have routinely interceded to secure a deal for Airbus. For example, when Airbus sold thirty-six airplanes to Turkish Airlines in July 2004, the announcement was made not by its CEO, Noel Forgeard, who was attending the air show in Farnborough, England, but by Jacques Chirac in Paris.

Although American presidents have rarely played that game, Bill Clinton did so in October 1995, and thereby probably headed off a bankruptcy filing by McDac. In doing so, he seemed to signal his administration's intention to do whatever it took to promote the sales of the country's major earner of foreign exchange.

The issue was which supplier would be awarded a contract for new airplanes worth $7.5 billion from Saudia Airlines. The Saudis were replacing their entire fleet with sixty-one new aircraft. Shortly before the Gulf War in 1990–91, Saudia had been on the verge of buying a number of Boeing aircraft. After the war, the talks resumed, but by then Airbus had become a major factor and seemed well positioned to capture the business.

Clinton strongly urged the Saudis, whose security had been bolstered by the war, to buy American. After tilting toward Airbus, King Fahd did change direction and chose to buy off the American shelf, partly because he knew that he was indebted to Washington and partly because of the savage violence in Bosnia. The rejection the year before by France and Britain of Clinton's proposal to lift the arms embargo in the former Yugoslavia angered Fahd, who had been financing a flow of arms to Bosnian Muslims.

Boeing and McDac were invited to begin negotiations in Riyadh on March 20, 1996. Given the wretched state of McDac's commercial operations, the entire award should probably have gone to Boeing. It didn't. An article in the *Seattle Times* in January 1994 warned readers that although Clinton had visited Boeing the previous winter, his administration's focus had shifted to Long Beach, California, where Douglas Aircraft manufactured its airplanes. California, the piece noted, "was crucial to Clinton's election."[34] Also, Missouri was a so-called swing state, and Saint Louis was headquarters for McDac.

In the end, Saudia bought twenty-three Boeing 777's and five 747-400's, twenty-eight aircraft in all. And it purchased thirty-three airplanes from McDac, four MD-11 freighters and twenty-nine MD-90's. As seen from Seattle, the good news—that Airbus was beaten on a deal it had expected to win—was mixed with having to divide the business with McDac. Some of Boeing's board members reacted angrily. "We have to take them off the street," one of them said.

Another Washington figure, Deputy Secretary of Defense (and later Secretary) William Perry, also played an indirect role in the merger. On a Friday evening in the summer of 1993, he gave a dinner for a dozen CEOs from the defense industry and told them they had to consolidate. There would have to be fewer such companies. Defense spending had been sliding for five or so years and was expected to fall much further. Mergers, defense buyouts, and sell-offs were under way, and the process would have to accelerate. "We expect defense companies to go out of business," said Perry afterward. "We will stand by and watch."[35]

It happened. Fifteen of the top defense companies became four. Perry's dinner is still talked about within industry and government circles—and usually referred to as "the last supper."

Phil Condit, who regarded himself as more of a strategic planner than a manager of operations, wanted to buy a major defense company. Boeing, he thought, should have two or more strings to its bow. Condit was a born diversifier. He wanted to take the company into other businesses—satellites, computers, and so forth. Above all, however, he wanted Boeing to become the world's largest defense contractor.

Compared to Lockheed and McDac, Boeing was then a lesser player in the defense business. It built bombers and the Minuteman missile system, but it didn't have "market breadth." Serious discussions between Boeing and Lockheed got under way, but they didn't go very far, mainly because Lockheed was too expensive and also insisted on preserving its name in any merged company. Boeing ruled out a hostile takeover.

Harry Stonecipher, McDac's CEO, was in charge of a company that was spiraling downward—fast. He was disinclined to allow funding for development of a new commercial airplane and, indeed, to fund research and development in that side of the house. McDac's existing commercial programs were a bust. For many years, the DC-10 had been a troubled aircraft that few carriers were prepared to buy. And the MD-11, a jumped-up version of the DC-10, hadn't tempted the market, not enough anyway, and the company had to take a $2 billion write-off on that plane.

In 1992, McDac disclosed a design for an airplane called the MD-12, a four-engine jumbojet with double-deck seating for up to six hundred passengers. Some months earlier, the company had announced its intention to sell 40 percent of its commercial aircraft business to Taiwan Aerospace for $2 billion. Quite clearly, the fortunes of the MD-12 and McDac itself were tied to a successful completion of those arrangements. In the end, however, Taiwan Aerospace backed off, and McDac shelved the MD-12.

Most of McDac's available resources were tied up in a strenuous competition with Boeing and Lockheed for the new joint strike fighter (JSF), a program that looked as if it might one day be worth $300 billion. But in November 1996, the Defense Department, in the curious idiom of the Pentagon, "deselected" McDac's design for the aircraft. Only Boeing and Lockheed remained. Lockheed won, and McDac was left high and dry.

An acquisition by Boeing of McDac had become the only workable solution for McDac, and Stonecipher was determined to make it happen. His thinking was fully shared by John McDonnell, the chairman, and by Phil Condit. Twice McDonnell and Stonecipher talked with Frank Schrontz about a "merger," the term both sides chose to call one company's purchase of another. Schrontz declined both times, partly because Stonecipher wanted an unacceptably large role in the combined company. In Seattle, he was seen as a potent, hard-driving figure who, unless controlled by another such figure, would take control. "Our chief concern was Harry," recalled one Boeing veteran who is still closely involved with the company. "He was feared—seen as a guy who in three years could become CEO. It took about that long."[36]

The price was another obstacle. "Harry wanted a very high price," said Larry Clarkson, one of Boeing's pivotal figures for several years. "He thought they'd win the first stage of the JSF and refused to acknowledge they might have to take a big write-off on the MD-11."[37]

Boeing had looked hard at McDac and twice crunched the numbers. Little, if any, due diligence was done during the initial discussion. Some was done during the second round of talks. Due diligence is a process by which the overall financial status of companies involved in mergers and acquisitions can be established. The practice, which typically lasts several months, extends well beyond checking documents, including annual and quarterly financial reports. It could be described as a search for hidden liabilities, and usually includes a letter of intent that says Company X intends to buy Company Y within a certain period provided there has been a thorough vetting of Company Y's finances.

Boeing had to be very careful, if only to avoid lawsuits that could have arisen if McDac was shown to have concealed data regarding its assets. But the pairing of Boeing with McDac would be trickier than most such arrangements, partly because Boeing wouldn't be entitled to examine the Douglas books until the deal was done; otherwise, Boeing would, in theory, have had a competitive advantage. Boeing would have to do due diligence afterward for the usual reason but also to demonstrate to the Justice Department that Douglas was indeed a failed company.

Later, several Boeing executives complained that too little due diligence was done because Condit had been in a hurry to complete the merger without a hitch. At least some of them didn't know that for a period of more than three years, Boeing's investment banker, First Boston, had been looking carefully at McDac's finances. According to Boyd Givan, "only about twelve people in the company were aware of that."[38]

There were other considerations, including Airbus, which, like Boeing, was aware that McDac was going to be rescued from itself in one way or another. A purchase of some of McDac's assets could have given Airbus a manufacturing base in the United States, and some American investment bankers did come to Toulouse to discuss the possibility of Airbus acquiring McDac's commercial business.

That conversation went nowhere, but Airbus was giving Boeing quite a lot else to think about. Stonecipher says, "We were in talks with Airbus. If the merger with Boeing hadn't happened, we'd be building Airbuses in Long Beach now."[39]

The European Commission could have vetoed the merger, and in doing so triggered a trade war. Boeing avoided a veto by making major concessions, one of which meant giving up an exclusive sales agreement with three of the world's biggest airlines: American, Delta, and Continental. Although the agreement had, of course, denied Airbus access to these carriers, it didn't really change anything. None of the three has since bought an Airbus.

After Boeing's board started urging Schrontz to take McDac off the street, he and McDonnell resumed talking from time to time. In December 1995, Schrontz, Condit, and Woodard met with McDonnell, Stonecipher, and someone else from McDac. The Boeing group continued to feel that the McDac people were asking for a lot more than their company was worth. Moreover, John McDonnell was pushing to have the company renamed the Boeing-McDonnell Company. Schrontz said no to a merger. McDac's deselection—its failure to make the cut—in the JSF competition reinforced the prevailing view in Seattle of a failed company, one that could no longer do the things it had once done well.

At about this time, Michael Sears, who was judged one of the two most capable of McDac's executives (and who would later go to prison for his role in a Boeing defense scandal), was dispatched to Long Beach, his mission to see if the Douglas company stood any chance of once again becoming a player in the commercial aircraft business. (The other executive was Michael Cave, who accompanied Sears to Long Beach and is now general manager of Boeing's commercial airplane programs.) After several months on the scene, Sears concluded that a new commercial airplane program would require two new models and new wings on two other aircraft. It would be a huge investment, at least $15 billion. McDac couldn't commit to a number nearly that high. McDonnell called Schrontz again, and the talks resumed; quite clearly, there would be at least some give in McDac's position.

The Pentagon and the White House strongly favored the merger, partly because they wanted stronger competition for Lockheed Martin. Also, combining Boeing and McDac would appear to confront Airbus with an even more formidable American adversary.

The board chairmen, Schrontz and McDonnell, authorized Condit and Stonecipher to meet and try to narrow differences on the key issues. On the morning of December 10, 1996, the two CEOs met for forty-five minutes in a suite at the Four Seasons Hotel in Seattle. They agreed on a range within which the price to be paid by Boeing would be fixed. And they drew most of the other issues within reach of agreement. Condit was later criticized by colleagues for not having had a lawyer in the room with him.

Four days later, members of Boeing's board and senior management met in the boardroom in Seattle. Their opposite numbers from McDac met in their boardroom in Saint Louis. Among the Boeing people taking part was C. Gerald King, who was to become the major Boeing figure in the process of making the merger happen. At the time, King was president of the Boeing Defense and Space group. He had gained wide respect in a variety of tough jobs and was seen as a potential successor to Condit. The following is his account of the meeting:

"McDonnell was still pushing for his version of what the company's name should be. Other issues were the price Boeing would pay and a job in the merged company big enough for Harry. As the talks wore on, the tough issues overhanging the room became the company name and Harry's job. I spoke up and said, in effect, that Boeing's name meant everything; that any change would compromise the general view of Boeing's integrity. Others chimed in saying similar things, but Boeing people were appalled at what might have been a near thing."

King was referring to what had been a sign of some give in a few board members' resistance to changing the company's name. Boeing lawyers saw the issue as a negotiating ploy. By saying, "We must not let our name disappear," the McDac side felt certain that Boeing would yield more in return for agreement on no change in the company name.

"The Boeing side," King continued, "wanted to have as little to do as possible with Stonecipher. He appeared to be on track to becoming the COO [chief operating officer] and president of the merged company, if the merger went through."

Stonecipher did get the role he wanted; the boards approved the merger. "Condit asked me to put it together," Jerry King continued. Although King had hoped to retire not long after this event, he agreed to stay on and spearhead a team of lawyers and engineers who would hammer out the agreement with their opposite numbers.

The process took eight months, and for King it was not an agreeable experience. "When we had a final wrap-up session in Colorado Springs," he said, "the McDonnell Douglas people gave me a plaque that made me want to throw up. It was the cover of the [current] *Economist*. It showed two camels fornicating, and the cover line was 'Who's on Top?' They gave it to me. I buried it in a closet and never showed it to anyone."[40]

The reactions were mixed. Those who had favored the merger saw a $35-billion company become a $48-billion company, its parts mutually reinforcing—each, in theory, cushioning a downturn in the other's market. Not the least of the gratified advocates were the financial markets, as reflected in the rise in share prices of the two companies. A few of the Wall Street analysts argued that the merger had saved Boeing, a company, they said, that had no cost controls and had forgotten how to run a business on cash.

Boeing Commercial's people lost no time in deploring the event. It was, they thought, a disaster. The due diligence was described as having revealed a negative number for Douglas. It would cost more to shut down that business than get out of running it, as McDac would now be able to do. That much was clear. "Douglas was riding the back end of its production cycle and, in effect, exiting the commercial business," said one of its executives who was there at the time of the merger.[41] In Seattle, a frivolous comment that stuck was "Let's sell Douglas to Airbus for one French franc."

Boeing had paid $13.3 billion for McDac. ("A smart guy," said one disgruntled Boeing executive, "would have let it fold and then bought up the pieces at ten cents on the dollar." Almost certainly, other parties, starting with the Pentagon, would not have let that happen.) For each share of McDac's stock they held, its shareholders were awarded a 0.65 share of Boeing stock. However, most Boeing people discovered virtually overnight that the company's two largest individual stockholders were now John McDonnell—no surprise there—and Harry Stonecipher, who also held numerous stock options.

The year of the merger, Boeing paid Stonecipher $3.5 million in cash, $4.1 million in restricted Boeing stock, and an additional $8.1 million in unrestricted Boeing shares. Included in the cash was $2.2 million to offset taxes on stock that would vest once the companies merged. Condit, by comparison, that year earned $1.3 million in cash and $204,000 in restricted stock.[42]

In a proxy statement issued in April 2002, at the time of an annual meeting of Boeing shareholders, John McDonnell was shown to hold just over 14 million shares. In second place was Stonecipher, with close to 2.5 million. The distant third was Condit, with about 816,000 shares.[43]

"So now Boeing had the two largest of its individual investors joined at the hip," recalls Richard Aboulafia, one of the aircraft industry's most highly respected analysts. "Both were now board members, and one was chief operating officer and president. This would make Michael Eisner blush. From a corporate governance point of view, it amounted to rank incompetence or something more sinister. In principle, there was no obstacle to the pair of them ripping the company apart for cash. In practice, that was unlikely, but the Stonecipher-McDonnell alliance could have affected Boeing's plans for the future, and not to the advantage of the Boeing Commercial Airplanes company."[44]

Not long after the merger, Larry Clarkson ran into T. Wilson, who said, "McDonnell Douglas has just bought Boeing with Boeing's money."[45] Wilson may have said it to others as well; in any case, his comment became the affair's epigraph. Wilson was privately appalled by the merger, telling various people that McDonnell Douglas brought nothing to Boeing. They had never won a head-to-head competition with Boeing, he would point out. Not since the early 1970s, he would add, had McDac itself designed the military aircraft that accounted for its success. "We got nothing out of that [the merger]," he told intimate friends. Wilson felt strongly that Boeing should confine itself to doing what it did best. "Boeing," he often said, "should not be interested in acquisitions and mergers."

"What badly troubled T. Wilson," said Jerry King, "was the strength on the board that the McDac side ended up with. There was Harry and his attitude that he would whip the Boeing people into shape." And, he continued, "Schrontz chose not to stay on the board. That took the heart out of it. His departure was the biggest mistake of all. Phil was left with no one to help him."[46] For King and other heritage Boeing people, Schrontz had been a source of strength and wisdom.

Many Boeing heritage people conceded that a shift in emphasis toward the military side would usefully balance the company's dominant commercial business. And while acquiring the second-largest military contractor looked like a big step in that direction, Boeing, as they saw it, was already expanding its defense and space business. Not long before the merger, it had bought Rockwell International's defense and space division for $3.2 billion and was on track to make other acquisitions.

The McDac people returned Boeing's contempt for their military programs. Their line on Boeing's focus on commercial aircraft was: Why bet on a high-risk, high-cost, low-margin business when you can depend instead on Uncle Sam?

Shortly after the merger, an experienced and currently serving Boeing engineer said, "Historically, McDonnell Douglas had a different culture. And that negative, predatory, autocratic culture has displaced Boeing's old problem-solving culture."[47] He and others in Seattle, using similar language, talked about how their company had taken on the "crude, shoot-the-messenger style" of their new acquisition. Until the merger, Boeing still boasted that it was "a company of engineers." But not after the merger. Its engineers became the company's most disgruntled element.

Everyone assumed, correctly, that Phil Condit, who hated making decisions and hated controversy, would be no match for Harry, who liked nothing better than making decisions and didn't mind controversy. Phil told at least one colleague that Harry Stonecipher would be there for no more than eighteen months.

AIRPLANE PROGRAMS are eyed with suspicion by stockholders. A new one will create a deficit. That is a certainty in a business that harbors few of them. The deficit may be erased—the sunk funds recaptured—as the factory floor comes down the learning curve and becomes capable of producing at manageable cost an airplane the market likes. Or the program stalls, and the company is stuck with another failed airplane program.

Although very different people, Condit and Stonecipher were aligned in their approach to company business. They had known each other since the mid-1970s, when Condit was the chief engineer on the 757 program and Stonecipher was selling GE engines. Shortly after taking the helm of this hard-nosed, dedicated airframe manufacturer, Condit spoke of taking it into "a value-based environment where unit cost, return on investment, shareholder return are the measures by which you'll be judged." He was intoning the Stonecipher creed.

As the second senior officer and a pivotal board member operating in tandem with John McDonnell, Stonecipher set about trying to change Boeing's corporate culture by edging the company away from the risks of commercial airplane building and toward a focus on defense and becoming a global services corporation.

Condit and Stonecipher were about as different stylistically as two high flyers could be. Condit was patient and preferred being called Phil by the people, high and low, with whom he worked. He had a cultural side, affected, said various Boeing people. Stonecipher was blunt and impatient.

On March 25, 1998, about nine months after the merger, Stonecipher gave a rough, biting critique of the Boeing Company in a speech delivered at the Rotary Club in Seattle. What he said was bitterly resented, and still is—it's still talked about within the company and the city.

In recalling what he called "the old Boeing," Stonecipher described a conversation he'd had with the retired T. Wilson. "I told him Boeing is arrogant. He [Wilson] responded: 'And rightly so.' There's a great difference between pride and arrogance," Stonecipher told his audience of businesspeople.

Regarding company operations, he said, "I can stop a lot of spears for Condit, and I can throw a lot of spears." He described himself as "profitability driven," adding that for years he had defended himself against the widely viewed perception that he was interested only in making money. "After a while I just said, 'You're right. I am.'"

He compared the company's financial status very unfavorably with that of GE and Coca-Cola. "We have returns that can't even see the bottom of Coca-Cola. That is not acceptable."[48]

Eight years later, reflecting on coming to Boeing, Stonecipher said, "Boeing people didn't know the cost of anything. No one there shared cost data with anyone. No one knew the unit cost of anything they built. They needed help."[49] He had a point, if perhaps overstated. Various Boeing watchers on Wall Street felt roughly the same way about the company as it was operated then.

But Boeing heritage people worried aloud about what they saw: a potent figure—stronger by far than Condit, their nominal leader—but one who made no distinction between Coca-Cola, or soap, and Boeing's bread-and-butter product. The jet airliner was not a commodity, they felt, but rather the nation's most significant export because it earned the most dollars and harbored a singular array of advanced technologies. A strong national interest, they continued to think, lay in its good health and viability.

Condit strongly opposed allowing commercial aircraft to remain the company's first-priority business. Some of the Boeing heritage people described his approach as "defend and extend," meaning, defend your legacy by protecting existing products like the 737, and slow down the other guy by pretending to embark on new airplane programs. Condit did invite controversy by turfing out numerous executive-level people and cutting employment. And he started talking about taking the company to Chicago. More important, Boeing was losing market share.

But the apparent upside received greater attention. Profits were rising, and costs starting to drop. Lean manufacturing had begun belatedly to take hold, although it was still costing Boeing more than it should have to build airplanes. For a time Condit was lionized in the business press.

Stonecipher, too, was considered good value, notably on Wall Street and in the boardrooms of companies that he had managed. His quarterly reports had normally shown a profit, and under his direction corporate shares had a tendency to rise. However, many, if not most, people in his trade who thought that staying competitive meant investing in R&D and financing new products worried about his unblinking focus on the bottom line.

Wherever he fetched up, Stonecipher was judged smart, capable, prodigious, and opinionated. He could try to cut back the erratic commercial aircraft trade. But he didn't sidetrack what since the mid-1960s had been the Boeing Company's core business.

CHAPTER SEVEN

The Very Large Airplane

AFTER THE AIRCRAFT industry's downturn in the early 1990s, it appeared that the only new airliner likely to be built for the next several years would be a superjumbo. A much bigger airplane, the argument ran, would increase the number of passengers who could be flown between major urban centers connected by the hub-and-spoke airlines. Seat mile costs had to come down, and only the very large commercial transport—the VLCT as it was then labeled—would allow airlines to accomplish that, provided, of course, they could fill all those seats.

The unknown but unavoidably huge cost of building the very large airplane, or VLA, as it was also known, was intimidating. All sides wondered whether the project would dictate cooperative arrangements. The superjumbo (another of its designations), many thought, might have to be built as a joint venture, or not at all.

Just how this airplane, known formally now as the A380, actually came about is a muddled and contradictory saga. Within the Airbus family, the story blends misjudgment with duplicity and corporate roughhousing. Within Boeing there was also misjudgment, mixed with evasiveness and a strong whiff of self-deception. On both sides, there were those who believed what they chose to believe, or wanted others to believe.

The idea of a bigger airplane was hardly new. "Boeing has been thinking about it for twenty years or so," said John Hayhurst in 1993.

Hayhurst, now retired, was a highly respected Boeing engineer and vice president, among whose tasks was managing what his company called large airplane development. "Most of our thinking was on stretching the 747—anywhere from ten or fifteen feet to fifty feet," he said. "But two years ago, we saw the need for something even larger by the end of the decade—something not just twenty percent bigger, but more. A few carriers helped with that decision." He cited United and British Airways as being among them. "They forced us to focus and get busy studying the project," he said.[1]

Airbus was looking at it, too, and was being pulled, or pulling itself, in various directions. Its leaders had convinced themselves that Boeing was making the larger part of its profits with the 747, thereby enabling it to sell the rest of its product line at giveaway prices. They were wrong. The most profitable airplane that Boeing ever made was not the 747; it was the 767-300—the extended-range version.

By 1991, Airbus had attained a secure foothold in the single-aisle airplane market with its A320. Also, the Gulf War had ended, and Airbus was beginning to deliver the first aircraft in its A330 and A340 series.

"By then," says Jean Pierson, "we had an aircraft product line ranging from a hundred fifty to three hundred seats. At the air show in 1999, we announced ourselves as serious competitors with the goal of obtaining fifty percent of the market. But to achieve that goal we couldn't leave Boeing with the high end. You have to span the market. You need a cash cow of your own. And that is why I said Airbus intends to launch a competitor to the 747."[2]

In Europe, there was concern that Boeing might be using the super-jumbo to divide and conquer Airbus. Frank Schrontz held discussions over a period of several years with Edzard Reuter, the legendary chairman and CEO of Daimler-Benz, about collaborative ventures; Daimler-Benz owned Deutsche Aerospace, an Airbus member company, known as DASA. Schrontz said that he and Reuter "talked repeatedly about a big airplane. It would be a very complicated program. But we could use our joint expertise."[3]

Schrontz and Dean Thornton, president of the commercial airplanes group, agreed to do a joint study if Airbus or its member companies were ready for that. As usual, Schrontz and Thornton saw the pros
and cons very much the same way and, on balance, favored going forward. However, Ron Woodard, the executive vice president of the
commercial group and Thornton's heir apparent, felt differently. "It all
changed when Woodard took over from Dean," said a closely involved
Boeing executive. "He was constantly working on Schrontz to do less
about this."

Early in 1992, Boeing and all four of the Airbus member companies
reached an agreement to do a joint study of the prospects for a superjumbo. By then, Edzard Reuter had turned the management of Deutsche
Aerospace over to an ultrahard charger named Jürgen Schrempp, who
knew nothing about making airplanes but was widely judged to have
set for himself the goal of unseating his famous boss and managing a
large conglomerate of which DASA was just one part. (Schrempp
reached his goal; he retired in 2005 as chairman of DaimlerChrysler.)
The four partners also agreed that Schrempp and Pierson would manage the talks for Airbus. But Pierson declined to take part.

Almost overnight, Schrempp became Pierson's bête noire. Pierson
called him "the new Führer." Schrempp, he said, was already planning
to replace Reuter by making himself a star in this new arena. He
intended to reshape the European aircraft industry by rebalancing it
in Germany's favor. According to Pierson, Schrempp saw the move
toward a joint study with Boeing as an opportunity for himself.[4] But
since a superjumbo would compete with the 747—the supposed cash
cow—Boeing's interest in helping to build one jointly impressed Airbus as suspect. Still, if there was to be a superjumbo, Boeing, it seemed,
might insist on having a large piece of the action. Otherwise, the better
part of wisdom for Boeing would lie in discussing the project with
other parties—the Europeans, the Japanese—and then doing nothing.

Boeing's strategy, although well understood by European players,
created serious divisions among them, notably between the French and
the Germans; British Aerospace, feeling itself too puny to play a seri-

ous role in the superjumbo game, actually nudged Boeing toward Deutsche Aerospace and Schrempp, by then a bitterly controversial figure.

It began in early 1992 when Schrontz and Larry Clarkson met at the St. Regis Hotel in New York with Richard Evans, who was British Aerospace's chief executive at the time. "He encouraged us to talk to Edzard Reuter and Jürgen Schrempp," said Clarkson, who managed the Boeing side of the joint study, along with Hayhurst. Clarkson was vice president for international planning and often described as Boeing's secretary of state. "We all agreed," he said, "that there wasn't room for two airplanes in the market and we should try to do it together. It was agreed we would work with the Airbus partners, not Airbus itself, to lessen the antitrust issues. Frank [Schrontz] believed strongly in the program. Woodard did not, as he 'feared' Airbus. At some point we brought in the three [Japanese] heavies. Schrempp made it clear that he was ready to go it alone if the French didn't want to take part. He thought he would become the leader of Europe's aircraft industry."[5]

A meeting of the Airbus board in Seville, Pierson said, "gave Schrempp an opportunity. He announced there that he had met with Frank Schrontz, who, he reported, had agreed that Germany could lead a European team on the very large aircraft study." Schrempp, Pierson continued, "then threatened to take Daimler out of Airbus. He turned to Henri Martin [his French counterpart], and said, 'Do you want to follow me, or not?' He seemed to be suggesting that it didn't matter. He had Boeing in tow. But no one was ready to confront the prospect of German withdrawal. That would have collapsed Airbus. But I knew the Boeing team. Why would guys who had a monopoly [of jumbo aircraft] share it with a guy who had twenty percent of the market and help that guy get to fifty percent?"[6]

A former Boeing executive who declined to be quoted by name and was one of the few figures closely involved in the affair said, "The Germans told us: 'We will take a leadership role in Europe if you, Boeing, will take responsibility for the U.S. and Japan.'" This meant that

Boeing, in effect, would survey the prospects for a superjumbo in both the American and the Japanese airline markets and try to enlist the eventual participation of Japanese companies in what seemed an enormous undertaking. "There's no question about it. We did start the talks with Deutsche Aerospace," Hayhurst said flatly.[7]

Alan Boyd was president of Airbus North America at the time. In various jobs, including secretary of transportation, he had made many friends within the industry and was well connected in Seattle. His account of Boeing's liaison with Schrempp runs as follows:

In February 1992, Schrempp went to New York to work something out with Boeing, and told his partners nothing. He let on nothing. And then, in the summer, at the Farnborough International Airshow, in Britain, the partners began talking about the big airplane. Jürgen pulled the Boeing people aside and said, "Remember, this is our first meeting." But he had been tracked. They knew what he'd been up to.

It was then agreed that the partners would talk with Boeing. Jürgen went and returned with a draft agreement to do market studies with Boeing. He wrote in a clause that Boeing agreed to and which said that neither of the parties would talk to anyone else. [Anyone else meant Japan's three "heavies."] Pierson hit the roof. "That blocks us out," he said. "Boeing is already in bed with the Japanese." So then Jürgen volunteered to remove the offending clause. And he said he had done so. But Boeing sent in another draft which showed that Jürgen had not talked to them, and that left a lot of mistrust of the German partner.[8]

Schrempp had not only been freelancing, according to Airbus people. He had given Boeing the Japanese card to play on its own. But Schrempp's partners would not yield that card—not without a struggle. "We talk to the Japanese bilaterally," said one Airbus executive at the time. "They are essential for what they can contribute financially and can contribute on the industrial side. We also want to co-opt the Japanese in order to discourage the possibility of a Japan-led Asian aircraft consortium striking out on its own."[9]

However, it was already a little late for Airbus. In January 1993, Pierson had the rug pulled from beneath him. He was in Tokyo negotiating with the three heavies on the very day that they and Boeing issued a statement announcing their intention to examine jointly the feasibility and potential market for a very large airplane.

Shortly afterward, tempers quieted. Boeing and all of the Airbus member companies reached an agreement on doing the joint study of a superjumbo. Still, no one thought that Schrempp would give up trying to gain a lasting advantage in his duel with the French. And in conversations with Boeing executives at the time, one drew the impression that they wished him well. "There are differences within Airbus," said Schrontz. "The Germans say, 'You can't give away airplanes.' For the French, market share is everything."[10]

And was Boeing fishing in troubled waters so as to sidetrack the superjumbo? "We are not stalling," said Schrontz. "We do not see this as an attempt to forestall Airbus on a very big airplane. It is not an attempt to break up Airbus and its products. But one consortium managing another consortium would be impossibly complex. We are serious. If there is a market [for the jumbo], we want to play in that market. I think there is a market. The question is whether it is big enough. There are interested airlines: British Airways, United, JAL, ANA, Singapore Airlines, Cathay Pacific, and Lufthansa." And what about that other consortium, the Japanese one? "We don't know whether the Japanese will take part [in building the aircraft]. We have kept them up to date. The question is what kind of airplane makes sense and in what time frame."[11]

Boeing and Airbus interpreted the outcome of the joint study differently. Airbus foresaw a market for 500 to 600 airplanes. Boeing envisaged sales of between 300 and 350. What was interesting, though, as Clarkson says, was that "both sides calculated the development cost to be $14.5 to $15 billion, with negative cash flow reaching $22 billion, all in 1992 dollars."[12] This meant that for some unknown period of time these airplanes, if built, would be sold for much less than it had cost to develop them because the various factories building them would not yet have come down the learning curve.

Still, Airbus's hierarchy, starting with Pierson, was convinced right from the start that it had to build a VLA, with or without Boeing or the Japanese heavies. It didn't take long for Pierson to get the better of Schrempp, and the Airbus commitment to the A3XX, as the big airplane was called in its developmental stage, remained intact, although there would be skirmishing periodically between the Airbus leadership in Toulouse and their colleagues in Deutsche Aerospace.

Boeing's attitude toward the big airplane is hard to disentangle from the divergent views of its executives. Some of them professed doubt that an airplane of that size would find a market large enough to justify the cost of creating it. Others, although attracted to going ahead, felt that the company had more than enough on its plate, given the ballooning costs of the 777 program and the need to modernize the 737. And then, in recent years various Boeing personalities have ascribed to themselves some artful forethought; their approach to the big airplane issue, they said, was to play for time—to allow Airbus to commit itself to a losing proposition. Boeing would "ambush" Airbus. Harry Stonecipher recalls saying to colleagues, "We must not do anything to drive them away from that airplane," because "we knew the market for it wasn't there."[13]

Did Boeing actually try to entrap Airbus with some crafty forethought? The answer almost certainly is no. What we know is that Airbus felt strongly pushed to complete a family portrait of its airplanes with a very big one and thereby prove that the company's improbable blend of corporate cultures and divergent methods could match Boeing's most conspicuous accomplishment, the 747.

As for Boeing, it did play for time, mainly because it lacked a strategy. Its management was divided. Curiously, none of the senior figures seems to have considered, at least not seriously, building the big airplane jointly with DASA, BAe, and the Japanese. Doing so would have greatly diminished, if not extinguished, Airbus, and Boeing would have become the leader of a huge international consortium and been able to offload a lot of the financial risk in building airplanes, large or small.

In buying time, Boeing's behavior seemed directed toward confusing the competition about its own intentions and thereby causing Airbus to slow down the A3XX program or even discontinue it. And if Airbus actually built the airplane, Boeing just might have already created a stretched version of the 747 to compete against it.

Boeing did quick-march an array of new versions of the 747 past airline customers. They heard about 747-500's, -600's, and -700's. Even today, people who should know—Boeing people past and present, industry analysts—can't say whether the company wanted to steer Airbus away from the A380 by talking the talk, announcing new programs that would not be pursued. Or did management flirt seriously with these paper airplanes and then allow its increasingly cautious instincts to cancel them, one after the other?

Some among the company's first- and second-tier executives feel that management was never going to build another jumbo airliner. Some were also certain that the world's airlines wouldn't be attracted to newly made-over 747's built around 1960s technology. And some echo Boeing critics who say that the company spent ten years trying hard but failing to divert Airbus from the A380.

In January 1997, Boeing proclaimed an end to its plans for new versions of the 747, citing a limited market that didn't justify the $7 billion cost of developing one.[14] Aside from British Airways, none of the airlines had shown an interest in another 747. Yet just a year later, Boeing was again talking the talk about a new 747 variant, one of which was designated the 747X. (The *X* stands for "experimental," and Boeing was actually discussing a bewildering variety of 747X's, a reflection of the company's highly tentative approach to what it was doing.)

In August 1996, an article in the *Wall Street Journal* reported that Boeing "has secured orders from Asian carriers for more than 30 of its new larger, longer-range 747 jumbo jets, paving the way for next week's expected announcement to proceed with production, according to executives familiar with the jet maker's sales effort." But the second half of the article undercut the first half: " 'The problem is that it's a very limited market and the investments are really big,' said Ronald Woodard, president of Boeing's commercial airplane group, in a recent interview. 'We're going to have a real struggle to come up with a sound business case.' "[15]

Among potential buyers, the most interested was Singapore Airlines. It probably would have been the launch customer for this new stretched 747 with a new wing, had Boeing gone ahead with it. Instead, SIA became the launch customer for the A380.

The airplanes that Boeing didn't build deserve attention partly because of their influence on two programs currently under way. One is called the 747-8 (known initially as the 747 Advanced), which comes closer to being a new airplane than most of the models that Boeing was waving around in the 1990s. This airplane, too, will have a new wing, and it will incorporate many of the features of Boeing's highly innovative 787, including the new light materials and the new higher-performance engines.

The other new program is the 787 itself. It was foreshadowed by the most heralded of the airplanes that Boeing didn't build, the so-called Sonic Cruiser. The tale of how this misconceived program led to the 787 is a reminder of how dicey and, indeed, accidental this business can be. On March 29, 2001, Alan Mulally announced cancelation of the 747X program. Customers, he said, had provided "clear direction . . . that the 747-400 [the then current model] will satisfy the majority of their large airplane needs." Instead, Boeing would build a new and faster airplane, one that, Mulally claimed, "could change the way the world flies as dramatically as did the introduction of the jet age." It would be called the Sonic Cruiser and would "fly at speeds of Mach .95 or faster over extended ranges."[16]

Just what Mulally and others had in mind with this notional airplane remains unclear. Lacking an explanation, many onlookers inside and outside Boeing wondered whether this, too, was a gesture aimed at buying time. Was Seattle still trying to confuse or divert Toulouse? Or confuse the airline industry?

The airplane's cruising speed was supposed to hover just below the threshold dividing subsonic speed from supersonic, a zone of especially high turbulence. The turbulence would create drag, thereby increasing the airplane's fuel burn.

According to Christopher Avery of Morgan Stanley in London, British Airways complained about the airplane to financial analysts, saying, "Boeing doesn't say what they are offering. Is it subsonic, or more than Mach 1 [supersonic]? Unless it goes over Mach 1, there is no point. It's too difficult. Mach 1 is an engineering wall. It must be exceeded."[17]

Several of the company's most experienced and knowledgeable figures had serious reservations. One of them was Joseph Sutter, the renowned aerodynamicist who designed the 747. Choosing his words carefully, he said: "The 747 cruises at Mach .85, so you don't save a lot of time going to Mach .98. But you'd be burning too much fuel and creating a design problem. It would have cost serious money to solve that design problem and allow the airplane to fly at that speed without the turbulence—soluble but very expensive. It took the company too long to acknowledge that."[18]

Another was Larry Clarkson, who besides having been for several years a widely admired member of Boeing's executive council, had previously been president of Pratt & Whitney's commercial jet engine division. "Trans-sonic is the hardest place in the world to be," he said. "It was a dumb idea, and a waste of two years. No one seems to know what lay behind it. Confusing the marketplace is as plausible as any other explanation."[19]

"We all said the Sonic Cruiser made no sense," said Richard Branson. "It offered only a twenty-five-minute advantage." (He was referring to Virgin Atlantic's transatlantic flights. Other estimates had the

Sonic Cruiser shaving thirty to forty-five minutes from that journey, although passengers might have had to pay a premium of 10–15 percent.) "Phil Condit made a mistake by not stretching the 747 and thereby making way for the A380. Boeing should have done something a long time ago."[20] He meant something sensible.

Airbus was as confused as Boeing's airline customers. "It was another mistake," said Gerard Blanc. "But they took it seriously. I talked to Mulally and to Walt Gillette [the Sonic Cruiser's program director and now chief of engineering]. They argued it could be done. But why would you want to do it?"[21]

Not even the Asian airlines were attracted to the Sonic Cruiser, even though they, unlike so many other carriers, were making money, and even though passengers on long-haul transpacific flights would have been the main beneficiaries of a modest improvement in speed. On December 20, 2002, twenty or so months after the unveiling of the Sonic Cruiser, Mulally told a media gathering that Boeing was canceling it in favor of a new and different airplane. "Our airline customers," he said, "see greater potential value and need for a more efficient airplane. The remarkable enabling technologies we've identified pursuing the Sonic Cruiser will allow us to take a significant improvement."[22] This was no exaggeration.

Neither would it be an exaggeration to say that the Sonic Cruiser would have embarrassed Boeing had it not led to a decision, painfully taken, to go forward with the 787. Two years after that decision, a senior Airbus executive said, "They [Boeing] have been living off our technologies for a long time. Now it's our turn to go to school on theirs."

BIGGER IS NO longer better, according to Boeing people. Airbus, they contend, made a strategic mistake by failing to recognize that the market had changed direction. Airbus rejects this thinking; its case for the A380 is based on the heavy growth in air traffic it expects to see. Although Boeing, too, has been projecting heavy growth, the joint study disclosed serious differences. "It was a marriage between a cat and a dog," says Gerard Blanc of Airbus. "It couldn't work. What would the production line look like? The cockpit? Guys would be fighting like hell."[23]

Actually, the parties had agreed on sharing costs of production, and they had agreed that the final assembly of the aircraft would be in the United States. They also devised an approach to the antitrust problem that any joint project would have confronted.

"By mid-1995, however, we said there are too many roadblocks," according to Blanc. "We agreed then with Boeing that there was no market [for the superjumbo], even though we knew there was a market, and we were determined to exploit it. We felt we had the competence and this was our missing piece."[24]

Its new airplane, Airbus decided, would be just as big as the state of the art would allow. The assumption was that no airline would want another 747 if there was a bigger and newer jumbo on offer—that is, unless Boeing decided to sell 747's at giveaway prices. Still, recalled Hanko von Lachner, a longtime Airbus board member, "we didn't really know at that stage who was right or wrong, ourselves or Boeing. In our business case, we assumed that we wouldn't be alone in this market for a long time. Boeing, we thought, would react with an improved 747. We even prayed they would spend their money on the wrong airplane.

"An argument in favor of the A380," he says, "was Boeing's 777. It was a better airplane than our A340. But we calculated that the A380 would help to protect the A340. An airline that bought the A380 would be unlikely to buy the Boeing airplane."[25] He was referring to the advantages of commonalty, from which Airbus has benefited with its family of airplanes that have many of the same features.

The interplay of the A380 with the A330, the A340, and Boeing's 777 sharply pointed up the pitfalls and the unknowns that can torment any commercial aircraft program. In designing the A330 and A340—two double-aisle airplanes—Airbus took a novel step that seemed very clever at the time. It built these two planes with the same fuselage and the same wing, thereby slicing costs. The A330 would have two engines, and the A340, Airbus's longer-range minijumbo, four engines. Boeing sat back, watched this happen, and then built a more advanced, slightly more comfortable minijumbo, the 777, one that could fly similar routes but with two fewer engines.

With hindsight, it seems clear that instead of creating its own jumbo—the A380—Airbus could have and probably should have built a bigger A340, one with a new wing and equipped with two fewer but more powerful engines. A bigger A340 could have been the 747's replacement aircraft, given the trend toward smaller, not larger, double-aisle airplanes. It could have bracketed both the minijumbo and jumbo segments of the market and, in doing so, have done some damage to the 777, the best airplane in Boeing's fleet. Stated differently, an A380 with 555 seats is likely to be a little too big for the high-end market, and the 777 a little too small. In that case, an airplane that fell somewhere between those two would be a better fit for that market.

In Toulouse, there was little if any support for launching the airplane that became the A340. Its deficiencies were seen clearly. The explanation for why the wrong airplane was built speaks volumes about the politics of Airbus—about the shoals its leadership in Toulouse must too often try to maneuver around with varying degrees of success. A big shoal in this case was Lufthansa Airlines, the major carrier of a major Airbus member state. Lufthansa wanted and got a four-engine airplane. Apropos, the A380 superjumbo is assembled in Toulouse, but the components are made in the factories of four countries and then sent there.

Airbus insists, naturally, that the A380 is the greatest people mover in the sky. It can, Airbus says, offer airlines lower seat-mile costs than any other aircraft, an advantage that will lower ticket prices by as much as 25 percent. And the passengers—all 550 of them in a filled-to-capacity flight—will travel more comfortably than they would in any of the other big double-aisle aircraft.

The A380, according to John Leahy, will convey a sense of being on a cruise ship. As they board, passengers will not confront a cramped galley but instead a wide staircase to the upper level, where the first-class and business-class sections are located. Each first-class seat will fold open into an ample bed. On the lower deck, the coach class will have seats that are estimated to be an inch wider than the current standard, although they won't have more legroom. Whether a cruise-ship feel is created will depend on how much money a customer can or will invest in various refinements envisaged by Airbus. These include cocktail lounges, waterfall lounges, and private suites, some with a minibar and private closet.[26]

Airbus argues that the A380 is a "ministep" up in size, as Pierson describes it, compared to the advent of Boeing's 747, an event that occurred thirty years ago. That airplane, Pierson noted, was 150 percent bigger than Boeing's own 707, the second largest airliner then. "We should treat the A380 as part of a normal evolution," he said. "It is thirty-five percent bigger than the 747-400." And in a standard configuration it would have 144 more seats. However, Pierson has worried about what he calls the big airplane's "parameters."[27]

If the A380 had a single prophet, the distinction would probably be accorded to Adam Brown, who until his retirement in 2005 exercised responsibilities that exceeded his title, vice president for customer affairs. "The A380 is ugly. [It has a bloated, snub-nosed look.] I concede that," he said. "It has to be, though. To be compatible with the parameters of airports, it is required to sit in an eighty-meter-square box. That box determines the geometry of the airplane. The wingspan must be less than eighty meters. Even a stretched version of the airplane will have to be less than eighty meters in wingspan."[28]

Moving that wing, which weighs thirty tons, along with fuselage sections and other components, to the final assembly line in Toulouse required Airbus to devise an entirely new transportation system. For existing Airbus double-aisle aircraft, the modules are flown to assembly sites in Toulouse and Hamburg in whalelike Beluga Super Transporters.

However, these aircraft couldn't possibly carry huge A380 pieces. Instead, they travel by sea, by river barges, and finally by road convoy to Toulouse. A roll-on-roll-off ship was built in China to collect modules built in Hamburg. The wing panels, which are made in Broughton in North Wales, are ferried on trucks and taken to barges in the Dee estuary. The barges take their improbable cargo to a huge cargo ship called the *Ville de Bordeaux,* constructed especially for transporting A380 components.

The fuselage sections, the wings, and the tail sections are then transshipped onto roll-on-roll-off barges for the journey of ninety kilometers up the river Garonne. They navigate beneath designated and specially protected arches with the help of global positioning satellites to align the boats precisely with the use of onboard sensors and sensors under the bridges. Four barge journeys are required to transport the six very large sections needed to produce one A380.

After debarking, the modules travel 240 kilometers on specially designed trucks to the assembly line outside Toulouse. France's transport ministry carried out a program of road widening and removing bottlenecks along the route, which involves only rural roads and avoids motorways. The convoys move only in the wee hours, with the roads closed in extended sections to public traffic. The journey takes three days.

According to Airbus, its five-hundred-meter-long final assembly plant is the biggest industrial building in Europe. The jigs are seven stories high. Elevators take the workers to the different levels of their workstations.

AERODYNAMICISTS, including some of Boeing's, regard the A380 as a major technological achievement—a marvel, some say. It can take off and land quietly, indeed all but noiselessly compared to other airliners of whatever size. Its capacity for tight maneuvers, even at low altitudes, is remarkable.

But the issues of whether the airplane is too big for the market or for existing airports, or both, haven't gone away. Airbus answers by stressing, first, the A380's presumably low seat-mile costs and, second, the need to increase the size of double-aisle airplanes, since there are limits on the number of flights into and out of airports in any one day. "We can't just keep putting people into more and more airplanes," one is often told in Toulouse.

For industry people with long memories, concerns expressed about the size of the A380 sound very like what was said about the 747 thirty or so years ago: how arduous and time-consuming it would be to process passengers and then unload them; how unprepared the airports would be; how the airplane's turnaround time couldn't be less than two and a half hours.

One who remembers all that especially well is Clancy F. Wilde, who during much of the 1970s and 1980s ran Boeing's worldwide marketing strategy for jet airliners and for a time was in charge of the flight testing and training necessary to introduce new equipment. "The 747," he said, "redesigned techniques for handling people and baggage. JFK was going to run out of slots, but the 747 saved the airport because it doubled its capacity. Pan Am's forecast for transatlantic travel was only fifteen percent of what it became."[29] With the 747, ticket prices went down, and air travel was there for more people.

The air-travel market and the A380 make a good match, Airbus contends, in part because major cities serviced by hub airports are where most people live and where they want to go. Also, the largest population growth, Airbus notes, is occurring in these urban centers. The company predicts that in twenty years airlines worldwide will be offering twice as many daily departures as they did in 2004. Reducing costs, airport congestion, and environmental impact, the argument runs, will require very large aircraft flying between major hubs.

"There will always be major hubs that need connecting and everyone wanting to leave them at the same time," says Morgan Stanley's Avery. "The time zones create a natural bunching up of flights. At midnight, for example, British Airways sends three 747-400's from Hong Kong to London, Cathay Pacific sends one, and Virgin sends one A340-600. That is five wide-bodies leaving between sixty and ninety minutes of each other at about midnight. There is no point in leaving before midnight because that would mean arriving before the overnight curfew at Heathrow is lifted. That route cries out for A380's."[30]

Dispatching two 747's from one airport to another within an hour or less of each other was standard procedure prior to the falloff in air travel post-9/11. United Airlines, for example, had 747's flying one just behind the other from Los Angeles to Tokyo. Much of the scheduling for long routes is aimed at travelers who are understandably concerned with being in bed at a sensible hour.

A big part of the argument for an airplane as large as the A380 arises from the pressure on airports to create more slots, build more runways, hence more terminals. In their business plans, airport managers have an incentive to show a smaller number of aircraft flying in and out. Responding to the argument that the A380 will produce two or three times as much car parking and continuous immigration snarls, Adam Brown says, "The problem is not the airplane. It is the traffic." And for support, he cites a statement by the Port Authority of New York and New Jersey: "We need to adjust not by adding flights but by adding bigger aircraft," said Pasquale DiFulco, a spokesman for the Port Authority. In April 2004, the Port Authority predicted that the A380 would bring 1,040 jobs and $82 million in annual economic activity to JFK.[31]

London Heathrow, the busiest international airport, is also promoting the A380 on multiple grounds. Its size will reduce airport congestion, and, because the airplane's engines run so quietly, it can, unlike other aircraft, comply with Heathrow's evening noise restrictions. "A bigger airplane that operates more quietly than two 747's offers the carrier a win-win situation," says Michael di Giralamo, deputy director for airport operations at Los Angeles International Airport (LAX).[32]

According to BAA, Britain's airports group, the A380 will account for one in every eight flights into and out of Heathrow—or sixty thousand takeoffs and landings a year—by 2016. It "will enable nearly 10 million more passengers to fly to and from the airport with no increase in flights."[33]

Aside from Heathrow and LAX, all of the top ten hubs from which the A380 will operate are in Asia; they include Singapore, Seoul, Kuala Lumpur, and Sydney. And of the top ten routes, only London's Heathrow and New York's JFK do not serve the Asia-Pacific region.[34]

Twenty-two airports around the world are ready for the A380—their runway-taxiway systems, their aprons, and access to gates will be fully compatible with the airplane. Passenger holding rooms and baggage claim areas in these airports are judged equal to the challenge. Among the twenty-two are most of the so-called Pacific Rim airports; some of them were recently completed or renovated and embody major design improvements. Beijing's airport is the sole exception, although the authorities intend to have it fully compatible with the A380 by the end of 2007 or early 2008, in time for the Summer Olympics in mid-2008. The other three Chinese hubs from which the airplane will operate—Shanghai, Guangzhou, and Hong Kong—are ready. Three major airports in Japan, starting with Tokyo's Narita, are also ready.

Elsewhere, however, some major airports have had to scramble to prepare for the A380, and some are less prepared than others. The least set is LAX, even though it had for a time been expected to have the most A380 operations of the world's airports. Several carriers, among them Singapore Airlines (SIA), Qantas Airways, Virgin Atlantic, Korean Airlines (KAL), Malaysia Airlines, Lufthansa, and also Federal Express, had said they would be flying into LAX. And that was hardly surprising, since it serves as the major gateway to Asia and, for Asian carriers, the major gateway to the States.

The airplane had been expected to begin commercial life with a fully loaded nonstop flight of ninety-two hundred miles between LAX and Singapore. That changed when SIA, the aircraft's first operator, decided that although LAX would be able to accommodate the airplane, it wouldn't be able to do so in a way that met passenger expectations. So SIA then announced that another route—Singapore to JFK—would come first. LAX no longer figures in SIA's planning.

Then Virgin Atlantic, another on the short list of early users of the A380, decided to delay delivery of the airplane, partly, it said, because "real concerns still exist about the ability of airports to meet the requirements of this aircraft." The A380's boarding times at LAX were cited as among these concerns. In May 2004, KAL also wondered anxiously whether LAX would be ready to receive the A380.

These airlines could hardly think otherwise. LAX isn't fully compatible with the A380 and won't be for some unknown period of time, largely because plans to modernize a relatively decrepit facility and prepare it for the A380 became embroiled in a master plan that, besides being remarkably foolish and hugely expensive, was unresponsive to the problems at hand. The plan was inspired by former mayor James K. Hahn and, in effect, scuttled the previous mayor's master plan, which was regarded as sensible.

The Hahn plan's price tag was $11 billion—the biggest of all airport projects ever, even though Hahn had pledged to cap airport growth at $78 million, another foolish notion. Denver spent $3.5 billion on the country's newest airport. San Francisco spent $5 billion on modernizing its airport.

"We couldn't get the politicians focused in time and consequently will not be able to handle the airplane efficiently," says Michael di Giralamo. Di Giralamo is highly respected and known in airport circles as LAX's "go-to guy." "We will be able to accommodate the airplane in terms of landing, taxiing, and parking," he says. "But passenger service will not be at the level that airlines want. Some airlines will say, 'Let's put it somewhere else.' The mayor [Hahn] said to me, 'Why are they building it [the A380], and who needs it?' "[35]

The Federal Aviation Administration is restricting operations of the A380 at LAX to one runway because it feels the airplane's 261-foot wingspan requires runways to be 200 feet apart. LAX has four runways, one of which is 200 feet wide. The others are just 150 feet wide, and the FAA has expressed concern about wingtip clearance on parallel runways. The more serious concern on all sides, including that of the FAA, is the incidence of runway incursions at LAX. Among the corrective steps to be taken will be creation of a center taxiway and moving one of the runways. Environmental issues have held up work on the center taxiway.

Airlines operating big airplanes such as the 747, 777, and the A340 out of LAX feel under more pressure there than they do elsewhere. Runway and taxiway standards are well beneath those of other hub airports. Work is under way to improve the taxiways, along with the concrete fillets that allow aircraft to turn corners. But most of the improvements won't be completed until 2010. Work on the runways has been held up, again because of environmental issues. Expanding the holding rooms will take until 2012.

The various problems that may discourage some carriers from flying the A380 into LAX could obviously hurt Airbus. "Airbus does not want to see the world's biggest and most modern airplane flying into an airport that isn't equipped to handle it," says Frank Clark, executive director of Laxtec Corporation, an association of airlines that use LAX's international terminal.[36]

The question, then, is which A380 operators may decide that, despite the airport's drawbacks, there is no better alternative. The region's financial and international business sectors are concentrated in Los Angeles, as are the major ethnic population groups that travel long distances with some regularity. That explains why KAL, after hesitating, has decided to operate its A380's from LAX.

A380 users who decide against the airport could fly the airplane instead into San Francisco. The city has worked hard at being chosen to receive A380 operators and thereby begin to displace Los Angeles as the major gateway. Its new international terminal is ready. Four of the gates have been modified for the A380. Each of them has dual bridges that allow passengers to be disembarked and loaded rapidly enough to keep turnaround time within reasonable bounds.

The runways at San Francisco are 750 feet apart, not enough to allow two A380's to take off side by side but enough for one to leave alongside some other airplane. Besides the new terminal, which was opened in December 2000, the airport created two new parking garages, new freeway ramps, and two new employee parking garages. The other up-to-date feature is a light rail system that connects the terminals, garages, rental car offices, and a Bay Area Rapid Transit (BART) station that is located at the entrance of the international terminal. Bus and auto traffic on surface roads has been reduced.

John Martin, the airport's director, sees it as capable of competing with LAX. "Through passengers prefer landing here," he says. "We have a much higher level of amenities, and are much more efficient. The customs service is a much better facility. We have better facilities in general, including better restaurants."[37]

Officials at LAX are cautiously optimistic that in the end A380 operators—most of them Asian—will conclude, or have already concluded, that access to the Los Angeles market must outweigh the clear advantages of flying into San Francisco's airport. Many incoming travelers from East Asia would be unable to make the connections they require at San Francisco. Indeed, a great many such connecting flights out of San Francisco, especially those on Southwest Airlines, depart from Oakland.

AIRBUS'S CHIEF CONCERN isn't the readiness of airports for the A380 but the readiness of the travel market. Skeptics abound. The turnaround time of an airplane that big, they say, could turn out to be two and a half hours. And who, they ask, would want to fly in such a huge aircraft? How could 550 or so passengers evacuate this huge double-decker, if it came to that?* And then, how will they all get out of an airport without interminable delays? Think of all those passengers retrieving all that baggage and navigating other potential shoals, includ-

*On March 26, 2006, Airbus successfully completed a passenger evacuation test, as required by the American FAA and the European Aviation and Safety Agency (EASA). The test, according to Airbus's announcement, "was the most stringent ever performed and the first ever on a passenger aircraft with two decks. The aircraft was fitted with a very high density cabin layout featuring 853 seats which were all occupied. In addition there were two flight crew members and 18 cabin crews from Lufthansa on board to manage the evacuation in a representative way. The trial was performed in darkness and filmed with infrared cameras. The doors and slides that were operative were not known before the trial."

ing customs. Will there be waiting rooms large enough? And what about parking facilities?

The argument for Boeing's much-admired new airplane, the 787, is that the international route structure is "fragmenting"—jargon pointing to the fact that people would rather fly directly to where they want to go without having to stop off along the way at some hub airport. "Everything is fragmented," says Alan Mulally. "Seventy percent of the people landing at Narita are not going to Tokyo," he argues. "The same is true of O'Hare and Chicago. These people are trying to get to some other place. The congestion is in the hubs, not elsewhere."[38]

Boeing's 787 and its still more recent Airbus counterpart, the A350, are aimed at this point-to-point travel preference, whereas the A380—twice their size—will be plying the hub-to-hub routes. The A380, its critics insist, was badly timed. The market won't be ready for an airplane that big for perhaps a decade, they say. Airbus's thinking, they continue, was rooted in the early 1990s, when the idea of flying very large airplanes between hub airports seemed to make great sense. What sells now, the argument goes, is frequency and fragmentation. Leisure travelers are likely to buy their tickets based on price, whereas the business traveler is able to choose convenience, even if that means paying more.

Airbus is not connecting the dots, its critics maintain. It is the business traveler who pays the bill, they say. The issue is not how many people can be jammed into the airplane, but how much revenue they produce. The front end of the bus generates more revenue by a factor of five on a normal long-haul route, according to the A380's critics. The spread, they say, is less on domestic flights.

Pierson's argument—that the A380 represents a natural evolution from the 747—has support, even among those who feel that its arrival is premature. So far, they say, the discussion has lacked perspective. Boeing and Airbus, they note, are both forecasting 5 percent annual growth in air travel. And that is 5 percent of a very big and rising number. Moreover, in the business plan for a new airplane, the company, whether Boeing or Airbus, will count on a production run of twenty or so years. But the point in that twenty-year cycle at which the airplane may be fulfilling the company's hopes for it is rarely apparent. The A380 may be a decade away from meeting Airbus's expectations. And it may be that only an enlarged version of the airplane will do that. It is capable of carrying 750 to 800 passengers. Indeed, its wing is optimized for an airplane bearing that kind of load.

There is talk of a baseline, nonstretched all-economy A380 carrying between seven and eight hundred passengers; but the economics are not there, say the skeptics, because, again, it's the pricier seats in the front of the airplane that pay most of the costs of the flight. "This long-haul, 'pack 'em in' approach has been tried and it has failed," says one airline industry analyst. "It's not the bodies that matter, it's the revenue."

Left to itself, the A380 might over time satisfy Airbus's expectations. But it won't be left to itself. Instead of talking the talk, Boeing, as noted, is developing the 747-8, an advanced version of its veteran jumbo. This airplane will be a better cargo carrier than the A380, and it can be sold for less. Boeing's calculation rests partly on an assumption that the A380, with 550 seats, is too large and that its own 777 is a little too small for the big plane market. If so, the argument runs, an all-new 747 with 450-plus seats will be a good fit.

Perhaps. Boeing is also keenly aware that the market for this version of the 747 will be limited, if only because it will be squeezed between the A380 at the high end and the 777 at the lower end. And the airplane will embody a thirty-five-year-old design. However, Boeing will be investing a lot less in its 747-8 than Airbus has already invested in the A380. Indeed, the real significance of the new 747 may be that every one that is sold will mean one less A380 sold.

CHAPTER EIGHT

A Challenge from Asia

OVER THE PAST five decades, Boeing has been the country's largest single exporter and earner of foreign capital, a major innovator of high-end technologies and a major user of them, the custodian of a tribal knowledge about designing and integrating the numberless systems and parts of which a modern airliner is made. No other American company has that knowledge. Elsewhere in the world only Airbus and Russian industry have it.

For now, many would say. Boeing has elected to outsource a sizable body of knowledge. The greater part of its new airplane, the 787, is being built elsewhere, with Japan's three major aircraft companies in the lead role. Boeing's close and productive ties with them have at times raised questions, although never to the same extent as now. Has Boeing tilted the playing field against itself? Could these companies use what they have learned from Boeing to build and market their own large commercial aircraft? Indeed, has Boeing, in effect, ceased to be a maker of large commercial aircraft? And if so, why?

The 787 program is stretching technology to its outer edge, starting with the wing, the *smart* part of any airframe—"the soul of the airplane," as British aircraft people say. In the art of making wings for commercial aircraft, Boeing, as noted earlier, has had few peers. Now it has outsourced the wing of the 787, the first to be made partly of composite material, to the three Japanese "heavies." They are also

167

responsible for a section of the all-composite fuselage. And Boeing has licensed the design and manufacturing technologies involved in composite materials to the Japanese.

Alenia of Italy and Vought Aircraft are producing the center and aft fuselage sections, along with the airplane's horizontal stabilizer—in all, 26 percent of the structure. Boeing itself is supplying roughly 35 percent of it, including the vertical fin, the fixed and movable leading and trailing edges of the wing.

Boeing and Airbus have always outsourced subcomponents and systems to suppliers. In the case of the 787, however, Japanese suppliers are acquiring so-called core competences, starting with wing technology and the new lightweight materials. A comment, possibly overdrawn, but increasingly heard, is that whoever acquires the manufacturing edge with these new materials will dominate the aircraft industry in the twenty-first century. Hence, critics say, Boeing is giving up its competitive edge by outsourcing the responsibility for producing major parts of the 787 with the new materials.

"The 787 composite wing and fuselage structure are new technologies—untried on this scale even by Boeing," says Stan Sorscher, a Boeing engineer. "Boeing developed much of the materials, manufacturing processes, tooling, tolerances and allowances, and other design features, which are then transferred to suppliers in Japan, Italy and elsewhere. Over time, institutional learning and forgetting will put the suppliers in control of the critical body of knowledge, and Boeing will steadily lose touch with key technical expertise."[1]

A great many industries save money by outsourcing jobs and tasks. In effect, they outsource to stay alive. Keeping an entire production line at home is no longer a sensible option. But the wide array of products built or assembled globally—cell phones, hard drives, hose clamps, or whatever—can't be equated with the large jet airliner in terms of their complexity and national importance. In Seattle, one hears that a Boeing airplane is forty-five thousand pieces flying in close formation.

Boeing, unlike Airbus, isn't concerned with creating jobs, and its management appears unconcerned with what becomes of the specialized capabilities it is sharing and others it is generating. Outsourcing, as management professes to see it, is unavoidable, the best and perhaps the only means of holding labor and structural costs within financially stable bounds. There is something to that, although the larger reasons for outsourcing on a major scale have been advertised as gaining market access and also sharing the financial risks.

The talk about market access and moving to cheaper labor markets is misleading. Also very important to Boeing is gaining entry to low-cost financing from the world's second-biggest economy. Why else locate the wing supplier for the new airplane five thousand miles from Puget Sound? Briefly, this outsourcing is mainly about cheap money.

There is no evidence, however, that Boeing is saving much money by outsourcing the 787's wing or sections of the fuselage. Japan is not a cheap labor market. To the contrary. Neither is Italy. But the outsourcing does send a message to the unions that Boeing deals with. It says: "If you mess too hard with us, we can always outsource your job to another place."

Early in the new century, Boeing began reacting to the Airbus surge and its own stumbles in the marketplace by searching, especially in East Asia, for "strategic partners." In return for aircraft sales in these countries, Boeing would allocate production and design work on its aircraft. In August 2002, an article in *Business Week* said, "Condit sees globalization as a way to both expand sales to nations that sign on as manufacturing partners and to tap into cheaper labor markets."[2]

For a company as versatile as Boeing and as endowed with exceptional resources, the alternative to making airplanes is assembling them. And that is what Boeing is doing with the 787. "Systems integrator" is the term being used in Seattle and elsewhere within the industry to define the company's current approach to the business. As practiced, it means shifting the financial risks to suppliers, especially those who, like the Japanese and Italians, are subsidized by their governments.

Under the leadership of Phil Condit and then Harry Stonecipher, the company's process of change accelerated; aversion to risk became embedded in Boeing's corporate culture. Condit and Stonecipher had a strong aversion to a business that was so vulnerable to fluctuations in the economy and the airline market.

The "first-tier" suppliers—Japan's three heavies, Italy's Alenia, and Vought—help to finance the 787 program, provide a chain of lesser suppliers, and build the systems. Boeing puts the systems together. "We are an assembler, an integrator," said Condit.[3]

In exercising its right as a first-tier partner to choose a second-tier supplier, Vought selected a German-based subsidiary of EADS, Airbus's parent, to build the 787's aft pressure bulkhead, a dome-shaped structural wall at the rear of the passenger cabin. "It's not a surprise to Boeing," said a spokesperson at that company.[4]

Boeing sees itself, in the words of a senior vice president, as "an internationally networked virtual company." That is Boeing's "answer," he said, to globalization. "The emphasis is on electronic communication—doing business on a networked basis."[5]

The issue of sharing advanced technology with Japan has been around for roughly a quarter century, and for most of that time its focus lay in Washington. In 1983, a page-one story in the *Washington Post* by Dan Morgan cited transfers of sensitive military technology that, the story said, "have enhanced the technical capability of an already expanding Japanese aircraft industry [and lie] at the heart of a spreading controversy in Washington about whether the United States has given away information vital to its security and commercial competitiveness."[6] The issue, however, turned on military, not commercial, aircraft.

The current controversy is a largely internal Boeing affair. It pits management against other sectors, especially the engineers. Not surprisingly, they take strong exception to the outsourcing of core components, since much of the work for which they would have been responsible has gone, and a great many jobs with it. That aside, many of them are convinced that the company has lost sight of its larger interests. Their worst-case scenario, in brief, envisages Japan designing airplanes and outsourcing some or much of the fabrication to Korea and eventually to China.

In January 2006, Dominic Gates of the *Seattle Times* cited what he described as a bombshell dropped some months earlier by a group of Boeing engineers working on the 787 program. (This newspaper covers Boeing closely, and its reporting on the company is read closely by the aviation industry.) These engineers, veterans of the B-2 stealth program, told an internal investigator that data from B-2 bomber technical manuals had simply been copied straight into 787 technical specifications. Boeing managers, Gates said, were caught by surprise: " 'We all underestimated the amount of screening we need to do for military technology,' said Walt Gillette, head engineer and president for airplane development on the 787.

" 'It is our clear intent to make sure we comply with the law,' " Gillette said. But, Gates wrote, "the underlying issue is whether Boeing's plan to outsource high-tech 787 composites manufacturing could put U.S. government technology in the hands of either enemies or potential future economic competitors. Yet Boeing's internal response," he continued, "suggests a reverse perspective: that the laws designed to protect military secrets create barriers to legitimate sharing of commercial technology, which executives see as essential in the globalized aviation marketplace."[7] It's an argument that can be used to support Airbus's contention that U.S. technology flows back and forth between the military and civilian sectors, with Boeing as the main beneficiary.

A disaffected view within the company runs like this: "Boeing has gone from a technology-driven culture to one driven by schedules and budgets," says one experienced engineer. "But the need to rely on the same kind of people for competence and attention to safety is no less. Can you run the systems integration process after you've outsourced the store? It's easier to integrate if you have a clear knowledge and feel for the pieces."[8] Stated differently, there is a concern that as Boeing "demanufactures" in the Puget Sound area, it could be squeezing out the U.S. aircraft industry's capacity to compete with other suppliers.

The engineers feel, probably correctly, that the highest form of technology transfer is people-to-people. In 1978, Japan's three heavies helped to create fuselage sections of Boeing's 767, and as many as 133 of their people traveled to Seattle to work on the program. These Japanese companies produced about 15 percent of the 767. In the early 1990s, the same companies had more than 260 people involved in building about 22 percent of the 777. Now a similar number are in Seattle working on the 787 program.

The 777 was the first computer-designed ("paperless") airplane. The system, known as CATIA, that made it possible was designed by Dassault Aviation in France. Japanese engineers sat side by side with Boeing counterparts in the mammoth plant in Everett. Other Japanese engineers in Japan had CATIA workstations connected to other CATIA workstations in Everett and in Seattle. This all-electronic system made possible a free flow of information between engineers and the factory floor. That was a first, one that saved a lot of time.

In 2003, a group of Boeing engineers circulated an unsigned, strongly worded memorandum of ten pages on their company's alleged "brain drain." Although the bias of the writers was obvious, parts of what they wrote reflected a point of view shared by numerous industry figures and analysts. It cited Phil Condit's definition of Boeing's "core competency" as "large-scale systems integration" and posed two questions: "How can Boeing hope to successfully be a 'large-scale systems integrator' if they don't have enough experienced, qualified engineers to do the integration? If Boeing's engineers no longer understand the technical aspects of the airplane's design and manufacturability, how can they integrate?

"Integration," the memorandum said, "takes place at the individual engineer level, which is where Boeing is cutting. The front-line engineer is where the rubber meets the road, but Boeing has made it clear that engineers are merely 'costs' to the company, not assets."[9]

Apart from assembling major components, Boeing and Airbus integrate black boxes and computerized flight decks with fly-by-wire components. Many experienced aircraft industry executives with engineering backgrounds do not doubt that Japan, too, could learn this black art. It currently manages the world's most integrated transportation system, a seamless network of high-speed and local trains, public and private rail and subway lines.

Other equally experienced people are skeptical. "It's hard to become what Boeing is," says a former vice president of GE's aeroengines group. "It's known as 'systems know-how.' Here's an example. The navy once wanted to hang a Pratt engine on the F-18, which had only GE engines. The navy wanted to see some competition, and so we were instructed to turn over the blueprints and all relevant documents to Pratt. Pratt tried and could not produce a good enough engine. They had everything that was needed except the know-how."[10] And so goes the discussion.

Since the mid-1980s, if not before, the Japanese have wanted to make the wing for a Boeing airplane. They tried and failed to persuade Boeing to let the three heavies build the wing for the 777. They are widely thought to put aerospace at the top of the industrial pyramid—ahead of electronics and automobiles—because it is judged to have the largest potential for benefiting other industries.

Within and beyond Airbus there is an awareness, as distinct from an immediate concern, that an Asian Airbus might one day emerge. A senior U.S. government bureaucrat who specializes in commercial aircraft agrees. "Japan would be the integrator," he says, "and South Korea would take a large role. There would be other players and one day China."[11]

Pierre Chao, one of the most carefully listened to among industry analysts, takes a balanced view.

Japan, theoretically the biggest of the potential competitive threats, has been constrained for the last two to three decades because Boeing has simply co-opted its industry. For years, various parts of the Japanese bureaucracy have wanted to develop an indigenous commercial aircraft product line, but industry has refused to go along because of their lower risk and more lucrative role as subcontractors to Boeing. There is certainly some danger of an Asian Airbus down the line that brings together China, Japan, Korea, and, who knows, Taiwan or even the Russians.

Russia certainly has all the technology needed, and China could produce the aircraft very cheaply. Boeing and Airbus absolutely do not want to see an Asian-based competitor exploding onto this market, especially if one accepts that commercial aircraft are becoming commodities in a mature marketplace.[12]

A fellow analyst, an Asia watcher, professes to see "a combination of Japanese technology and low-cost Chinese productivity producing an Asian Airbus." He can, he says, "envisage an alignment of Fuji and Kawasaki with Honda," which "is doing serious things with [aircraft] engines."[13]

Among Airbus people, one hears little concern, at least so far, about outsourcing jobs, but there are executives in Toulouse who do see their company as running a risk of helping to create an Asian competitor. No one used to think that China, despite having planned a regional jet airliner (the ARJ), had the technology or know-how to do more than contribute its low-cost production to a major joint venture. And talk of a Sino-Japanese arrangement still sounds far-fetched, given the demons in their relationship that would have to be silenced. In Washington, the prevailing view is that strategically Japan is very vulnerable. For Japan to compete with the United States in the world airline market—Boeing turf—would carry the risk of harming relations with its only reliable ally.

A former Boeing CEO who declined to talk on the record about a competitive threat from Asia feels strongly that Japan will not step up to the challenge but that China will: "The risk-averse Japanese culture will discourage that temptation," he said. "But the Chinese will eventually be there." He disagreed that China couldn't overcome the technological barriers. "They have twice put a man in orbit, and some of the best aerodynamicists in the world are Chinese."[14]

In discussing a potential threat from Japanese industry, most Boeing people are dismissive, contending that the business of reading the airline market, selling airplanes, and providing after-sales service globally is another and even trickier black art, one that Japanese companies are unlikely or reluctant to learn. Airbus, they say, mastered the art (and did so with disparate companies), but it took them thirty years.

Along with numerous other skeptics, the Boeing people, like their former leader, note that Japan has a risk-averse business culture, and making airliners is a high-risk business—one that can do ruinous damage to a balance sheet, and one where the financial benefits are fugitive. Japan's Ministry of Economy, Trade, and Industry (METI), according to one of its officials, "would like to see the aircraft industry become a big player in this business, partly because of budgetary pressures on the defense side. So we see the commercial side as the way to go. But there are big obstacles. You cannot compare selling consumer products to selling airplanes. That involves one professional dealing with another professional. It's very difficult to establish trust."[15]

For now, the conventional wisdom supports the skeptics. Risk-averse Japanese suppliers do have a very good deal with Boeing, and they might be content to await a new cycle in technology, one that showed signs of moving industry toward a cost-effective supersonic airliner. "We have to decide whether to take a bigger part in engine development, or whether to leapfrog the current generation [of aircraft] and jump ahead to the supersonic technology, since the U.S. and the Europeans are ignoring this sector," said one industry executive.[16]

Suppose that Boeing, for whatever reason, ended its privileged association with Japan. Would Airbus abandon one or more of its "centers of excellence" so as to acquire similar arrangements with Japan's aircraft industry? We are unlikely to know, since it's unlikely to happen and hard to imagine, unless, that is, Japan should elect to develop a supersonic airliner and choose a partner, like Airbus, that can draw on direct financial help from partner governments. Meanwhile, Airbus will continue to do what it has always done—outsource a huge array of components and subsystems, many of them to American and Chinese suppliers.

Until recently, the received wisdom was that Airbus, unlike Boeing, wouldn't outsource core competences, partly because of the jobs that would leave and partly because of a reluctance to help any supplier become a competitor. But the dynamic and overarching importance of the Asian airline market has altered a few basic assumptions. China is a huge market, and demands technology in return for granting access to it. Airbus is not outsourcing just work to Chinese industry but an increasingly big share. The scale of the outsourcing doesn't compare to what the three Japanese heavies are currently doing for Boeing, at least not yet. But the pattern so far appears to be roughly similar.

Four Chinese manufacturers are making a wide range of wing components for Airbus aircraft. According to an Airbus "backgrounder," dated September 2005, the company "has undertaken to transfer to China the technology required for the manufacturing of the complete wing of the A320 family aircraft." Two Chinese companies were already producing the leading and trailing edges of that aircraft's wing. Six such companies are making landing gears, a major component, for the A320. In June 2006, Airbus disclosed its plan to build an assembly plant for A320's in the coastal city of Tianjin.

The same document reported a joint venture between Airbus and China Aviation Industry Corporation I (AVIC I) establishing an engineering center adjacent to the offices of Airbus China. The center is described as intended "to develop a close relationship between Airbus and the Chinese aerospace industry, with a view to China becoming a full risk-sharing partner in a future Airbus program for new-generation aircraft. A risk-sharing partner takes complete responsibility for a part of a program, from design to manufacturing, including the corresponding investment and profit sharing."

In late 2005, Airbus served notices on suppliers that it had tightened its criteria for contractors with whom it works—including a requirement that major suppliers (known as tier-one suppliers) outsource a minimum amount of work to companies in Asian countries such as

China and India. "Those who don't comply will face 'significant penalties,'" said Claude-Henri Hereus, the company's vice president of procurement strategy. The mandate was described as part of a broader global "action plan" in which Airbus is seeking partnerships in China, Russia, and elsewhere, specifically for development and production of the A350.[17]

In pondering what lies ahead, the aircraft companies can't take much for granted. Their industry may change direction abruptly. The companies—Boeing and Airbus now—may confront dilemmas of the kind occasionally churned up by the marketplace. For example, neither wanted to venture into the market for regional jets; it didn't impress them as viable. So two other companies, one Brazilian, one Canadian, jumped in with aircraft of sixty to eighty seats built around stretched business jet fuselages. Now they dominate a segment of the market that may grow.

The Brazilian company, Embraer, has become the fourth-largest airplane company in the world, and is prospering, although it used to be said that Brazil could not build an airliner. Embraer was initially established by the government as an aeronautical engineering school, grew into a private company, and is now listed on the New York Stock Exchange. It is Brazil's largest exporter. JetBlue, as noted, bought one hundred of Embraer's latest aircraft, the E-190, which seats one hundred passengers, and has options for another hundred.

The next big battleground will be the market for single-aisle aircraft. The two big players will replace their current models—Boeing's 737 and Airbus's A320—with new aircraft that are expected to be built around the new technologies being used for the 787 and the A350. A large question turns on whether Embraer and its Canadian competitor, Bombardier, will join the fun and develop aircraft of, say, 125 seats or larger versions of existing models.

Someone has compared what may happen to a regatta, with two boats tending to worry about each other, behaving accordingly, and then watching the other boats sail by them. In this case, the regatta analogy is not likely to stand up. Embraer and Bombardier won't be building new airplanes—at least, not for a long time—with the new lighter-weight materials that Boeing and Airbus are using, because they don't have the technology. Also, in any aircraft pricing war with Boeing and Airbus, these smaller companies would be swiftly subdued.

All parties will be closely watching the Chinese airline market. The bulk of the growth there is likely to be in the small, single-aisle aircraft. If an Airbus Asia should actually lie ahead, this market could hasten its arrival.

WHEN JACK WELCH was running GE, he accelerated the trend toward outsourcing major technology-centered products. Transferring the heavier costs of production by moving down the supplier food chain appeared to be much the simplest solution to the rising problems of making these items at home. For Harry Stonecipher, who had worked for him, Welch's business model was the one to emulate.

In the mid- and late 1990s, Boeing sharpened the pace of shifting production and design work abroad. While trying to widen market access for its airplanes, Boeing Commercial's leadership had to clear away, or go around, various labor-management disputes, the most serious of which was a strike called against the company by the International Association of Machinists (IAM) in September 1995. It lasted sixty-nine days and ended with groundbreaking job security provisions, including a formal "make-buy" process whereby the IAM would have the opportunity to review all significant outsourcing and make proposals to keep the work in-house.

The settlement's other effects included the start of formal offset arrangements between China and Boeing Commercial Airplanes group; six Chinese factories began churning out parts for Boeing commercial aircraft. Offset arrangements with Japan that had begun twenty or so years earlier were more informal until the 787 arrived, at which point the role of the three heavies changed from being suppliers to risk-sharing partners, and Boeing gutted most of the make-buy process.

In the year following the terrorist attacks of 9/11, with Condit and Stonecipher at the helm, Boeing laid off nearly thirty thousand people. *BusinessWeek* commented that if Condit "can use the window of opportunity opened by the layoffs, Boeing could be transformed into a global enterprise that's much less dependent on the U.S. for both brawn and brains."[18]

Struggles with the two key unions—IAM and SPEEA (Society of Professional Engineering Employees in Aerospace)—drove the outsourcing process into higher gear. The unions argued that globalization would do a lot more harm than good, mainly by draining the company of the skills and resources it needed. They also complained about a company decision to spend $10 billion on repurchasing shares instead of investing that money in a new aircraft. This opinion was widely shared within the industry and a source of puzzled speculation within Airbus, which had built two new models and several derivatives in a period when Boeing did little other than upgrade its 777.

Within the Puget Sound area discordant feelings ran high. Even elements within Boeing's management were troubled by a change of direction that appeared capable of seriously weakening the company in the middle or long term. By outsourcing so many systems, would Boeing also be outsourcing the markups? While it was absorbing overhead, would the profit margins be created by the suppliers? If a supplier marked up parts by, say, 20 percent, how could the company do likewise?

In building the wing and much of the fuselage of the 787, the Japanese companies will refine the manufacturing process by coming down the learning curve. The curve develops on the factory floor. There is very little money to be made on the first airplane, or unit, or even the next few. The margins develop with the units that follow, because by then the factory floor has "learned" how to make and assemble the parts, or core components, with greater competence and in less time.

The aircraft industry is especially captive to the learning curve dynamic, because the cost per unit is high and comparatively few units are produced. Other products—running shoes, automobiles, televisions, and countless more—are turned out in large quantities, so the curve flattens out quickly. With airliners, the curve remains steep for much longer, unless or until the airplane is selling briskly.

A few years ago, a case against outsourcing was made by Dr. L. J. Hart-Smith in a paper delivered at a Boeing symposium in Saint Louis. Dr. Hart-Smith, it's worth noting, was and remains a Boeing senior technical fellow. Drawing on thirty-five years of experience in the industry, first with McDonnell Douglas, he said, "It was the suppliers who made all the profits on the extensively outsourced DC-10, not the so-called systems-integrating prime manufacturer. The same thing," he added, "has happened on aircraft assembled by Boeing, in Seattle." By comparison, Douglas's more successful DC-8, according to Hart-Smith, "was manufactured and assembled almost entirely within the Long Beach plant."

Further along, he says, "If the prime manufacturer, or systems integrator, cannot make his fortune by giving all his work away, who does benefit? The subcontractors, of course. They have a guaranteed profit margin if they write the contract properly. They have access to free technical advice if they encounter problems, because the systems integrator cannot allow them to fail."[19]

Boeing can argue that sharing the financial risks with another company is very different. Risk sharing is really revenue sharing. Japan's three heavies have become risk-sharing partners instead of suppliers. With this arrangement, Boeing negotiates a fixed percentage of the revenue with each partner. And the partners must each share a larger portion of the costs of developing the airplane.

Although it's a beneficial arrangement for Boeing, there can be some downside. If and when an overseas partner determines that no other supplier can do the same work for Boeing as well or cost-effectively, that company is certain to insist on a larger share of the revenue. At that point, Boeing would find itself paying foreigners to do what it could have done itself, or what it might have paid domestic suppliers to do; however, the money would be flowing abroad instead of staying within the country.

"I see considerable risk in the business and the technical issues," says a knowledgeable Boeing engineer. "For instance, I'll be very interested to see how much leverage the suppliers have with their sixty-five percent equity in gaining favorable terms for future use of the technology."[20]

Boeing didn't need to acquire risk-sharing partners to build the 787. Boeing was aware that the financial markets would have funded development of the airplane, an admittedly more expensive option. But the option that Boeing selected is hardly the ideal way to reduce risks, especially long-term risks.

Boeing isn't Wal-Mart, a globally integrated company that has amassed great economic power on its own terms. Its products, like those of numberless other companies with global networks, are commodities. A used-up tube of toothpaste or a worn bath towel is swiftly replaced. But Boeing operates in a different supplier-integrator environment. The company may get ten thousand calls per year from customers operating a product that will have cost $120 million or so and will require maintenance and technical analysis of component parts that are five or fifteen or twenty-five years old. An open question is whether a company with those responsibilities can fulfill them if it loses touch with the methods and procedures being used to make its product, especially an airplane that is built around an all-composite fuselage and wing.

IN 1992, Boeing's share of the world market for airliners was 70 percent. But with American carriers starved for funds and canceling or postponing equipment orders worth many billions of dollars, Boeing had become heavily and increasingly dependent on sales to foreign airlines, especially those in East Asia, where economic growth and power were by then concentrated.

Japan and China, along with British Airways, had become Boeing's two largest overseas customers. Air travel within and into China was growing exponentially—by nearly one-third in 1991 alone. Rapidly expanding regional airlines were sprouting up, and new airports were being built from scratch. "It is a mushrooming economy with a weak transportation infrastructure," Condit said at the time. "It needs airplanes. The same is true of Indonesia with all those islands. It's pretty exciting. Our guess is that the intra-Asian traffic growth will be greater than in the U.S. for the first time in the history of our forecasts."[21]

China was giving Boeing's leadership a lot to think about. In competing with Airbus—an aggressive but still small player—Boeing had advantages; it was the dominant supplier of commercial aircraft, and its role as a major defense contractor underlined its political importance in Washington. To buy Boeing might help to promote Chinese access to the huge American market that beckoned.

For both Boeing and Airbus, but especially for Boeing, political issues with China would always have to be reckoned with. In the 1990s, Boeing felt that its commercial presence in China was always at risk in Washington. The issue then was whether to keep extending most-favored-nation, or MFN, treatment to China in trade. Then as now, China was running a heavy trade surplus with the United States, but without MFN the surplus would have shrunk significantly. It was equally true that if China had chosen to buy the majority of its jet airliners from Airbus, the U.S.-China trade deficit would have been very much larger.

So it was that when Boeing executives were asked what they wanted most from Washington, the anxious and emphatic response was that continued, unconditional MFN for China comes first, second, and third on the wish list. Each year, certain members of Congress attacked MFN for China, citing its poor record on human rights as well as a predilection in Beijing for flogging weapons to some of the world's least stable places.

An experience of a former Boeing representative in Beijing, Thomas Lane, left a strong impression on the company. Sometime in 1991, Lane found himself in the unusual position of being invited to a dinner given by Prime Minister Li Peng and seated on his host's right.

In an after-dinner talk, Li Peng observed that China was ready to buy a lot of Boeing airplanes, but wouldn't do so if there was trouble about MFN. Richard Albrecht, who was then Boeing's president, said, "When the Chinese tell us to go tell our government not to interfere [with MFN], we mention weapons sales and human rights, and each of them says, 'That's not my area of responsibility.' "[22]

The Chinese were hardly subtle in their use of aircraft deals as leverage in the campaign for MFN renewal. Late in 1992, United Airlines, Boeing's biggest customer, announced it was postponing delivery of 122 Boeing airliners worth $3.6 billion; the list included 777's, Boeing's new airplane, for which United was a launch customer. On April 7, 1993, United, a typically hard-pressed and overcommitted U.S. carrier, disclosed that it was deferring delivery of another 49 Boeing aircraft worth $2.7 billion and also including 777's; by then, Boeing had committed several billion dollars to the 777 program. But on April 9, just two days after the second blow from United, China placed an order worth $800 million for 20 Boeing airplanes, all narrow-bodies. And from Beijing there also came a strong hint of a follow-on order for a similar number of the pricier wide-bodies, both 767's, and, yes, the 777's on which the company thought its future might depend.

Boeing began selling airplanes in China in 1972, in the midst of the Cultural Revolution and six years before Washington and Beijing opened formal diplomatic relations. After acquiring a dominant position, Boeing began to be perceived by its hosts, along with other Western companies operating in China, as taking the market there for granted, ignoring those of its own people who knew better, and, in general, showing little sensitivity to the business culture in which it was operating.

A long and well-documented article in the *Seattle Times* in June 2005 described the ins and outs of the Boeing-China relationship over a period of several years; Boeing, it concluded, "may be pulling itself out of its decade-long downturn in China." Still, regaining its dominant role in China, the article said, "may require corporate leadership that is more nimble, humble and ethnically diverse."[23] Boeing has since begun to get that kind of leadership.

From its early days as a small player, Airbus had the Asian market in its sights. Building on a small foothold, its share increased steadily. And while sales by Airbus to Chinese airlines have continued to lag behind Boeing's, each of China's chief long-distance carriers—Air China, China Eastern, and China Southern—are now buying aircraft from both suppliers. Boeing remains well ahead in sales to Air China, the flagship carrier, which is based in Beijing, although China Eastern, centered in Shanghai, is purchasing more planes from Airbus. China Southern, which is operated from Guangzhou and is the country's largest airline, is now acquiring roughly equal numbers of Boeing and Airbus aircraft, although Boeing still holds a sizable lead in their fleet.

Each side can report good news. Two-thirds of the aircraft delivered to China in 2004 were from Airbus. But in sales of airliners with a hundred seats or more, Boeing had roughly 70 percent of the Chinese market at the end of 2005, Airbus 30 percent. The stakes are seen as immense. In the next twenty years, Chinese airlines are expected to triple their fleets, adding twenty-three hundred aircraft worth nearly $200 billion.[24] As in the past, China is seen by Boeing and Airbus as *the* growth market.

Still, there are China watchers within the industry who show some skepticism born of experience. "It's always next year with China," they like to say. The country's massive rural labor force lacks mobility, and, many would argue, needs it. Sales of aircraft in the Chinese market have never been an accurate reflection of demand, still less of potential demand. The market was what the government said it was. An airline might sometimes have to take airplanes it didn't want or forgo those it did want. (Air traffic control as recently as the early 1990s was chaotic. It lacked positive radar control, except on three routes. An airliner's departure time would be noted and keyed to an announcement that in X number of minutes another flight would depart.)

Airplane salesmen, whether from Boeing or Airbus, liked to say,

"There is just one buyer of aircraft in China. Never mind whose logo is on the tail." That comment has become a little clearer than the actual truth as, gradually, the interplay of suppliers, airlines, and central political authority loosens. Boeing and Airbus try to acquire nonbinding commitments from an official body, CASC (an acronym for the government agency that manages China's aviation industry), which in turn reports to the State Council. It still does, and the State Council must still approve CASC's recommendations of aircraft purchases. The carriers, too, try to maneuver their preferences through or around CASC. But more often than in the past CASC's recommendations are approved, with the government then allocating the aircraft to various airlines. However, the carriers are no longer required to take delivery, in which case the airplanes in question may not be built at all.

The relaxation of official control reminds some China watchers of another saying, "The mountains are high, the emperor is far." According to a senior industry executive with long experience in China, "It all comes down now to politics and price. It used to be just about politics. Now it is about politics and economics. Not so long ago, the leadership took these decisions [on aircraft procurement] without any attention being paid to the economic analyses that were always provided. Not anymore. Now the people at the top who make these decisions do read the analysis, partly because the numbers have gotten so high. Their decisions have to show some appreciation for the money involved, as well as making sense politically."[25] Put differently, the big Chinese airlines now have more to say about aircraft selection and procurement, while continuing to need the central government's approval.

As before, gaining official approval depends heavily on external politics. Any rumor, however vague or tenuous, that points toward a new arms package earmarked for Taiwan can harm Boeing's prospects if the supposed source is American. Or (less likely) if it's European, Airbus will be the loser.

On this point, contacts between China and France are instructive. Their relations are normally close. Both countries see themselves as centers of civilization, and both have highly centralized administrations. The year 2005 was called "the year of France" in China, while 2004 was "the year of China" in France.

In January 2004, China's president, Hu Jintao, made a state visit to France during which he went to Toulouse and was shown a cabin mock-up of Airbus's A380. His host, French president Jacques Chirac, made some comments about Taiwan designed to please Hu, and in doing so he went well beyond what his staff had expected him to say. In turn, Hu noted a purchase by China Southern of some A320 family aircraft a few days earlier.

The meeting probably led to an order by the Chinese six months later for twenty A330's, Airbus's midsize aircraft. The purchase agreement was signed by France's prime minister, Jean-Pierre Raffarin, and the Chinese vice premier, Zeng Peiyan. The authorities in Beijing divided the new aircraft between China Eastern and China Southern.

In October, four months later, Chirac returned the visit. China was widely expected to announce the purchase of several A380's while he was there. But that didn't happen, very probably because France's government had been unable, or hadn't tried, to lift an arms embargo imposed in 1989 as punishment for the Chinese leadership's crushing of the democracy movement at Tiananmen Square. "Of course, these two issues are connected," an official with Air China told the *Wall Street Journal*. "China always places political concerns first when making big orders for aircraft."[26] In January 2005, three months after Chirac's visit, China did make the long-awaited purchase of five A380's.

Long-distance air travel had become a more immediate concern for the Chinese, largely because they would be hosting the Summer Olympics in July 2008 and appeared to feel a need for more airplanes, today and tomorrow. Airbus and Boeing did what they could to make the most of the moment. Airbus pushed to expand sales of its entire family, from the A320 at the low end to the superjumbo A380 at the high end. Boeing competed hard against the A320 with its 737, but its larger effort, some of it visible, some much less so, was directed toward selling sixty of its new airplane, the 787, to China in a single package, or "block deal."

Given its long range, midsize, and highly tempting performance guaranties, the 787 seemed an ideal fit for the Chinese market. But for Boeing, the path to agreement held some traps, the first of which was Japan's heavy involvement with the airplane. Its content would be 35 percent Japanese, and the launch customer was All Nippon Airways. Also, Boeing stood accused of having taken the Chinese market for granted, whereas Airbus had taken nothing for granted. And of course, Airbus was planning to compete against the 787 with a new and similar airplane, the A350. Granted, the A350 wouldn't be available until two years or so after the Summer Olympics, but Chinese decision makers had to worry that despite Boeing's assurances, its new airplane might not be ready in time either. Indeed, the first deliveries of the 787 had been scheduled for the summer of 2008, at just about the time the Olympics would begin.

Boeing's strenuous efforts to sell the package to China were waged in Washington as well as in Beijing. The U.S. presidential campaign was under way, and Boeing was trying to conclude the 787 deal with China before the election. Predictably, both candidates had echoed Boeing's claims to the high ground in its duel with Airbus over subsidies for new airplane development.

The White House went further, according to a senior Boeing executive, who said that in October 2004, President George W. Bush contacted President Hu Jintao and requested that a purchase by China of 787's be approved for announcement prior to the U.S. elections. That didn't happen, but two weeks later, at a meeting in Chile of leaders of Asia-Pacific states, Bush and Hu did discuss the 787 package. In late January 2005, the package was approved. Six Chinese airlines would receive 787's.

China's leadership likes to announce large acquisitions of Boeing airliners during high-level American visits in order to ease, if temporarily, Washington's unhappiness with China's huge trade surplus.

During Bush's visit to Beijing in November 2005, China signed an agreement to buy seventy Boeing 737's and announced that an order for another eighty would follow.

JAPAN IS a market unlike any other, partly because it is one of the few countries in which planes and trains compete. Two highly efficient travel modes apparently generate so much intercity traffic that both prosper. Yet despite the high-volume rail travel, Japan has carriers that fly jumbo airliners, notably Boeing 747's, on flights between neighboring cities that last no more than an hour and are normally filled. The world's three most heavily traveled routes, according to a JAL official, are, first, Tokyo-Haneda-Sapporo; second, Tokyo-Haneda-Fukuoka; third, Haneda-Osaka. (Japanese travel buffs point out that Air France canceled its Paris-Brussels service when France's high-speed rail service began connecting these two cities and their airports.)

Japan's singularity afflicts Airbus. The company competes strongly in China, but not in Japan, where politics and habit conspire in Boeing's favor. In a large sense, Boeing is seen as family, having been a presence in Japan for more than a half century. Airbus didn't become a presence there until May 2001. Also, Boeing has the advantage of being American. Thanks to America's more sympathetic treatment of Japan in the nineteenth century, and to the long and productive business relationships that lasted well into the twentieth century, the Japanese put aside the bitterness created by their defeat in World War II more rapidly than had been expected.

In 2003, Airbus competed against Boeing for the sale of single-aisle aircraft to All Nippon Airways. Although ANA's selection of Boeing 737's over Airbus's A320's was predictable, Airbus complained that political pressure had steered the decision away from ANA's preference for the A320's. This move by Airbus angered various interested parties in Japan, not least ANA's management, and further weakened Airbus's position. Its CEO, Noel Forgeard, felt obliged to visit Japan and issue an apology to Yoji Ohashi, president and CEO of ANA.[27]

Not long afterward, ANA decided to replace its entire fleet of Airbus airplanes—A320's and A321's—with Boeing aircraft. "We haven't helped ourselves by the way we have dealt with the Japanese," said Christian Scherer, a highly regarded senior vice president of Airbus. "We learned marketing from the U.S., but this Anglo-Saxon marketing model doesn't work in Japan. It does work for Boeing."[28] He was alluding to Boeing's special relationship.

Although Airbus has tried to learn from its mistakes in Japan, it feels that Boeing continues to benefit from official intervention on its behalf. The alleged pressure from on high is cited as most often indirect. "We have discovered that MHI [Mitsubishi Heavy Industries] has on occasion pressured JAL [to buy from Boeing] when its airplane was competing against us," an Airbus vice president says flatly. His term "its airplane" reflected MHI's strong involvement with Boeing aircraft, along with the heavy subsidies it receives from the Japanese government.

Early in 2005, Airbus decided to try to avoid hitting bottom in Japan. It was holding little more than 1 percent of the market there, and that share was heading toward zero. Airbus's declaratory goal (probably romantic) was not just breaking Boeing's monopoly in the world's second-largest airline market, but gaining a half share by 2010.[29]

The prospects for Airbus in Japan are not good. The company won't be selling A350's to ANA or JAL; both are fully committed to Boeing's 787. At the lower end—the single-aisle market—Boeing's 737 will remain the aircraft of choice for both JAL and ANA. In June 2004, Ohashi announced that ANA would create a new low-cost airline. He withheld the details except to note that the aircraft to be used would be 737's.

For some time, Airbus has professed to believe that in the end JAL, Japan's largest long-distance carrier, would ignore the local pro-Boeing ambiance and buy the A380. Airbus's calculation was that eventually JAL would see its competitors—Korean Airlines, SIA, and others—flying seven A380 flights in and out of Narita every day and would do the simple math: the cost of flying five hundred or so people on the long routes would be less with A380's than with Boeing 747's. So the question

(Airbus thought) would not be whether JAL would buy the A380 but when. Then, toward the end of 2005, Boeing began offering the 747-8, a bigger and highly improved version of its own jumbo. This aircraft seemed capable of prospering in various Asian markets, including, most important, Japan's.

IN 2004, people in the United States were averaging about 2.2 trips by air annually, according to Airbus calculations. The corresponding figures for China and for India were 0.05 and 0.02 trips, respectively. More people in India, it turns out, were traveling on the railways in a single day than they were by air in a year; the use of air transport in India works out to about 1 percent of air travel in the United States and other mature markets.[30]

That may be changing. In February 2005, the *Seattle Times* reported that "Indian airlines old and new are shopping for jets"; that "the Indian government is liberalizing aviation regulation and moving to rapidly upgrade airport infrastructure"; that "Boeing's biggest handicap may be not having enough of the right jets available when the market wants them." The article went on to report that air travel in India grew by 20 percent in the preceding year.[31]

This growth will nearly match and possibly exceed that of China over the next twenty years. India has a larger middle class than China, and is widely seen as the most underserved country by the airlines. "India is the hottest growth market on the planet," said Richard Aboulafia, vice president of the Teal Group and among the most respected industry analysts. The market there is said to be growing at 25 percent annually.[32] And, Aboulafia says, "India is also the better China. To sell planes to India, you don't need to go through a state purchasing agency that makes drama queen pronouncements about not buying anything for a year. There's no asinine talk of the need for a home-grown regional jet . . . just straightforward A320 and 737 purchases."[33]

Still, not until recently was either Boeing or Airbus selling many airplanes in the Indian market. According to a Boeing strategy paper, Air

India had ordered just thirty of the company's aircraft between 1963 and 2005.[34] But only a few months later, in January 2006, the paper was abruptly overtaken by Air India's purchase of sixty-eight Boeing planes, including twenty-three 777's and twenty-seven 787's. The sale was an event, a major victory for Boeing, a hard blow for Airbus, especially since, a year earlier, the prior Indian government had seemed strongly in favor of buying the equivalent Airbus models.

Left to itself, Air India might very well have decided in Boeing's favor, but it wasn't left to itself. Boeing benefited from a strenuous campaign led by senior players in the Bush administration, starting with the president, aimed at persuading India's government to steer the deal toward Boeing. There is nothing uncommon about deploying this sort of influence; major commercial transactions are increasingly linked to side deals arranged by officials. France's Jacques Chirac did much the same for Airbus, mounting a similar full court press; five members of his cabinet and thirty CEOs traveled with him to India. Airbus then sold sixty single-aisle aircraft to Indian carriers.

Among the issues at play was nuclear technology. In July 2005, President Bush agreed to sell civil nuclear technology to India, thereby reversing a policy that had been in place since India's test of a nuclear device in 1974. Much of the foreign policy community in Washington, including former government officials and members of Congress, strongly opposed the move, arguing that India is not a signatory to the Nonproliferation Treaty and does not accept internationally agreed safeguards designed to prevent the diversion of these technologies. Although the deal may greatly weaken efforts to prevent proliferation, Chirac lost no time in supporting Bush's initiative.

Boeing and Airbus both acknowledge having underestimated the Indian market. It is expected to add 5 million passengers between 2005 and 2010. In 2005, Jet Airways had an initial public offering that was sixteen times oversubscribed. Its founder and chairman, Naresh Goyal, thinks that between 2005 and 2010 Jet Airways' revenue will triple. "It should be around $3 billion," he says. India "is a captive market. No other country . . . has so many nationals living overseas. Also, last year

[2004], eighteen million people traveled into and out of India, and the Indian carriers' share was under twenty-five percent. So more than seventy-five percent of the traffic goes to foreign airlines into and out of India. We can change that."[35]

Although some financial analysts feel that Jet Airways is rushing its expansion, Goyal, an exuberant character, is not expected to change course. His goals include raising Jet Airways' service standards to the lofty levels of two carriers—Singapore Airlines and Cathay Pacific Airlines—that he regards as the world's best. "I can tell you," he has said, "that nobody has ever seen the kind of things that we are planning."[36]

India's low-cost carriers are thriving; they are described as "democratizing" air travel. They offer flights for the cost of a first-class rail ticket, thereby cutting a one-day train journey from, say, Bangalore to Delhi to two and a half hours. Still, the number of Indians traveling by air in a year—15 million—is the same number estimated to go by train in a day. "A small percentage of that [train traffic] going into airplanes is just going to phenomenally increase the growth," Dinesh Keskar, Boeing's sales chief for India, told the *Seattle Times*.[37]

In a brief period ending in 2005, a number of mostly no-frills Indian carriers were launched. They included Kingfisher, Indus Air, East West, GoAir, SpiceJet, Air One, and Visa Air. First on the scene was Air Deccan, which has offered fares as low as $11 and provides service in the hinterlands as well as connecting big cities. G. R. Gopinath, the carrier's founder and co-director, has said, "I didn't want to connect just Bombay and New Delhi. I wanted to link across the country, leave my footprint."[38] Other no-frills start-ups lie in the wings.

Kingfisher started a trend, first with personal in-flight entertainment systems and then with special valets at the airports it uses. "The passenger will not have to worry about lugging his baggage as the special valet will take care of his luggage from the point of his arrival at the airport," says Girish Shah, the airline's general manager for marketing. The service, he added, "is not limited to our passengers. [It] also helps passengers of rival airlines in handling their baggage."[39]

Naresh Goyal's high opinion of SIA and Cathay Pacific is widely shared. "SIA's management is very professional," says Paul Kiteley, Airbus's senior vice president for customer affairs, Asia. "When buying an airplane, they make a thorough evaluation, and that process becomes a reference point—a stamp of approval within the industry. The process is very precise and very tough. They are very demanding—the people who run the process.

"The SIA cabins," he continues, "are always very attractive. They have the latest seats and in-flight entertainment, including video on demand—a huge array of audio and visual. The cabin crews are very well trained. No one ever complains. It is a consistent service throughout the fleet. They retire the young women early. SIA is not required to keep those who are no longer young."[40]

Kiteley takes a similar view of Cathay Pacific's service, which he deems "extremely well run and very consistent."[41] He and others also give high marks for service to Emirates Airline, which was created in 1985 by the government of Dubai and uses SIA as a model. Emirates is one of the world's fastest-growing carriers. It claims to have received two hundred international awards for excellence and to take passengers to "destinations in Europe, the Middle East, the Far East, Africa, Asia, Australasia, and North America." These include nonstop flights between the United States and Dubai and between Sydney and Dubai.

With its extensive route system, Emirates also stands accused by other carriers of siphoning off their traffic. It can do so, they say, because of hidden but heavy subsidies it receives from Dubai's leadership. A widely held but as yet unproved charge is that Emirates is spared having to pay for much of its fuel. Rival airlines see Emirates as being used to make an international hub of Dubai, its airport serving a huge region also served by less-well-off European carriers.

The loudest outcry against Emirates is made by Qantas. Australia lies at the end of the route system. Travelers have to want to go there, and Qantas has developed the most profitable routes serving Australian cities. Efforts by Emirates and also by SIA to gain access to these routes have provoked Australia to raise the "national interest" issue. In

August 2005, Peter Gregg, the Qantas CFO, used a keynote address to the Asia Pacific Aviation Summit to do that much and more.

"State-controlled carriers like Emirates and Singapore Airlines," he said, "benefit from an aggressive corporatist approach by their governments that is aimed at promoting growth through their hubs. Among the advantages this bestows are favorable accelerated tax regimes and lower cost of debt financing, by virtue of their near-sovereign risk status, that make it cost-effective to continually acquire aircraft to keep their fleet age down and to increase capacity.

"Moreover, Emirates," he continued, "as an instrument of an oil-based state, has an additional advantage when oil prices are high. That is because . . . the higher revenues from oil help to offset any additional costs incurred by the airline."[42]

In February 2006, the *Financial Times* carried a page-one piece on the vaulting ambitions of the Emirates' government under the headline "Dubai Spreads Its Wings into Aerospace." "Dubai," the piece said, "plans to channel $15 billion into aerospace manufacturing and aviation services, aiming to make the Gulf emirate a leading force in the global aerospace sector within a decade."[43]

The struggles between Boeing and Airbus in 2005 to get the better of each other in crucial Asian markets provided some of the most intense moments in the quarter-century period during which they had competed head-to-head. Boeing won each of the battles that mattered most. December was a pivotal, all but climactic month. It began with a order from Cathay Pacific for twelve 777's, plus options for twenty more. Then came the pitched battle over a sale to Qantas, with Boeing's 787 matched against Airbus's A350.

Over a period of forty or so years, Qantas had been a "Boeing airline." Then, in late 2000, Airbus broke Boeing's hold by selling twelve A380's to Qantas, with an option for twelve more. "Airbus made an unrefusable offer," said a senior Australian official. "Qantas couldn't say no and maintain its credibility with its board."[44]

Five years later, Boeing regained the upper hand, but only after a frantic back-and-forth, hour-by-hour tussle in which, as the *Financial*

Times noted, "best and final offers were followed by even better best and final offers. The Qantas board, summoned last week to make the decision, was unable to make the call, as the two aircraft makers further shaved their bids."[45] In the end, Qantas bought 115 787's in a package worth $18 billion at list price and before the heavy discounts.

"We were low, but they didn't want the A350," said an Airbus official, sounding partly puzzled, partly awed.[46] Within the industry, there was some speculation that what may have tipped the scales in Boeing's favor was a continuing resentment by Qantas of the sale of forty-three A380's to Emirates Airline. As Qantas saw this transaction, Airbus was, in effect, subsidizing Emirates by selling the huge airplanes at allegedly giveaway prices. More to the point, these are the airplanes that Qantas regards as being capable of cutting most heavily into many of its prize routes.

However, other more relevant issues lay closer to the decision by Qantas to buy Boeing. Its 787 had acquired more credibility in the marketplace; it was expected to be available sooner than the A350; there was a question about whether Airbus could develop the A350 within a reasonable period of time, given the drain on the company's human resources, especially its pool of engineers, caused by the heavy commitment to the A380. Finally, Airbus was hurt by problems that some of its customers were having with the A340; it was being compared unfavorably with the 777, which had been exceeding its performance guaranties.

In 2005, Airbus and Boeing sold more commercial airplanes than either had sold in any past year. Although unit sales of Airbus aircraft amounted to 52 percent of the market, Boeing captured 55 percent of the dollar value, according to Airbus estimates, largely because of its edge in the most lucrative segment, double-aisle long-haul airplanes. Indeed, Boeing may have created a hold on the market in Asia for these airplanes.[47] In Seattle, the feeling, perhaps overly optimistic, was that Boeing had redrawn the competitive landscape. In mid-December, the company's share price rose to $71.98, a historic high.

Neither Airbus nor Boeing expects its business to be equally gainful in 2006. But for both, the year 2006 began in much the way that the previous year had ended. Six months later, SIA, the industry's bellwether, concluded a long negotiating process with the rival teams by choosing the 787 over the A350.

The betting is that Airbus will do what needs first to be done: make a strong effort to turn the A350 into a fully competitive program. That cannot be made to happen overnight. Far too large a part of the company's resources had been committed to the A380. Sales of this super-jumbo will continue to lag for some years, but sooner or later an expansive market may need an airplane of that size. In the 1990s, Airbus surged and gradually traded places with Boeing. The companies have now traded places again, at least in the market for double-aisle airplanes, but in the space of only one year.

CHAPTER NINE

Muddling Through, More or Less

ON MARCH 21, 2001, Boeing's labor force and the city of Seattle were shocked to discover that the company's headquarters would shortly be moved to the Chicago, Dallas, or Denver metropolitan area. Moving away from Seattle, Boeing said, would allow management to distance itself from commercial aircraft operations and put that division on a more equal footing with the military and space units.

Each of the three cities in contention worked hard to prevail, offering millions of dollars of tax breaks and other incentives. Chicago got the nod. The announcement was made on May 10. Boeing's management and 250 or so employees would commence operations there on September 4.

The decision to move was driven by Phil Condit, who would say to insiders, "We don't want to be off in a corner of America. We should be close to our customers and in a big international city."[1] Three days before the company told the world where its new headquarters would be, Harry Stonecipher was promoted to the position of vice chairman. He agrees that he and Condit wanted to improve customer access and adds, "They wanted to see Phil and me. We didn't want to appear commercial-airplane-centric."[2]

It's unclear whether he and Condit may also have calculated that locating Boeing's headquarters in a district that bordered the one represented by J. Dennis Hastert, the Speaker of the House of Representatives, might help the company. The proximity certainly didn't hurt, as events—troublesome ones—would show.

Dallas had been fairly confident of winning, given its tie with the new president, George W. Bush. Texas right-to-work laws were seen as another advantage. For Seattle, of course, the move created a painful wound. The Puget Sound area had been Boeing's home base since it began life in 1916, and its importance to Seattle could hardly be overstated. Recent layoffs had already demoralized the workforce of seventy-eight thousand, and a downturn in the technology sector was hurting the city.

In looking back, a columnist for the *Seattle Post-Intelligencer* noted that "Boeing's move . . . reflected a corporate mindset largely based on the General Electric/Jack Welch model, 'we're indifferent to what businesses we're in, just so long as we make a lot of money in the businesses we are in.' In order to coolly, dispassionately evaluate the businesses they're in, Boeing corporate executives didn't want to be physically close to any of them."[3]

For Condit, the appeal of the GE model—a lean upper tier separate from company businesses—was probably encouraged by Stonecipher, who had been molded by Jack Welch. Airbus had already begun to worry about what it saw as an increasing convergence of Boeing and GE interests. For one of the two major suppliers of the engines used by Airbus and Boeing to be seen as favoring either customer was sure to sharpen tensions and suspicions that are always present anyway and often exaggerated. Stonecipher's role fueled Airbus's concern. He and Condit were seen as bent on changing Boeing's corporate culture. Management would acquire values that infused GE's methods.

"Taking a page from Welch's playbook," *Business Week* noted, "Condit is making the three key operating units—commercial airplanes, military aircraft, and space and communications—accountable to tough new performance standards. He is giving the heads of those units new CEO titles and the freedom to run their businesses as independent companies."[4]

The flaws inherent in this management model were widely judged to far outweigh its benefits. The driving principle—making money on every deal—excluded a sharp focus on gaining or protecting market share. By contrast, Airbus, which seemed then to be doing everything right, was all about market share. In the five years preceding 9/11, it had erased Boeing's dominance and pulled even in aircraft sales.

In late July 2003, the *Economist* zeroed in on Boeing in a long and highly critical piece. "Boeing," it began, "this week reported a net loss of $192 million in the second quarter, due largely to a $1.1 billion write-off in its space business. This is the latest misfortune to hit the firm, which has been remarkably accident prone since moving its head office to Chicago from Seattle in September 2001, days before its civil aviation business was thrown into crisis by the terrorist attacks. The move was supposed to symbolize its strategy of diversifying into defence, space and aviation services markets, such as air-traffic management.

"The latest troubles, though, concern a business that was to offer relief from the woes of civil aviation. Boeing has poured $5 billion into its space business since the mid-1990s, assuming a boom in satellites and launcher rockets as demand for broadband communications grew. The telecoms bust ended that boom before it began. Boeing is now shrinking its satellite business and focusing on government contracts."[5]

By the spring of 2004, the Puget Sound area had lost a hundred thousand jobs. By then, Boeing was being widely seen as peripheral, "an ex-spouse who is still hanging around the neighborhood," as some people described the relationship. For them, Boeing's transplanted headquarters were better suited to an investment bank; there were no airplanes to be seen in downtown Chicago, none of the large interior spaces in which aircraft are assembled.

BOEING'S AFFAIRS were actually less bleak than they impressed Seattle as being. The company was holding huge reserves of cash and marketable securities, even while spending heavily to shore up its pension plan. However, the Seattle-based Boeing Commercial Airplanes group

(BCAG) had been steadily losing ground to Airbus and was widely seen as mismanaged.

In looking hard at BCAG, a few investment banks saw company strengths, real and potential, as more than offsetting obvious weaknesses. That view was held by the IAM (International Association of Machinists), a persistent critic/antagonist of Boeing Seattle. The union's leadership felt that BCAG lacked direction and was being underfunded by management. Transferring the company's headquarters to Chicago struck the IAM as a move aimed, in effect, at demoting the company. The IAM felt that it could do a much better job of running it.

In the fall of 2003, the union's leadership had discussions with one investment bank, Merrill Lynch, about looking into the merits of separating the commercial group from the defense and space parts of the company—in effect, undoing the mergers, since nearly all of the people in those divisions were products of McDonnell Douglas or from Rockwell International, which Boeing had acquired in 1996. As seen by various Wall Street analysts, separating the Boeing Commercial group would amount to reaffirming its commitment to building airplanes. Serious doubts had been planted. The move would also detach Boeing Commercial from heavily politicized Defense Department budget allocations and the high-profile struggles for contracts to build weapons. The thinking was that an independent enterprise could achieve cost savings that would not be possible if it remained part of a conglomerate.

Besides Merrill Lynch, the union spoke with a private equity group that knew the aerospace business (and insists on anonymity). "We talked to the Wall Street people about equity and debt management," recalls Steve Sleigh, IAM's director of strategic resources. "The analysis showed that Boeing Commercial was a tremendously undervalued asset. At the time, Boeing stock was trading at $35 per share. Boeing Commercial's contribution to that valuation was less than $3. So we thought, 'Spin Boeing Commercial off and create new value for it and restore its focus.' We believed that this plan would get a lot of support on Wall Street."[6]

It did. The private equity group was prepared to write a check for $1 billion then and there as an earnest of its intention to invest seriously in the venture. The spin-off of BCAG, if agreed to by Boeing's leadership, would mean buying very cheaply the aviation industry's preeminent name and one of its two remaining suppliers of big airliners.

IAM's president, Thomas Buffenbarger, discussed the proposal with Condit, who said he would take it to the board. But Condit was deposed within a few weeks of the meeting. Asked about the IAM proposal, he said, somewhat guardedly, "In the long run, the commercial [business] will always be cyclical. It's always undervalued at the bottom and overvalued at the top. I always listened carefully to any proposal."[7] He declined to elaborate.

Once he had replaced Condit as leader, Stonecipher's third phone call, he says, was to Buffenbarger; he wanted to get off on the right foot with a very powerful union. Stonecipher recalls that, at a breakfast together, Buffenbarger "asked me to look at the proposal." Condit had not mentioned it to the board, of which Stonecipher, of course, was a member, or to him privately. Stonecipher reviewed the proposal and rejected it. He remembers saying, "I am the second-biggest individual shareholder. This company has a great future. [He meant Boeing Commercial.] It can become a lot better than it has been. If the company is undervalued, I intend to demonstrate that to the shareholders."[8] Stonecipher is not evasive. He is unsubtle and direct, a lot more so than many of the senior people whom he worked with at Boeing. He is described as having said, "This would have been a great idea with Phil running the company, but I think I can run it a lot more productively than he did."

"Our investors were very disappointed," said Sleigh. "They thought the Boeing Commercial group would be a great asset. We all thought the merger [with McDac] produced the worst possible synergy. What did Boeing get? Granted the stock has gone up, and granted the company had deeper pockets to fall back on. But what it also got was the move to Chicago and military scandals."[9]

IN 2001, Boeing lost the F-35 combat fighter award to Lockheed Martin. It was the biggest defense contract ever. Then, over the summer of 2003, the company began reeling from a series of setbacks in the military and space sectors. After it had just expanded its space business at a cost of $5 billion so as to build in an offset for losses on the commercial side, overcapacity in both the satellite and the launch markets dictated a heavy cutback in the space sector. In July, a grand jury indicted Boeing executives for swiping twenty-five thousand pages of proprietary documents belonging to Lockheed Martin during bidding for rocket contracts from the air force. The air force reacted by stripping about $1 billion from Boeing in current and future rocket business.

Condit then took the questionable step of sending an open letter of apology, a corporate mea culpa, that was published in several newspapers. Calling attention to the affair was seen by a number of people in and out of the industry as a mistake. Pointing up the incident, they felt, could further threaten the credibility of Boeing's efforts to reduce its heavy dependence on commercial aircraft sales by diversifying into military hardware.

In the past, Boeing hadn't invited serious trouble of this kind because it had taken steps to avoid it. In the mid-1960s, Boeing had shifted its priorities away from the Pentagon to the commercial airplane business, after deciding that the U.S. government was not a reliable customer for its airplanes because of the arbitrary, if not outrageous, manner in which the winners of major military airplane programs were chosen. In changing direction, Boeing took a gamble on the commercial sector to a degree unmatched by any other American company.[10] And as it began to dominate the market for LCA, Boeing's leadership took steps to insulate its commercial sector from corrupt practices that were endemic in the defense sector.

But that scrupulous leadership style began to change in the late 1990s, or more exactly, after the merger with McDonnell Douglas in

1997. What was destined to be an awkward marriage was worsened by the contempt in which two very different entities held each other.

Actually, McDonnell Douglas did in an earlier time conceive and manage some first-rate military programs, but it had not done so for many years. It had become identified with the incestuous relationship in which the military services operate with defense contractors and are indulged and protected by tame members of Congress. "The Iron Triangle" is a term widely used to describe parties whose collaboration greatly benefits an industry where the margins are good, the profits and shareholder security high.

A weapons program is normally managed by a so-called integrated product support team. And it is a team. There is a corporate product manager and a government product manager. They work together as team players. Suppose they are working on a combat aircraft and the air force's project manager, possibly an experienced and fast-track colonel, sees the program falling short of agreed performance benchmarks. Should he flat out complain? He isn't expected to. Complaining carries the risk of being seen as a non–team player, a judgment to be avoided, especially if he takes the complaint to OSD (Office of the Secretary of Defense) or Congress.

This air force colonel may be approaching retirement age and thinking about sustaining or, even better, raising his income level. The cost of educating children may be a concern. Holding his opposite number too closely to the program's specifications might weaken his chances of being offered a postretirement job by the prime contractor. Under rules aimed at discouraging conflicts of interest, the colonel could not upon retiring turn up there working on a program that he had been managing. But he could acquire a role in another of the company's several military programs. (In June 2004, the Project for Government Oversight found that since 1997 Lockheed Martin had made the largest contributions to the campaign funds of political parties of any federal contractor and had hired fifty-seven senior government officials as executives or lobbyists. Pete Aldridge, former undersecretary of defense for acquisition, became a director soon after approving a contract for F/A-22 fighter planes from the company. Boeing came second on the list of the top twenty contractors that had hired senior officials.)[11]

There is no clear dividing line separating the interests of government and those of defense contractors, at least not as seen from the Pentagon, either by its uniformed or civilian components. The system's vulnerabilities are not a source of serious concern, unless, that is, something goes very wrong.

In October 2003 something did go very wrong, and it happened to Boeing. The company was charged with having manipulated an air force plan to upgrade its fleet of aerial refueling tankers. Boeing had assumed, as did all interested parties, that the air force would award Boeing a contract worth $23.5 billion to replace the existing tankers with a hundred modified 767's. Boeing was counting heavily on the deal. That and probably nothing else would allow the company to keep open the 767 line, and the proceeds could be used to help with developing the 7E7, its first new airplane in a decade.

But like so much of what had befallen Boeing in recent years, the tanker deal was derailed by the company's gaffes, in this case very serious ones. Boeing had maneuvered the deal into the $87 billion appropriations bill for Iraq. And earlier Michael Sears, the company's chief financial officer (and judged a potential CEO), had offered a job to Darleen Druyun, who was about to retire from the air force, where for many years she had been an influential procurement official. Sears had previously discussed Ms. Druyun with her daughter, a Boeing employee, who had contacted him to discuss her mother's postgovernment employment prospects.

Unfortunately for Boeing, Senator John McCain, the popular and on occasion relentless Arizona Republican, got on the company's case. McCain was serving then as chairman of the Senate Committee on Commerce, Science, and Technology. For him, the shabby jet tanker deal amounted to corporate welfare, and he said so. At times, in fact, he appeared to like nothing better than to talk about the matter. And in doing so, he was particularly harsh in describing what senior Boeing and air force people did. The deal was temporarily put on hold.

"This was all cooked up by Boeing, the Defense Department, and Congress," he told a visitor in February 2005. "It's the Iron Triangle. These are massive scandals. The corruption extends to Congress, too. It involves a lot of campaign donations. They act as if DOD [the Department of Defense] has done nothing wrong. But the most guilty is DOD. They are far more culpable than Boeing. Boeing was trying to make money. The people at DOD are supposed to have standards and ethics."[12]

The process of defining the specifications for the new tanker was, McCain said, one example of what he was talking about. "Boeing was allowed to define everything," he said.[13] The air force, according to official documents, gave Boeing five months to rewrite official specifications for the tankers so that its 767 aircraft would get the contract. In doing so, Boeing eliminated nineteen of twenty-six capabilities the air force originally wanted, and the air force went along to keep the price down.[14]

In this kind of transaction, the Pentagon would normally require an analysis of alternatives (AOA). But a report by the Defense Department's inspector general showed that procedure to have been bypassed, in this case on the instructions of Air Force Secretary James Roche. "Don't even begin to start an unnecessary AOA," he wrote to a deputy. "All this would do is give enemies of the lease an excuse from DOD to delay."[15]

According to McCain, the tanker deal was inserted into an appropriations bill by a fellow Republican stalwart, Senator Ted Stevens, who was then chairing the Appropriations Committee. The record supports this contention, as does Stevens himself. In a hearing of McCain's committee, he took credit for his lead role, indeed expressing pride: "I challenge anyone about my backroom dealing or anything else. We offered that amendment. It was right in front of God and everybody. It was in the bill when it was reported. It was there to be debated. As a matter of fact, there was some debate about it."[16]

Among the hard questions spilling out of the affair is why so many people in Washington—people with voices that carried—played this hand so crudely and risked so many ugly consequences. The explanation, according to some knowledgeable staff people on Capitol Hill, is that President Bush let it be known that he wanted the Boeing–air force deal done. In October 2002, he said as much in a meeting in the Oval Office with House Speaker J. Dennis Hastert, one of the arrangement's most strenuous advocates, and he then instructed Andrew Card, White House chief of staff, to become his point man in the struggle that lay ahead.

Bush was indebted to Hastert, who not long before had guided the first of the president's massive tax cuts through a divided and rather skeptical House of Representatives. The two actually met twice to discuss the Boeing–air force problem. Helping Boeing was important to Hastert, according to his spokesman, if only because the company's headquarters lay close to his district and a number of Boeing people lived there. "Yes, the speaker goes to bat for Illinois and he's been personally involved in this; he makes no secret of it," his spokesman, John Feehery, told the *Washington Post*. But Hastert's interest in the deal, Feehery said, was more than pork-barrel politics: "He's not just fighting for the sake of his constituency, it's also for the country's sake."[17]

"This state of corruption won't change until we start putting people in jail," McCain said early in 2004.[18] Within a year, two of the people he probably had in mind were there. Darleen Druyun was tried and sentenced to nine months in prison for having negotiated a job with Boeing while serving as the air force's second-ranking procurement officer. In tears, she admitted to having boosted the price on the tanker deal as a "parting gift" to Boeing. She also acknowledged steering other contracts to Boeing over a four-year period, influenced by prospects of a job for herself and the fact that she had succeeded in obtaining positions for her daughter and son-in-law at the company. She also told about having warned Boeing several times that a competing bid by Airbus on the long-range tanker deal was significantly lower per plane than the company's own proposal, although one Boeing e-mail noted:

"Meeting today on price was very good, Darleen spent most of the day bringing the USAF price up to our number."[19]

Druyun damaged the system of which she had been a part and gave it a bad name, although not so much because of what she did as because she got caught doing it. Mike Sears, who had been seen as a likely successor to Condit, was fired in November 2003. Fifteen months later he was tried and convicted for having recruited Druyun while she was handling military contracts. Sears drew a four-month jail sentence and a fine of $250,000.

Thanks to the pressure from McCain, assorted colleagues in the Senate, and heavy press coverage, the tanker deal was canceled. The Pentagon then dealt an additional blow to Boeing by announcing that any decision to upgrade the air force's aerial refueling fleet would be reopened to competition.[20] Airbus then could see itself as a serious competitor for the tanker deal. The A330, having once chased Boeing's 767 from the middle market, would be the Europeans' contending airplane and, it appeared then, a stronger candidate.

A backward look at the terms of the discredited jet tanker deal points up sharply not just the flaws in the procurement system but some of what had gone wrong at Boeing. Instead of selling the 767's outright, Boeing was going to transfer them under a lease-purchase agreement, which allows the buyer, in this case the air force, to pay for the new aircraft incrementally and thereby be positioned to buy more new hardware. Leasing can be described as a method by which buyer and seller can improve the terms of a transaction with smoke and mirrors. The leases are usually not funded by the procurement budget but in O&M (operations and maintenance).

Since Congress pays far less attention to the O&M budget than to the procurement budget, a leasing agreement can and usually does leave the consumer better positioned to buy new systems. In the end, it can and usually does require the government to pay more for the equipment than had it been purchased outright. But it's a win-win arrangement for the buyer and seller. Only the public interest loses. The report from DOD's inspector general, cited above, noted that the Boeing jet tanker deal, if it went forward, could cause the government to spend $4.5 billion more than necessary. Both the Congressional Budget Office and the Office of Management and Budget, when asked, reported that the lease would have cost more than a purchase agreement.

Some leasing deals are more devious than others, and the one that Boeing and the air force were conspiring to make happen was at the high end, more so than most. They were structuring it in a way that would hide debt. Boeing would not have had to report the debt it was taking on in its financial reports. And the air force would not have recorded the lease as a line-item request in the president's budget.

The bad odor of the scandals didn't reach Seattle, and people there began to think a little less harshly about the move to Chicago and to point out that no one involved in the jet tanker scandal and other defense-related misdeeds belonged to "old Boeing," that is, to Boeing heritage; that without exception, the people responsible for behavior ranging from dubious to deplorable came with the merger.

After the merger, Boeing began to reposition itself around the Pentagon. But management went too far. It blurred the line separating the company from the government and instead of concentrating on the hardware, as it once had, Boeing crossed the line.*

Among the stiff challenges confronting James McNerney, who assumed full control of Boeing within a year of the tanker deal's demise, was how to rid the country's second-largest defense contractor of its bad habits. Posting a code of ethics aimed at governing behavior wouldn't do. Harry Stonecipher had tried that and was himself seen by the board not long afterward to have violated the spirit, if not the letter, of these precepts.

McNerney took a more robust and ingenious approach. The setting he choose was Boeing's annual leadership retreat. The time was early January 2006, with 260 of the company's top executives gathered in Orlando, Florida. There, Boeing's general counsel, Douglas Bain, who

---

*The penalty for crossing the line included a settlement with the Justice Department that required Boeing to pay $615 million to avoid criminal and civil charges. It was the largest penalty ever paid by a defense contractor.

was also a senior vice president until he retired in 2006, delivered a savage indictment of reprehensible behavior routinely practiced. His speech was leaked to Dominic Gates and Alicia Mundy of the *Seattle Times,* and they quoted numerous passages.

McNerney was in the audience, and Bain began by saying, "As I walked up here, I think I heard Jim McNerney mutter, 'Here comes Dr. Death.' "[21] No one there was in any doubt about who had staged this show.

"Was there a culture of win at any cost?" Bain asked his audience. "We now know what that cost is." Boeing, he noted, faced possible indictments by U.S. attorneys on both coasts, and the Department of Justice assessment of damages exceeded $5 billion. Also, Bain added, Boeing could be barred from government defense contracts or denied export licenses for both military and commercial sales. He reported that fifteen company vice presidents had been pushed out for various ethical lapses in recent years. "I found that to be an astronomically high number," he said.

"There are some within the prosecutors' offices that believe that Boeing is rotten to the core," Bain said. "The U.S. attorney in Los Angeles," he said, "is looking at indicting Boeing for violations of the Economic Espionage Act, the Procurement Integrity Act, the False Claims Act and the Major Frauds Act. The U.S. attorney in Alexandria, Va., is looking at indicting us for violation of the Conflict of Interest laws. And both are looking to throw in a few conspiracy and aiding-and-abetting charges, for good measure.

"These are not ZIP codes," he said, as he read off the federal prison numbers of Darleen Druyun and Mike Sears. "How come in the year 2000 nobody said, 'Should we really be hiring the relatives of our chief procurement officer of the largest customer we have on the defense side?' " Possible impending penalties, he said, include "a presumed denial of export licenses . . . both on the commercial and the government side," as well as "loss of security clearances, a possible resuspension on bidding for space contracts or even total debarment from all government contracts on the defense side."

Bain ended with three questions: "Do we have a culture of silence? Where was management throughout this? Is the problem the rank and file? Or is the problem us?"[22]

AFTER SERIAL SCANDALS someone had to go, and this time it had to be Phil Condit, although there was no evidence linking him to what had happened. Then sixty-two, he had survived, barely, other bad patches, notably the production meltdown in 1997, for which Ron Woodard was chosen—by Condit—to take the fall.

Boeing's reputation had suffered as never before on Condit's watch. He probably should not have outlasted the misappropriation of Lockheed Martin's documents, or that combined with the space systems debacle. He had to have been either miscast or indifferent to ethical standards. Whichever was the case, he should have been removed.

Condit was a complex character whose behavior led, among other things, to indiscreet womanizing, a tendency that would have had no importance or relevance had it not become a public matter and, for the company and its board, an awkward one. Around this time he was going through a tough divorce proceeding, his third—this one with a first cousin who was likely to have the best of it in court.

Curiously, it was T. Wilson, Condit's polar opposite in just about every way, who made possible his early advancement. Wilson must have seen what various other executives saw—a gifted engineer, highly intelligent and more well-rounded than others in his peer group. These qualities, plus a collateral gift for climbing the corporate ladder, did the rest. They also attracted a kind of Condit group at Boeing Seattle, people for whom Phil was the smartest and wisest. They ignored or forgave his reluctance, or inability, to make decisions, a managerial flaw that curiously never seemed to get in the way.

Although an odd couple, Condit and Stonecipher were able to work together, partly because they had similar views. They had skeptical attitudes about the commercial aircraft business. They wanted to make

Boeing a preeminent defense contractor. And they wanted to diversify and acquire high-technology properties.

They also shared the experience of having merged their two companies, although Stonecipher, who was hardly negotiating from a position of strength, drove the transaction; he had even managed to saddle Boeing with his company's albatross, the commercial aircraft division. From then on, the McDac part of the enlarged company (a Stonecipher–Mike Sears nexus) drove the decision-making process. Numerous McDac people who had been expected to move on after the merger connected themselves to the enlarged company and, in many cases, acquired authority.

A strong hint of what could lie ahead occurred on June 1, 1998, just six months after the company posted its first operating loss in a half century. A piece in the *Seattle Post-Intelligencer* reported Condit telling "stunned managers" that his second in command, Harry Stonecipher, "would be in charge of the commercial recovery."[23]

A cultural change, already under way, acquired momentum. Veteran Boeing watchers saw a company once run by engineers giving way to youthful products of business schools. "They understand process—which buttons to push," said a senior executive with a major Boeing supplier. "But they don't know shit. They don't know what they don't know. And there's no passion. They would be just as much at home with Procter & Gamble making soap."[24]

Stonecipher decided to retire four years later, in June 2002. (He had wanted to leave a year earlier, but the board asked him to stay on for a bit.) He appeared to have wanted to take life easier, and as one of Boeing's two largest individual investors, his influence was certain to continue radiating, especially with John McDonnell, the single biggest investor, still a board member.

In any case, Stonecipher wasn't gone long. Fifteen months later, in December 2003, Condit left under a cloud, and Stonecipher was now president and CEO. As boss in his own right, he created several admirers as well as detractors—predictably. He had allies on the board other than McDonnell. His heavy stress on cost cutting did not go down well with a large part of a company that was unaccustomed to tight fiscal discipline. It did go down well—very well—on Wall Street and with shareholders. Boeing's shares rose more than 50 percent on his watch.

Stonecipher's known misgivings about the commercial aircraft business caused concern. With him at the helm, would Boeing do something about its aging product line—at long last build a new airplane, maybe—or would he put the company's chips elsewhere and thereby begin to edge away from the commercial business in small steps?

Boeing Seattle had to worry. Eight months after taking charge, in an interview with the *Seattle Times,* Stonecipher laid heavy emphasis on his bottom-line focus: "The moment that we can't make money in this [commercial aircraft] business, we will not be in it," he said. "The only thing I do, the only reason I'm hired, is to make money."[25] In a company with a tradition of betting all that it had on a new airplane, talk like this was unsettling, at least to its commercial aircraft people and the city of Seattle.

There was a new airplane—the 7E7—awaiting a decision on whether to build it. The board's two most powerful members, Stonecipher and John McDonnell, were reported in the *Wall Street Journal* as having said this might not be a good idea. They expressed concern about the airplane's cost and said they might move to block the project unless company engineers could develop it much more cheaply than previous aircraft.[26]

But they could hardly do so, if only because the 7E7 (renamed the 787) would be designed around engines that did not yet exist and a combination of novel methods and technologies for building a long-range airliner. Stonecipher and McDonnell, according to the *Journal,* argued that Boeing "should focus on maximizing profit from its existing jetliner models and continue expanding its defense, aerospace and finance businesses."[27] According to Stonecipher, he keeps a copy of this piece in his desk and occasionally teases the reporter, Lynn Lunsford, about it, because, he says, "the piece was wrong, one hundred percent wrong. I told that to the editors of the *Wall Street Journal* whom I met with. I have been and still am a big fan of Lynn Lunsford's. But he was dealing with people [at Boeing] who didn't know what was going on."[28]

"Harry never teased me about the piece," said Lunsford, who likes and respects Stonecipher, and regards him as among the strongest figures the industry has produced in recent years. "He did say, 'I'd love to talk about this over a beer sometime.' But that never happened. I was in the room with him in the meetings he had with our editors. He never told them the story was wrong."

Boeing's board had not authorized a new model since it approved the 777 in 1989. A decision against going forward with the 7E7 would invite gloomy comment about where the U.S. aircraft industry was headed. The United States had pioneered commercial air travel and developed a dominant role, but nothing fixed that role as a permanent feature of international life.

Signs had appeared that several of the big Asian airlines, including some that were already buying Airbus's A380, were attracted to the smaller Boeing airplane. It, too, would be a double-aisle aircraft with improved comfort. And it would fly about as far as the A380 and do so point to point, rather than hub to hub. An airplane that would spare travelers the inconvenience and uncertainties of relying on connecting flights was certain to have broad appeal.

In the fall of 2003 and the first part of 2004, experts disagreed on whose concept—Boeing's or Airbus's—the market would like best. "It's not an either/or case," said John Pleuger, president of the International Lease Finance Corporation (ILFC), the biggest lessor of wide-bodied aircraft. "But the major traffic flows will be between major city pairs—hub to hub."[29] Gradually, however, the argument for flying point to point became the more convincing.

A voice to which close attention was paid was that of Steven Udvar-Hazy, chairman and CEO of the ILFC. In April 2003, he advised Boeing via the *Wall Street Journal* (and perhaps privately) "to leapfrog Airbus the way that Airbus leapfrogged them."[30]

A good argument for going ahead with the 7E7 was made not just by Boeing Seattle but also by some of the most carefully watched aerospace analysts on Wall Street. As they saw things, Airbus's engineering and financial resources were tied up with the A380 program. This meant that in a renewed struggle with Boeing for the biggest share of the middle market, Airbus would be competing with its A330, which would be a middle-aged airplane when the 7E7 became available.

In December 2003, Stonecipher and his board approved going forward with the 7E7 provided enough airlines from various regions ordered it. But in April 2004, Stonecipher points out, "even though we had only one customer for the airplane, we launched it." The airline was All Nippon Airways.

What actually happened was the following: The 7E7 team was frustrated. Its people knew the company had to find an answer to Airbus's A330 or simply forget about the middle market. And they knew that whatever they did would have to be done in a way that satisfied Stonecipher. He told them, in effect, "You will have to cut development costs and manufacturing costs. You'll have to get the airplane out the door smarter and faster." The team responded by recruiting the 787's risk-sharing partners: the three Japanese heavies, plus Alenia and Vought.

The process of financing and developing the 7E7 got under way. Not going forward with it would have amounted to a signal that Boeing was indeed exiting the commercial airliner business, a move that would have made the U.S. government very unhappy. Stonecipher was well aware that the government would go to great lengths to avoid having the country pushed out of the commercial airliner business. It's a symbol of American primacy that reaches into its past. The United States and its airline industry might have recoiled from the prospect of being at the mercy of one supplier.

Nor is it lost on various government agencies that the aircraft industry operates at the cutting edge of more high technologies than any other and its product historically earns more foreign exchange than any other single U.S. export. Given Boeing's dependence on Washington, starting with the Pentagon, Stonecipher had to think very carefully about the 7E7, especially in the light of the mess that his company had been making of its military programs.

Fifteen months later, in March 2005, Stonecipher had left again, this time involuntarily. The board told him to step down because of his "improper relationship" with a female executive of the company. "The board determined that his actions were inconsistent with Boeing's code of conduct" was the statement's starchy conclusion.

The code had been put together as part of a broad effort dictated by Stonecipher and aimed at mainly discouraging behavior of the sort that had gotten the company into trouble with the Pentagon. Moreover, the woman in question did not report to Stonecipher, and their affair—consensual—had been of brief duration.

At first, the board seemed to have overreacted and in doing so made itself look foolish, if not hypocritical. Within much of the company, many people, whatever their view of their leader, were incredulous. "This news is awful," said one executive in an e-mail to a friend. "It will make us look foolish, which we are, and puritanical. . . . If you want your CEO to resign over an issue like this, why not be a bit more dignified about it and just state he resigned for personal reasons? Why crucify him with his pants down?"

As more of the story dribbled out, it appeared that the board had actually been left with no other alternative. Highly explicit e-mails between Stonecipher and his inamorata, written on Boeing computers, bore a risk of being intercepted and embarrassing the company. It was a harsh end to a career that lasted had forty-five years, during most of which Stonecipher had operated at the center of various large companies' affairs.

Stonecipher was to the executive suite born. He was smart, capable, and resourceful. He was decisive and opinionated. Along with Airbus's John Leahy, he was one of the two most widely talked about of the industry's figures. He was his own best PR director. The press liked him. He was brutally frank and used the top job as a bully pulpit from which to tell all interested parties how to think about the issues affecting the airline industry.

Business Week Online carried a long article on the sacking of Stonecipher under the headline "Why Boeing's Culture Breeds Turmoil." The article cited Boeing insiders as describing "an ongoing culture of unrestrained excess that dates back to the Condit years. The lack of restraint also led to rampant political infighting among senior managers. . . . Executive-suite shenanigans and infighting are hardly unknown in Corporate America, but the degree to which they pervade Boeing is rare. For a company that must negotiate with governments and take responsibility for the safety of the flying public as well as sensitive military contracts, the distractions are particularly troubling."[31]

Stonecipher operated in what he saw as being the tradition of Jack Welch. In emulating Welch, some of what he did helped Boeing. Welch, for example, had created a management development institute in Crotonville, New York. He recruited a number of professors from leading business schools and paid them corporate salaries. GE executives who were judged to have potential were required to attend the course. Shortly after Boeing's merger with McDonnell Douglas, Stonecipher set up a similar institute with the same sort of people running it. Executives from both GE and Boeing are convinced that management in both places has been strengthened by the training that these institutes provide.

THANKS TO SALES OF aircraft by Airbus, its parent company, EADS, was able to record its best ever financial performance in 2005. And operating profits were expected to grow by more than 12 percent in 2006, given a forecast of "sustained high deliveries" by Airbus.[32]

Still, the company had little reason to rejoice. Its middle- and long-term prospects were clouded by a competition in which Boeing held much the stronger hand. At the high end of the market, Boeing would be launching its new jumbo, the 747-8, for a fraction of what Airbus had invested in the A380 (about $16 billion). Airbus misled itself in thinking there would be a large market for the A380. It isn't likely to develop, at least not for several years and maybe never. Airbus still thinks it may be able to sell somewhere between three hundred and five hundred A380's;

the numbers fall well beneath the company's rosier forecasts. Moreover, Airbus may continue to be harassed by the airplane's problems, one of which is weight. Being overweight, of course, drives up the airplane's operating costs. In any case, very large airplanes are no longer popular with airlines. After 9/11 and the SARS epidemic, people became less disposed to fly in them.

Boeing may find itself in the enviable position of having two new airplanes—the 747-8 and the 787—ready to begin operating in the current decade. The 787 is scheduled for delivery in mid-2008, the 747-8 in 2010. It won't matter much if these delivery dates slip, as they well may. The 787's production line is sold out for 2008–10.

With its deservedly popular minijumbo, the 777, Boeing bought time. The airplane was designed in the 1980s, entered service in the early 1990s, and will probably be a major revenue earner for another few years. However, Boeing talks about replacing all versions of the 777, except for the longest-range version, with longer-range models of the 787, a smaller airplane.

In the middle market, Airbus's A330 is likely to continue selling for a few more years, but will be pushed aside by the 787, once deliveries are under way. For a time, Airbus tried persuading itself and the airline industry that the widely popular A330 would remain the prudent choice for years to come. With fuel prices the issue, Airbus claimed that the operating costs of an improved A330 would probably be as low, or nearly so, as those of the supposedly superefficient 787. And then, Airbus observed, an improved A330 would cost a lot less than Boeing's innovative new airplane. Was it perhaps too innovative?

The airline market was unimpressed by the Airbus argument. Many carriers wanted new equipment, especially in Asia, and they could afford it. Boeing's claim that the 787's operating costs would be 20 percent lower than the A330's resonated. The carriers wanted more range from the next middle-market airplane. The 787 offered that. And point to point sounded right.

All sides then watched Airbus struggle with the question of how much to invest in an improved A330. But the very different operative question was when its management would swallow the reality: competing against the 787 would dictate a new Airbus model, not a derivative. The next question then was how much the company could invest in developing this new airplane, the A350, with so much of its engineering talent, not to mention financial resources, committed to the A380 and also a new military transport, the A400M. How advanced could the A350 be made to become? How much new technology would it need to compete against the 787?

These were hard questions. They confused and lengthened the process of designing the A350. Airbus found itself offering different versions, occasionally at the same time. The designers were asked, in effect, to create an airplane whose performance characteristics would compare favorably with the 787's, yet do so without embodying quite as much new technology *and* also manage somehow to offer a few advantages of its own.

The thinking was that a larger airplane than the 787—with a 10 percent higher seat count or even more—would better suit the needs of various carriers in East Asia, the Middle East, and Europe than the 787 would. Emirates Airline, rapidly growing and with a global route structure, became a target of this thinking. And so the A350 got bigger—big enough, Airbus thought, to be able to compete against not just the 787 but also its larger sibling, the 777. "We are positioning our program to be a 777-200ER killer," said Olivier Andries, the A350 program manager.[33] (The 777-200ER is the long-range version of the airplane.)

In designing their new airplanes, Boeing and Airbus had to satisfy the airlines' all but overwhelming priority: lower operating costs. That meant lighter aircraft and stronger engines. In building these new models Airbus and Boeing planned to rely mainly on lightweight composite materials. But they diverged on just how much of these materials would be used in place of aluminum, and exactly which ones to rely on. Boeing chose layered CFRP (carbon fiber reinforced plastic). It is the lightest, strongest, and most resistant to corrosion. But the carbon fiber raises questions, the first of which is cost. Working with carbon fiber is very labor-intensive, hence expensive. Using it in load-bearing surfaces is a calculated but real risk; the lamination must be perfect. Moisture is the enemy. It causes the spaces inside the layers between the material to expand; these layers are called honeycombs.

Another problem lies in the tendency of ground service equipment to bump into sitting airplanes on occasion and cause some damage. "Ramp rash" is the term for this nuisance. Depending on its location, the damage, or dent, can become a problem if not properly repaired. With carbon fiber, the damaged skin swiftly recovers its seamless surface and disguises the effects of whatever damage may lie beneath. With aluminum, of course, the damage shows and can be swiftly repaired and the aircraft's downtime minimized. The vulnerable parts of an airplane are the wingtips, slats, and flaps—anything that is hanging down or sticking out from the lower belly can be hit by a vehicle, a jet bridge, or a de-icing boom.

Airbus pioneered the use of carbon fiber on commercial aircraft in the mid-1980s with the tail fin of its A310. Company officials cite a step-by-step increase in the use of composite materials, each new application becoming a learning experience. Early in 2006, an Airbus spokesman declared that "Boeing has missed the boat on several smaller steps in using composites, so it is trying to do it in one giant leap."[34]

Airbus has planned to make the A350's wings from carbon fiber, but not the fuselage. That would be a bridge too far, according to one company official. The Airbus position was that by using an alloy known as aluminum lithium in the fuselage, the weight-saving benefits would be nearly as great as with carbon fiber but without the same risk of maintenance crews having to make tricky repairs in a pressurized environment. Aluminum lithium also costs significantly less, although that is not one of the advantages Airbus has cited. But ramp rash continues to be mentioned by the same Airbus executives as an argument against an all-composite fuselage.

Asked to comment on Airbus's position, a Boeing spokesperson said: "Based on our knowledge and experience we believe that CFRP is a better choice for primary structure. Airbus does not have the same level of familiarity with this material—though they do use it. Our evaluation of materials included a review of durability, strength, weight, cost, manufacturability and reparability. . . . Remember, we have developed proprietary manufacturing solutions that enable us to see cost benefits, manufacturing benefits and reparability benefits that are unique to Boeing. A company looking to make a material decision without the benefit of our unique solutions might not be able to understand the full value behind selecting CFRP as the material of choice for primary structure."[35]

What the Boeing statement didn't say was that the benefits "unique to Boeing" and the "proprietary manufacturing solutions" were drawn from the company's experience with CFRP when it was closely involved with developing the B-1 and B-2 stealth bomber programs. Airbus, of course, had no such experience.

FOR ABOUT THIRTY YEARS, the feverishly fought-over middle market was a preserve, held first by Boeing and then by Airbus. There are roughly three thousand aircraft currently serving this market, mostly Boeing's 767's and Airbus A330's, which will be replaced by 787's and A350's over the next twenty-five years. Boeing, of course, has regained a sizable lead, but these are early days. In the years ahead, Airbus isn't likely to catch up, but should acquire a respectable share of that market. Some of the airlines that fly the A330 will no doubt buy the A350 so as to save money by preserving "fleet commonalty."

At some point, however, the focus of the duel will shift from the middle market to the lower end, where Boeing and Airbus will compete for advantage in the even bigger replacement market for the next generation of single aircraft; these will be the successors to each company's runaway best seller: Boeing's 737 and Airbus's A320. Together, these single-aisle airplanes comprise close to 70 percent of the market as a whole. Moreover, they are fully amortized; each sale is pure profit. Neither side is in a hurry to replace these two airplanes, since sizable orders for both continue to arrive with all but clockwork regularity. "Why shoot the golden goose?" asks Harry Stonecipher in retirement. Why indeed? And then, announcing a replacement aircraft would cause all those orders to evaporate.

Still, the estimable 737's and A320's will begin to be replaced in a few years—between the early and middle part of the next decade. And here again, it's advantage Boeing. Sometime in 2008 or 2009, Boeing can, if it chooses to, announce the launch of its replacement aircraft. It will be described as a new-generation model, built around the 787's technology.

A similar announcement by Airbus will come later, but how much later is unclear. Airbus is overstretched. It is bedeviled by problems with the A380, and both its engineering and financial resources are spread thin by the effort to build an A350 that will attract airlines that haven't yet ordered 787's. Stated differently, Airbus ought to preempt Boeing—begin sooner to develop its A320 replacement aircraft. But it can't, not right away.

Briefly, Boeing would appear to be in a position to tilt the playing field and gain a two- or three-year advantage in the epic struggle for dominance of the market for thousands of new single-aisle aircraft. The question is, will Boeing shoot the golden goose and gain an edge in this bread-and-butter market, or will it rest on its current laurels, as it did before and as Airbus then did?

The appearances may be deceptive. The reality is that neither company is likely to have a new single-aisle airplane before 2014 or 2015. Besides offering lower operating costs, the new models will have to be reliable enough to assure that turnaround time on the ground not exceed twenty minutes. More important, the so-called next-technology engines that will power these airplanes probably won't be available before 2014. Each of the three engine companies is working flat out to make what amounts to a huge leap in technology. "The mother of all battles" is a term used by some of the people directly involved to describe the engine competition they see lying ahead.

After building the 777, Boeing pulled away from its core business and flew on automatic pilot for a decade or so. The performance of Boeing's leadership during those years is a reminder that it may be better to be lucky than to be smart. Boeing was lucky. Its new version of the 747 may be a successful program, although less so than had it been built in the late 1990s, when it was for a time being exposed to the airlines. By then Boeing had most of the technology that is now built into the 787, about which its board was for a long time hesitant.

Boeing's Sonic Cruiser, an idea that preceded 787, was a long step away from reality, but one that Boeing pushed hard to advance and that ended ignominiously. Yet much of the technology intended for the Sonic Cruiser made possible the 787. Put differently, the notional Sonic Cruiser led straight to a sensible variant that may have saved Boeing Commercial.

Over the past twenty years, Airbus invested far more heavily in research and development than Boeing. Taking some recent years, 2000 through 2004, Airbus spent more than $8 billion on R&D. Boeing spent less than half that. Yet Boeing is marketing the most technologically advanced of airliners, thanks in part to the smart defense programs it worked on.

Airbus was neither lucky nor unlucky. It was building very good airplanes and doing so less expensively than Boeing, and with a smaller labor force. Indeed, Airbus was doing many more things right than Boeing had been doing. As the new century began, Airbus was becoming pleased with itself. It then began mixing complacency with an arrogance of the kind usually associated with Boeing. As it forged ahead of Boeing, Airbus's style shifted from being collaborative to high-handed, on occasion even punitive. Another page from the Boeing book.

Besides overhauling the champ, Airbus decided to build not just a jumbo à la Boeing, but a superjumbo. A case could be made for such an airplane, but it drew on a strategy from which others, including Boeing, were distancing themselves. Their own revisionist strategy was based on the assumption that since the new technologies made possible aircraft that could take people where they wanted to go, not just to some major metropolis, the better part of wisdom lay in building such an airplane. Airbus's strategy of putting most of its chips on a jumbo aircraft bigger and better than Boeing's came to resemble the thinking of generals who always wanted to fight the new war with the tools of the last one.

IN THE EARLY SPRING of 2006, Airbus's plight was forcefully driven home, first by the two biggest customers for large commercial aircraft, then by Chew Choon Seng, the boss of Singapore Airlines, another big buyer, the envy of the airline pack and role model for several carriers. The setting for the first blow was a resort outside Orlando, Florida, where seven hundred figures from the International Society of Transport Aircraft Trading were holding their annual conference. On March 28, Steven Udvar-Hazy, ILFC chairman and one of the two preeminent customers, called on Airbus to scrap its existing design for the A350 and start over with a new airplane, one with *a new fuselage* as well as a new wing.

By staying with the airplane's current design, Udvar-Hazy warned, the company would probably gain no more than a 25 percent market share against the 787. He then admonished Airbus to do an equally radical remake of its larger A340, an aircraft that the market had been disdaining. Henry Hubschman, who is president of GECAS, the largest lessor of airplanes, told an interviewer that he agreed "completely" with Udvar-Hazy. "We're not interested in a Band-aid reaction to the 787," he said. Airbus, he added, should develop a new family "that incorporates even more of the new technologies [than] the 787 is doing."[36]

In his shot across Airbus's bow, Udvar-Hazy conveyed a sense of urgency, noting that Boeing's 787 had a lead of two and a half to three years; that a decision to remake the A350 would have to be announced before the Farnborough Air Show in July—then just four months away.

A week later Chew Choon Seng echoed Udvar-Hazy and Hubschman, saying that Airbus, "having gone to the trouble of designing a new tail and introducing a lot of new composites, . . . might as well go the whole way and design a whole new fuselage as well instead of using something old. It would make it more directly competitive with the 787."[37]

Because their own interests were centrally involved, these three movers and shakers had been studiously blunt. It's not complicated. The buyers do not want to leave most of the market for midsize wide-bodied aircraft to one supplier. They require competitively priced models, and that means aircraft that offer similar advantages.

Among those in Orlando who listened to Udvar-Hazy telling Airbus what to do was John Leahy, the company's sales chief. A little earlier, Leahy had given an upbeat presentation of Airbus's competitive position that must have struck all or most of the audience as far distant from his real thinking. In Toulouse, an autocritique had been under way for several months. It included a lot of badmouthing of senior people by other senior people. Leahy himself had bundled most of the complaints into a letter he sent to Gustav Humbert, Airbus's boss in Toulouse, and four other senior managers. His letter was then leaked to *Der Spiegel*, the German newsmagazine. "In the view of investors, Boeing has taken over the leadership in all airplane categories," the letter said. Leahy then suggested a major public relations campaign to win back lost territory. "Our strategy is very weak in comparison to Boeing," the letter continued. Leahy, according to *Der Spiegel*, "relentlessly denounced failures and strategic mistakes."[38]

The autocritique embodied in the leaked Leahy letter clearly pointed to the presence of a dissident faction in Toulouse. And Udvar-Hazy's performance at the trade meeting in Orlando aroused suspicion that he had been encouraged to tell Airbus what it needed to do by some of its own executives, a few of whom were in the audience. Something was—is—going on either chez Airbus or between Airbus and its parent company, EADS. A divorce won't happen. EADS owns Airbus, and Airbus provides most of its parent company's cash inflow. But the guessing post-Orlando was that an Airbus cabal was trying to embarrass EADS into spending the $8 billion to $10 billion it would take to do what should be done.

The leadership at EADS belatedly did what had to be done, perhaps because of the maneuvering by Leahy and like-minded colleagues. Still, whether the cabal would have prevailed had not the Airbus crisis of June 2006 dictated going forward with an A350—and soon— is unclear. The new model was unveiled one month later at the Farnborough International Air Show, where all parties were awaiting a sign of renewal at Airbus. The airplane was officially designated A350XWB, for "extra wide body."

Just over a third of the A350 will consist of composites, most of which will be built into a new wing. The rest of the airplane will combine aluminum lithium with traditional metals. It will have new engines. A new wider fuselage is intended to provide a cabin that will exceed the comfort level of the 787, with roomier seats in rows nine abreast. Airbus is promising more width at eye level, shoulder level, and at the armrest.

Given its size, however, the A350 appears designed to go after the market currently dominated by Boeing's 777, less so the 787. Airbus will offer three versions, with the number of seats ranging from 270 to 350. The market for these so-called minijumbos is smaller than the market for the 787, but amounts to nearly the same in dollar volume. And it is growing rapidly.

Airbus got itself back on track by deciding to couple its future with this new airplane. The A350 is intended to begin carrying passengers by 2012, at which time it will become the flagship airplane, more important certainly than the superjumbo. It will take travelers just as far as the A380, in greater comfort perhaps, and at lower seat mile costs.

"This will be a good airplane," said Jean Pierson a week or so after it had been unveiled. People in Toulouse had been consulting him quietly in preceding months about the design. "I recommended it," he continued. "The nine-abreast seating is what it should have. I am confident. I'm sure it will be competitive. Singapore Airlines bought the airplane because it will compete with the high end of the 787 [the longer-range version] and the 777—both of them."[39] Many airlines, of course, had hoped to see a new Airbus that would compete on price with the 787.

The first of the big problems was finding an engine for the new airplane; there was nothing usable on the shelf. The best of the current designs were ten years old, and none of the engines based on those designs would meet the thrust and performance characteristics required by the new Airbus. However, Rolls-Royce lost little time in committing to a new engine that would produce up to ninety-five thousand pounds of thrust, enough for the largest version of the A350 and usable in each of its three versions. GE is expected to create an engine that will work with two of the versions, but not with the largest. That version will be competing against Boeing's extended-range 777, an airplane for which GE is the exclusive engine supplier.

Finding $10 billion to develop the A350XWB became the tough but soluble question—soluble provided the binational EADS management agreed to give the airplane priority over the distressed superjumbo program. Boeing, too, has questions to think through—questions that are unavoidable in this business. Management will have to decide when to shift the company's focus to the new-generation single-aisle airplane. More immediately, there have been design problems with the 787; weight is one of them. "We worry about it [the 787] every day," said Jim McNerney, Boeing's boss, during the Farnborough show. "Only the paranoid survive when you are doing airplane programs."[40] McNerney must also think about the flawed corporate culture of a company that began losing its bearings in the mid-1990s.

Boeing's luck was shown to be holding when McNerney changed his mind and agreed to take the helm. All sides agree that he is an exceptional talent with no apparent weaknesses and that Boeing is capable of coherent, unitary decision making. Conversely, EADS-Airbus is a jumble of moving parts, too many figures of authority in different places. In Paris, Noel Forgeard, before he was shorn of his role as co-chairman of EADS, had said that Airbus didn't need launch aid from governments for the A350. Then he said that Airbus would take the aid anyway. Talk like that creates confusion. Communication about

Airbus issues between Peter Mandelson, the EU's commissioner for trade, and Airbus member governments is often rancorous. That, too, has created confusion in the market for Airbus products, especially the A350.

The intimidating question for Airbus and its patrons had become how much to spend on remaking the company's products and how soon. But the larger and persistent question is about leadership—about corporate restructuring; about whether, and if so how, the conflicted Airbus-EADS family can create a management style that, like Boeing's, is based on strong, unitary leadership, or some close approximation. If, under pressure, it does so, the company will one day recover its balance. Interested parties—customer airlines, engine makers, and others—will take comfort. They need two healthy airplane suppliers, as do airline passengers.

NOTES

All unattributed quotations come from personal conversations with the author.

CHAPTER ONE. BEING NUMBER ONE

1. Conversation with Robert Kiley, May 9, 2004.
2. Conversation with anonymous GE executive, July 15, 2005.
3. Conversation with Jean Pierson, June 13, 2004.
4. Conversation with Robert Alizart, June 9, 2004.
5. Kevin Done, "The Big Gamble: Airbus Rolls Out Its New Weapon in Its Battle with Boeing," *Financial Times,* January 17, 2005, p. 15.
6. J. Lynn Lunsford and Daniel Michaels, "New Order: After Four Years in the Rear, Boeing Is Set to Jet Past Airbus," *Wall Street Journal,* June 10, 2005, p. A1.
7. Chew Choon Seng, interview, *Focus* (German language), August 8, 2005.
8. Paul Betts, "Airbus Chief Prepares for EADS," *Financial Times,* December 4, 2004, p. 21.
9. David Gauthier-Villars, "France Studies Steps to Fix Airbus Problems," *Wall Street Journal,* June 22, 2006, p. 6.
10. Conversation with Robert Alizart, July 22, 2006.
11. Conversation with Jean Pierson, July 26, 2006.
12. Jonathan R. Laing, "The Right Stuff," *Barron's,* March 13, 2006, pp. 24–27.
13. Conversation with Bob Conboy, April 29, 2005.
14. Conversation with Jean Pierson, June 13, 2004.
15. Conversation with Henri Courpron, June 27, 2005.

CHAPTER TWO. TRADING PLACES

1. Caroline Daniel, "Boeing Places a Cautious Bet on Rival," *Financial Times,* December 16, 2003, p. 15.

2. David Bowermaster, "Boeing, Japan Say Aerospace Deals Now Official," *Seattle Times*, May 27, 2005, http://seattletimes.nwsource.com.

3. Conversation with Gordon McKinzie, May 2, 2005.

4. Conversation with Jeff Shane, April 12, 2004.

5. Christopher Buckley, e-mail to author, September 23, 2004.

6. Conversation with John Patterson, September 30, 2004.

7. Conversation with Christopher Buckley, September 23, 2004.

8. Conversation with David Neeleman, April 6, 2004.

9. Conversation with Christopher Walton, September 2, 2004.

10. Conversation with anonymous Airbus executive, September 5, 2005.

11. Conversation with anonymous, October 19, 2004.

12. Conversation with anonymous Boeing vice president, December 23, 2004.

13. J. Lynn Lunsford, "Dog Fight—Behind Slide in Boeing Orders: Weak Sales Team or Firm Prices?" *Wall Street Journal*, December 23, 2004, p. A1.

14. Conversation with anonymous Boeing executive, January 7, 2005.

15. Conversation with Harry Stonecipher, July 27, 2006.

16. Conversation with anonymous Boeing executive, January 7, 2005.

17. Lunsford, "Dog Fight."

18. Ibid.

19. Conversation with anonymous Boeing executive, January 14, 2005.

20. Lunsford, "Dog Fight."

21. Communication with anonymous Airbus executive, January 19, 2005.

22. Lunsford, "Dog Fight."

23. "Lucky 8 Pays 60 in Boeing Deal," *New York Times*, January 29, 2005, p. C2.

24. Conversation with Scott Carson, May 4, 2005.

25. Conversation with anonymous, April 24, 2004.

CHAPTER THREE. FOLLY AND HYPOCRISY

1. Conversation with anonymous Boeing executive, March 17, 1993.

2. Conversation with Frank Schrontz, March 18, 1993.

3. David Greising, "Arming for Trade War: Boeing Sleuths Seek Proof of Improper Subsidies to Airbus Series," *Chicago Tribune*, May 20, 2005, pp. 1, 12.

4. R. Jeffrey Smith, "Emails Detail Air Force Push for Boeing Deal," *Washington Post*, June 7, 2005, p. 1.

5. Stanley Holmes, "Boeing vs. Airbus: Time to Escalate," *BusinessWeek Online*, March 21, 2005, http://www.businessweek.com/bwdaily/dnflash/mar2005/nf20050321_4418_db046.htm.

6. Greising, "Arming for Trade War," p. 12.

7. Conversation with Henri Courpron, June 27, 2005.

8. Conversation with anonymous, February 10, 2005.

9. Richard Aboulafia, newsletter, June 2004, http://www.richardaboulafia.com/shownote.asp?id=164.

10. Conversation with anonymous vice persident of GE Aeronautics, August 18, 2004.

11. Conversation with anonymous, September 17, 2004.

12. Tobias Buck, "Bush Fuels US-EU Aircraft Subsidies Dispute," *Financial Times,* August 16, 2004, p. 6.

13. John Gapper, "Boeing Has Not Mastered the Art of Griping," *Financial Times,* September 9, 2004, p. 13.

14. Ibid.

15. Jeffrey Garten, "How to Head Off a Battle of Aerospace Titans," *Financial Times,* January 10, 2005, p. 13.

16. David Armstrong, "In-Flight Online Systems Take Off: Airlines Install Broadband Connections," *San Francisco Chronicle,* October 31, 2004, p. D4.

17. Dominic Gates, "U.S., EU Resolve to Settle Dispute," *Seattle Times,* January 12, 2005, p. E1.

18. Kevin Done, "Airbus Asks European States for A350 Aid," *Financial Times,* January 13, 2005, p. 1.

19. Peter Mandelson, "Not an Issue for the WTO," *Washington Post,* April 1, 2005, p. A27.

20. Edward Alden, Daniel Dombey, and Ralph Minder, "Zoellick Accuses Mandelson of Using Spin in Dispute over Aircraft Subsidies," *Financial Times,* April 7, 2005, p. 1.

21. Conversation with anonymous Airbus official, July 25, 2005.

22. Elizabeth Becker and Mark Landler, "Fortunes Are Reversed in a Dogfight at the Airshow," *New York Times,* June 15, 2005, p. C10.

23. Michael Mechan, "Range Wars," *Aviation Week,* June 13, 2005, pp. 64–65.

24. Ibid.

25. Conversation with Larry Clarkson, May 26, 2004.

26. Conversation with Henri Courpron, February 7, 2006.

27. Kevin Done, "Boeing Chief Hopes Talks Can Resolve Airbus Dispute," *Financial Times,* July 20, 2006, p. 5.

CHAPTER FOUR. MARKET SHARE — THE AIRLINES' ENEMY

1. Adam Brown, "Airbus' View of the Future," keynote speech delivered at International Air Transport Association Conference for the 21st Century, Frankfurt, Germany, May 26, 2004.

2. John Newhouse, *The Sporty Game* (New York: Alfred A. Knopf, 1982), p. 14.

3. Ibid., p. 15.

4. Conversation with Edward Colodny, February 16, 2005.

5. Kevin Frieberg and Jackie Frieberg, *Nuts!: Southwest Airlines' Crazy Recipe for Business and Personal Success* (New York: Broadway Books, 1996), p. 49.

6. John Newhouse, "The Battle of the Bailout," *The New Yorker,* January 18, 1993, p. 42.

7. Ibid., p. 46.
8. Ibid., p. 51.
9. Micheline Maynard, "Lenders and U.S. Tighten Screws on Struggling Airlines," *New York Times*, December 7, 2004, p. C2.
10. Susan Carey, Kathryn Kranhold, and Melanie Trottman, "GE's Bailouts of Troubled Carriers Divide Airline Industry," *Wall Street Journal*, March 31, 2005, p. B1.
11. George Hamlin, presentation to Transportation Research Board, January 11, 2005, p. 3.
12. Robert L. Crandall, address at 57th Annual Wright Memorial Dinner, December 17, 2004, p. 4.
13. Conversation with Louis Miller, March 11, 2005.
14. Claudia H. Deutsch, "For Many Pilots the Thrill Is Gone," *New York Times*, October 15, 2004, p. C1.
15. Caroline Daniel, "The Death of a Golden Goose: US Airlines and Unions Clash over Pay and Benefits," *Financial Times*, December 28, 2004, p. 7.
16. Ibid.
17. Ibid.
18. Norma Cohen, "Pension Safety Net's $78bn Hole," *Financial Times*, November 19, 2004, p. 21.
19. Caroline Daniel, "Losses Mount for US Carriers Despite Cost-Cutting Efforts," *Financial Times*, February 7, 2005, p. 18.
20. Dan Roberts and Kevin Done, "Delta Goes Head-to-Head with Low Cost Rivals by Cutting Air Fares Up to 50%," *Financial Times*, January 6, 2005, p. 1.
21. Micheline Maynard, "Big Fare Cuts Made by Delta Turn Industry on Its Head," *New York Times*, January 7, 2005, pp. C1, C6.
22. Frieberg and Frieberg, *Nuts!*, pp. 57, 98.
23. Conversation with David Neeleman, April 6, 2004.
24. Barbara S. Peterson, *Blue Streak: Inside JetBlue, the Upstart That Rocked the Industry* (New York: Portfolio, 2004), p. 15.
25. Ibid.
26. Ibid., pp. 15–16.
27. Ibid., p. 39.
28. Ibid., pp. 39–40.
29. Conversation with with Benoit Debain, June 11, 2004.
30. Conversation with Richard Branson, June 15, 2004.
31. Caroline Daniel, "Airlines Reveal Merger Details," *Financial Times*, May 20, 2005, p. 20.
32. Caroline Daniel, "Southwest Aims at 10% Expansion," *Financial Times*, March 22, 2005, p. 23.
33. Micheline Maynard, "Latest Target of Airline Cuts: Number of Seats," *New York Times*, March 29, 2005, p. C4.
34. Conversation with Hubert Horan, March 11, 2005.

CHAPTER FIVE. PLAYING THE GAME

1. Conversation with Jean Pierson, June 13, 2004.
2. Ibid.
3. Conversation with Richard Branson, June 15, 2004.
4. Conversation with John Rose, June 4, 2004.
5. Conversation with Alan Boyd, August 16, 2004.
6. Conversation with Jean Pierson, June 13, 2004.
7. Conversation with John Leahy, June 14, 2005.
8. Conversation with Jean Pierson, June 13, 2004.
9. Conversation with Clyde Kizer, March 4, 2005.
10. Conversation with Gerard Blanc, June 9, 2004.
11. John Newhouse, *The Sporty Game* (New York: Alfred A. Knopf, 1982), p. 50.
12. Conversation with John Hayhurst, April 27, 2005.
13. Conversation with Stanley Little, March 14, 2004.
14. Conversation with Jean Pierson, June 13, 2004.
15. Conversation with Robert Alizart, June 8, 2004.
16. Conversation with Jean Pierson, June 13, 2004 .
17. Conversation with Robert Alizart, June 8 2004.
18. Conversation with Gerard Blanc, June 10, 2004.
19. Stephen Aris, *Close to the Sun: How Airbus Challenged America's Domination of the Skies* (London: Aurum Press, 2002).
20. Conversation with Jean Pierson, June 13, 2004.
21. Conversation with Alan Boyd, August 16, 2004.
22. Conversation with Steve Rothmeyer, April 21, 2004.
23. Ibid.
24. Bill Richards, "Boeing Plots Course; Schrontz Foresees a Rough Ride If Economy Slows," *Seattle Post-Intelligencer,* September 21, 1990, p. A1.
25. Conversation with Gordon McKinzie, May 2, 2005.
26. Conversation with Clyde Kizer, March 4, 2005.
27. Conversation with Alan Boyd, August 27, 1993.
28. Conversation with Frank Schrontz, March 18, 2003.
29. Conversation with Jean Pierson, June 13, 2004.
30. Ibid.
31. Conversation with Alan Boyd, August 16, 2004.
32. Conversation with Jean Pierson, June 13, 2004.
33. Conversation with Jack Schofield, May 24, 2005.
34. Teal Group, presentation, Boeing 777: Program Briefing, p. 6.
35. Conversation with Boyd Givan, March 15, 2004.
36. Conversation with John Leahy, June 14, 2002.
37. Conversation with Dean Thornton, March 18, 1993.
38. United States and Europe, Rolls-Royce Subsidies from the UK Government, p. 1.

39. Conversation with anonymous GE executive, March 29, 2004.
40. Conversation with Jean Pierson, June 13, 2004.
41. Conversation with anonymous GE executive, April 20, 2005.
42. Newhouse, *The Sporty Game*, p. 56.
43. Conversation with anonymous GE executive, April 20, 2005.
44. Newhouse, *The Sporty Game*, p. 53.
45. Conversation with anonymous former Pratt executive, July 31, 2005.
46. Conversation with anonymous GE executive, April 20, 2005.
47. Conversation with anonymous Pratt executive, January 24, 2004.
48. Conversation with anonymous GE executive, April 24, 2005.
49. Newhouse, *The Sporty Game*, p. 53.

CHAPTER SIX. MELTDOWN AND MERGER

1. Conversation with retired Boeing executive, May 3, 2005.
2. Stanley Holmes, "Boeing's Sonic Bruiser," *Business Week Online*, July 2, 2001, http://www.businessweek.com/magazine/content/01_27/b3739179.htm.
3. Conversation with Gordon McKinzie, May 2, 2005.
4. Conversation with Frank Schrontz, March 18, 2005.
5. Conversation with Mike Little, March 16, 1993.
6. Conversation with Phil Condit, March 15, 1993.
7. Conversation with Ron Woodard, March 6, 2003.
8. Conversation with Mike Little, March 16, 1993.
9. Conversation with James Johnson, March 1993.
10. Conversation with anonymous Boeing vice president, August 4, 2004.
11. Conversation with Phil Condit, March 15, 1993.
12. Conversation with Mike Little, March 16, 1993.
13. Conversation with Alan Mulally, March 1993.
14. Ibid.
15. Conversation with Ron Woodard, March 6, 2003.
16. Conversation with Boyd Givan, March 15, 2004.
17. Conversation with Gerard Blanc, June 8, 2004.
18. "Boeing Rival Airbus Won't Rest on Laurels," *Bloomberg News*, September 29, 1999.
19. Conversation with James Womack, March 2004.
20. Conversation with anonymous, April 19, 2004.
21. Conversation with Larry Clarkson, May 26, 2004.
22. Conversation with Ron Woodard, March 6, 2003.
23. Conversation with Jean Pierson, June 13, 2004.
24. Conversation with anonymous, April 2004.
25. Conversation with anonymous, April 4, 2005.
26. Stanley Holmes and Mike France, "Boeing's Secret," *Business Week Online*,

May 20, 2002, http://www.businessweek.com/magazine/content/02_20/b3783001.htm.

27. Conversation with Stanley Holmes, August 11, 2005.

28. Ibid.

29. Class Action Complaint for Violations of Federal Securities Laws, U.S. District Court, Western District, Seattle.

30. Holmes and France, "Boeing's Secret."

31. Stanley Holmes, "What Really Happened," *Business Week*, December 15, 2003, pp. 35–39.

32. Paul Proctor and Anthony L. Velocci Jr., "Woodard Ousted in Boeing Shake Up," *Aviation Week*, September 7, 1998.

33. Conversation with Phil Condit, December 5, 2005.

34. Richard M. Weintraub and Byron Ocohido, "Boeing May Get Less of Big Saudi Jet Order," *Seattle Times*, January 28, 1994, p. 1.

35. John A. Tirpak, "The Distillation of the Defense Industry," *Air Force*, July 1998.

36. Conversation with anonymous Boeing executive, May 2005.

37. Conversation with Larry Clarkson, May 3, 2005.

38. Conversation with Boyd Givan, April 19, 2005.

39. Conversation with Harry Stonecipher, March 25, 2006.

40. Conversation with Jerry King, March 16, 2004.

41. Conversation with Jerry Niklesburg, October 28 , 2004.

42. Patricia Callahan, "So Why Does Harry Stonecipher Think He Can Turn Around Boeing?" *Chicago Tribune*, February 29, 2004, p. 6.

43. Boeing Company, Proxy Statement, Annual Meeting of Shareholders, April 29, 2002, p. 11.

44. Conversation with Richard Aboulafia, May 24, 2004.

45. Conversation with Larry Clarkson, May 3, 2005.

46. Conversation with Jerry King, March 16, 2004.

47. Conversation with anonymous Boeing engineer, April 16, 2004.

48. Karen West, "Boeing's Arrogant Image Must Go," *Seattle Times*, March 26, 1998, p. 1.

49. Conversation with Harry Stonecipher, March 25, 2006.

CHAPTER SEVEN. THE VERY LARGE AIRPLANE

1. Conversation with John Hayhurst, March 1993.

2. Conversation with Jean Pierson, June 13, 2004.

3. Conversation with Frank Schrontz, March 18, 2005.

4. Conversation with Jean Pierson, June 13, 2004.

5. Conversations with Larry Clarkson, March 1993 and September 2005.

6. Ibid.

7. Conversation with John Hayhurst, March 1993.

8. Conversation with Alan Boyd, May 1, 1993.

9. Conversation with anonymous Airbus executive, March 1993.

10. Conversation with Frank Schrontz, March 18, 2005.

11. Ibid.

12. Conversation with Larry Clarkson, May 3, 2005.

13. Conversation with Harry Stonecipher, March 4, 2004.

14. Richard Aboulafia, "Boeing 747," Teal Group report, July 2005, p. 10.

15. Jeff Cole, "Boeing Lands over 30 Orders from Asian Carriers for New 747's," *Wall Street Journal*, August 29, 1996, p. B6.

16. Boeing announcement, March 29, 2001.

17. Conversation with Christopher Avery, June 1, 2005.

18. Conversation with Joseph Sutter, April 20, 2004.

19. Conversation with Larry Clarkson, May 3, 2005 .

20. Conversation with Richard Branson, June 15, 2004.

21. Conversation with Gerard Blanc, June 10, 2004.

22. *Boeing News Now* (online), December 20, 2002.

23. Conversation with Gerard Blanc, June 10, 2004.

24. Ibid.

25. Conversation with Hanko von Lachner, June 10, 2004.

26. Sara Kehaulani Goo, "Airbus Hopes Plane Will Take Off, Beat Boeing," *Washington Post*, December 19, 2004, pp. 1, 22.

27. Conversation with Jean Pierson, June 13, 2004.

28. Adam Brown, "Airbus' View of the Future," keynote speech delivered at International Air Transport Association Conference for the 21st Century, Frankfurt, Germany, May 26, 2004.

29. Conversation with Clancy Wilde, March 15, 2004.

30. Conversation with Christopher Avery, September 20, 2005.

31. Reuters, May 18, 2004.

32. Conversation with Michael di Giralamo, September 21, 2005.

33. Kevin Done, "Infrastructure Must Improve Rapidly," *Financial Times*, July 19, 2004, p. A32.

34. Ibid.

35. Conversation with Michael di Giralamo, September 21, 2005.

36. Conversation with Frank Clark, March 11, 2004.

37. Conversation with John Martin, October 4, 2004.

38. Conversation with Alan Mulally, May 6, 2005.

CHAPTER EIGHT. A CHALLENGE FROM ASIA

1. E-mail exchange with Stan Sorscher, October 14, 2005.

2. Stanley Holmes, "Boeing's High Speed Flight," *BusinessWeek Online*, August 12, 2002, http://www.businessweek.com/magazine/content/02_32/ b3795088.htm.

3. Ibid.

4. Dominic Gates, "Airbus Parent to Build Key Part of Rear Fuselage for Boeing 787," *Seattle Times*, October 18, 2005, p. 3.

5. Conversation with anonymous Boeing vice president, August 4, 2004.

6. Dan Morgan, "Is It Sharing Know-How or Selling the Store?" *Washington Post*, May 4, 1983, p. A1.

7. Dominic Gates, "Separation Anxiety: The Wall Between Military and Commercial Technology," *Seattle Times*, January 22, 2006.

8. Conversation with anonymous, April 23, 2004.

9. "The Downfall of a Great American Airplane Company—An Insider's Perspective," pp. 6–7.

10. Conversation with anonymous former vice president GE Aircraft Engines, August 18, 2004.

11. Conversation with anonymous U.S. government official, July 14, 2004.

12. Conversation with Pierre Chao, February 24, 2005.

13. Conversation with anonymous, April 2, 2004.

14. Conversation with anonymous former Boeing CEO, December 5, 2005.

15. Conversation with anonymous Japanese official, October 21, 2005.

16. Conversation with anonymous, October 20, 2005.

17. "Airbus Tells Suppliers: Outsource to Asia," *Aviation Week*, November 21, 2005, p. 20.

18. Holmes, "Boeing's High Speed Flight."

19. L. J. Hart-Smith, "Outsourced Profits—the Cornerstone of Successful Subcontracting," Boeing Third Annual Technical Excellence Symposium, February 14–15, 2001.

20. Conversation with anonymous Boeing engineer, May 21, 2004.

21. Conversation with Phil Condit, March 15, 1993.

22. Conversation with Richard Albrecht, March 17, 1993.

23. Kristi Heim, "Boeing Stumbles in Race for China," *Seattle Times*, June 5, 2005, http://seattletimes.nwsource.com/html/boeingaerospace/2002307265_boeing china05.html.

24. Ibid.

25. Conversation with anonymous industry executive, October 17, 2004.

26. Charles Hutzler and Daniel Michaels, "Airbus Struggles to Get Chinese Order," *Wall Street Journal*, December 3, 2004.

27. Conversation with anonymous industry executive, October 17, 2004.

28. Conversation with Christian Scherer, June 11, 2004.

29. Mariko Sanchanta, "Airbus Sets Out to Break Boeing Hold on Japan," *Financial Times*, February 10, 2005, p. 15.

30. Adam Brown, "Airbus' View of the Future," keynote speech, International Air Transport Association Conference for the 21st Century, Frankfurt, Germany, May 26, 2004.

31. Dominic Gates, "Boeing High on India," February 22, 2005.

32. Manjeet Kirpalani, Stanley Holmes, and Carol Matlack, "Dogfight over India," *Business Week Online,* May 2, 2005.

33. Richard Aboulafia, *Teal Group Briefing Book Series,* February 2005, p. 2.

34. "Details of Boeing's Outsourcing Strategy," Boeing strategy paper, July 15, 2005, p. 8.

35. "Jet Propelled," *Airline Business,* November 21, 2005.

36. Ibid.

37. Gates, "Boeing High on India."

38. John Lancaster, "India Is Fertile Soil for Airlines," *Washington Post,* February 22, 2005, p. E1.

39. Byas Anand, "Airlines Trying Hard to Woo Customers," *Economic Times,* September 12, 2005, http://economictimes.indiatimes.com/articleshow/1227696.cms.

40. Conversation with Paul Kiteley, June 9, 2004.

41. Ibid.

42. Peter Gregg, keynote address, Asia Pacific Aviation Summit, Sydney, Australia, August 9, 2005.

43. Kevin Done, "Dubai Spreads Its Wings into Aerospace," *Financial Times,* February 20, 2006, p. 1.

44. Conversation with Senior Australian Official, February 27, 2004.

45. Kevin Done, "Qantas Order Sees Boeing Claw Back Share from Airbus," *Financial Times,* December 15, 2005, p. 21.

46. Conversation with Airbus official, January 10, 2006.

47. Mark Landler, "Airbus Edge in Sales in '05 Comes with an Asterisk," *New York Times,* January 18, 2005, p. C1.

CHAPTER NINE. MUDDLING THROUGH, MORE OR LESS

1. Conversation with Phil Condit, July 13, 2004.

2. Conversation with Harry Stonecipher, March 27, 2006.

3. Bill Virgin, "Oh, Won't You Come Home, Boeing?" *Seattle Post-Intelligencer,* March 29, 2005, p. C1.

4. Stanley Holmes, "Boeing Attempts a U-Turn at High Speed," *Business Week Online,* April 16, 2001, http://www.businessweek.com/magazine/content/01_16/b3728103.htm.

5. Rachael Horwood, "Boeing Versus Airbus," *Economist,* July 24, 2003.

6. Conversations with Steve Sleigh, April 2 and 11, 2004, and February 27, 2006.

7. Conversation with Phil Condit, December 5, 2005.

8. Conversation with Harry Stonecipher, March 2, 2006.

9. Conversations with Steve Sleigh, April 2 and 11, 2004, and February 27, 2006.

10. John Newhouse, *The Sporty Game* (New York: Alfred A. Knopf, 1982), p. 23.

11. Caroline Daniel and Demetri Sevastopulo, "Inside the Iron Triangle," *Financial Times*, December 7, 2004, p. 21.
12. Conversation with Senator John McCain, Feburary 5, 2004.
13. Ibid.
14. Joseph L. Galloway, "Tanker Bid Was Tailored to Boeing," *Philadelphia Inquirer*, March 28, 2004, p. 1.
15. R. Jeffrey Smith, "Roche Opposed Review of Alternatives to Plane Deal," *Washington Post*, July 30, 2004, p. 6.
16. United States Senate, Committee on Commerce, Science and Technology, meeting transcript, p. 14.
17. Jeffrey H. Birnbaum, "Boeing Has a Powerful Ally with Hastert," *Washington Post*, July 18, 2004, p. A10.
18. Conversation with Senator John McCain, February 5, 2004.
19. Daniel and Sevastopulo, "Inside the Iron Triangle," p. 21.
20. *Financial Times*, November 23, 2004, p. 4.
21. Dominic Gates and Alicia Mundy, "Boeing's Lawyer Warns of Company's Legal Peril," *Seattle Times*, January 31, 2006, p. A1.
22. Ibid.
23. James Wallace, "Hard-Nosed Stonecipher Retires at Boeing," *Seattle Post-Intelligencer*, June 1, 2002, p. A1.
24. Conversation with anonymous executive, March 3, 2004.
25. Dominic Gates and David Bowermaster, "Blunt Boeing CEO Bullish on Company's Prospects," *Seattle Times*, August 2, 2004, p. A1.
26. J. Lynn Lunsford, "7E7 Facing Powerful Resistance," *Wall Street Journal*, April 22, 2003, p. C1.
27. Ibid.
28. Conversation with Harry Stonecipher, March 25, 2006.
29. Conversation with John Pleuger, March 26, 2004.
30. Lunsford, "7E7 Facing Powerful Resistance," p. C1.
31. Stanley Holmes, "Why Boeing's Culture Breeds Turmoil," *BusinessWeek Online*, March 21, 2005, http://www.businessweek.com/magazine/content/05_12/b3925039_mz011.htm.
32. Kevin Done, "Airbus Delivers Record Profit for EADS," *Financial Times*, March 9, 2006, p. 15.
33. Robert Wall, Michael Mecham, and Andy Nativi, "Airbus Redesigns A350," *Aviation Week*, May 23, 2005.
34. James Wallace, "Airbus to Use Composites," *Seattle Post-Intelligencer*, January 10, 2006, p. C1.
35. Boeing Company, "Statements on CFRP vs. Aluminum Lithium," August 18, 2005.
36. Dominic Gates, "Airplane Kingpins Tell Airbus: Overhaul A350," *Seattle Time*, March 29, 2006.

37. "Airbus Should Redesign the A350, Singapore Airlines Says," *Bloomberg News Online,* April 7, 2006.

38. Dinah Deckstein, "Fiery Letter from the Chief of Sales," *Der Spiegel,* February 6, 2006.

39. Conversation with Jean Pierson, July 26, 2006.

40. James Wallace, *Seattle Post-Intelligencer* Aerospace blog, July 19, 2006.

ACKNOWLEDGMENTS

I am grateful to Bruce Blair, the president of the World Security Institute, as well as my friend and colleague, for letting me write this book on WSI's premises. That helped a lot.

I must thank Victoria Garcia and Holly Mackey for finding documents that otherwise would have been adrift in cyberspace, and for helping in other ways, including organizing notes.

I am also grateful to Andrew Wylie and Jeff Posternak for the sound advice and support they provide in representing me.

Lastly, I want to thank Ash Green, my editor on this and three other books, for his friendship and support.

INDEX

A NOTE ON THE TYPE

Pierre Simon Fournier le Jeune, who designed the type used in this book, was both an originator and a collector of types. His services to the art of printing were his design of letters, his creation of ornaments and initials, and his standardization of type sizes. His types are old style in character and sharply cut. In 1764 and 1766 he published his *Manuel typographique*, a treatise on the history of French types and printing, on typefounding in all its details, and on what many consider his most important contribution to typography—the measurement of type by the point system.

COMPOSED BY STRATFORD PUBLISHING SERVICES, BRATTLEBORO, VERMONT

PRINTED AND BOUND BY BERRYVILLE GRAPHICS, BERRYVILLE, VIRGINIA

DESIGNED BY ROBERT C. OLSSON